C000247259

George Whitefield MA
Field-Preacher

*"Every one hath his proper gift.
Field-Preaching is my plan;
In this I am carried as on eagles' wings;
God makes way for me everywhere."*

JAMES PATERSON GLEDSTONE

AMBASSADOR

BELFAST ◆ **GREENVILLE**
NORTHERN IRELAND   SOUTH CAROLINA

GEORGE WHITEFIELD
Field-Preacher

This Ambassador Edition 1998

ISBN 1 84030 038 8

Ambassador Publications
a division of
Ambassador Productions Ltd.
Providence House
16 Hillview Avenue,
Belfast, BT5 6JR
Northern Ireland

Emerald House
1 Chick Springs Road, Suite 203
Greenville,
South Carolina 29609, USA

www.emeraldhouse.com

To

MY WIFE,

AND

TO MY DAUGHTER

MAY,

MY FELLOW-HELPERS

IN MAKING THIS BOOK

PREFACE

THE favourable reception which was given to my 'Life and Travels of George Whitefield' published in 1871, now long out of print,[1] and the need that was felt in certain quarters for a briefer life of the great field-preacher, which nevertheless should be full, though without excess of detail, have led me to prepare this book. The main idea is the same in both books, viz.: 'To reveal a great heart, stirred with the purest emotion, ever desiring absolute perfection in goodness and unintermittingly seeking it, resolved to leave nothing undone by which others might become partakers with itself of the great salvation, and impatient of all impediments, whether ecclesiastical or social, that threatened the consummation of its hopes.'

I. The greatness of Whitefield's labours is not easily realised, and not even a three-volume life could outline it. One month's labours are recorded in this brief sentence—'he preached to ten thousand persons every day for twenty-eight days.' That fact will bear a great deal of analysing. The far-reaching influence of his preaching can only be imagined by remembering that his vast congregations were often gathered together in thinly populated districts—*e.g.* Haworth

---

[1] See extracts from some reviews at the end of this volume.

on the Yorkshire moors, Cambuslang the Scotch village, the backwoods of the American settlements—persons coming long distances, at great cost of time and trouble, to hear him. He said of his forest-preaching—'I am hunting after poor sinners in these ungospelized wilds. People are willing to hear, and I am willing to preach.' He mounted his horse, and rode to a point where he and they could come into contact.

II. It will be noticed that, although Calvinism is generally supposed to have a deadening influence upon the hearts of its disciples, Whitefield was always aggressive and in advance of his brethren in the adoption of new methods of doing good. He led the way in field-preaching, in the employment of laymen as preachers, in organising the new Welsh converts into a General Association of Methodists, and he seems also to have been the first to prepare a hymn-book for his congregation at the Tabernacle. He was a pathfinder. His zeal, courage, and faith kept him foremost.

III. Some suggestion may be found in this life as to the relation of evangelistic to pastoral work. Whitefield was frequently invited to labour in given districts; and, in the main, with very satisfactory results. It is true that his work was fiercely assailed, and that he passed through a storm of obloquy, but it is also true that the storm abated towards the close of his life, and that his opponents and he came nearer together. They had been stirred by his contagious zeal, and both he and they had mellowed in charity. In multitudes of instances he went uninvited, and his work, done on the race-course, in the field, or in the market-place, just left its results for the settled pastor to gather; which was perhaps the easiest method.

IV. The ethical value of his work was individualistic during his life; the social and political appeared afterwards. He worked for the units; the units in their aggregation must work for the body politic. It were as idle and unjust to blame him for not personally inaugurating large reforms as to blame the Apostle Paul for not procuring the franchise for Roman Christians. He was in the line of progress, and his labours continue in new forms of usefulness. He aimed at making new men, the new men must make the new State. And no doubt the social and political and international success of Christianity would come sooner and be greater were Christians to labour more zealously for personal conversions. To get a man a new home is a good thing; to get him a new heart is better. ' This ought ye to do, and not to leave the other undone.'

V. No careful student of his life will conclude that he had no formative influence because he was neither a constructive theologian nor the founder of a sect. He was more and better than either of these. He was the means of calling multitudes from death unto life; and then they formed themselves into societies and churches as they saw best. In the coming days of Church union it may appear that the greatest heart of the evangelical movement was far before his time, when, as a young man of twenty-seven, he said:—'I am persuaded there is no such form of Church government prescribed in the book of God as excludes a toleration of all other forms whatsoever.' 'O that the power of religion may revive! Nothing but that can break down the partition wall of bigotry.' Or, in other words, nothing but that can unite Christians as such. Is not that the ideal of Christian fellowship toward which all the churches are moving? As regards sectarianism Whitefield was a centrifugal force, as regards true Christian union he was centripetal. He lived for the larger idea as it is to be realised and embodied by love.

VI. The secret of Whitefield's marvellous influence has been and always will be a problem of absorbing interest. It cannot be given on the page of a book, but might perhaps be discovered by one who should reverently, prayerfully, and sympathetically travel with him day by day through his mighty labours for the salvation of souls, and watch with him in his hours and days of prayer. A rapid reading of this or of any other book will not discover it. Imagination, sympathy, fellowship, and imitation must be employed. He was a mystic. His was a 'life hid with Christ in God,' pouring itself out in loving service through an organism perfectly adapted to the work of preaching. As his oratorical genius was in full bloom as soon as he began to preach, so also was he wholly consecrated to the will of God and filled with the Spirit from the time of his new birth. The outward demonstration never exceeded the inward reality, hence there never was a halt, never a break, never a decline. 'He went from strength to strength, until he appeared before God in Zion.'

As we read the fierce and scornful language in which he was assailed from so many quarters, and notice, on the other side, the multitudes of all classes, including crowds of the aristocracy, some of them Christians of the warmest devotion, who came to hear him, it suggests the inquiry whether, by all the means used, the English people, rich and poor, but especially the titled, are as deeply and as widely influenced by the gospel now as they were a hundred and fifty years ago. If the intensity of the hatred and opposition directed against him accurately indicated the enormous influence which he wielded, as it certainly did, is the prevalent indifference of to-day to the preaching of the gospel the measure of the feebleness that is neglected? One thing is certain: the whole Church of God needs a fresh baptism of the Holy Spirit; and thankful shall we be, if it be soon given.

CONTENTS

CONTENTS

CHAPTER I

1714-1735

THE Rev. Samuel Whitefield, a clergyman of the Church of England, who first held a living in Wiltshire, and afterwards one at Rockhampton, in Gloucestershire, was the great-grandfather of George Whitefield. Samuel Whitefield had five daughters—two of whom were married to clergymen— and two sons, one of whom, named after his father, succeeded to the living at Rockhampton. The other son, Andrew, described as 'a private gentleman,' had a family of fourteen children, the eldest of whom was Thomas. Thomas was established as a wine-merchant in Bristol, where he married Elizabeth Edwards, of that city; afterwards they removed to Gloucester to keep the Bell Inn, now the Bell Hotel. They had seven children—one daughter and six sons; their youngest, George, was born in the Bell Inn on December 16th, O.S. (December 27th, N.S.), 1714. Some time about Christmas, 1716, the father died, and his fair-haired little boy was left without one remembrance of him. The mother had a tender, faithful heart, commendable prudence, a great desire for the welfare of her children, and much willingness to deny herself for their sakes. George always held her in reverent affection. With the fondness of a mother for her last-born, she used to tell him that, even when he was an infant, she always expected more comfort from him than from any other of her children.

Only one event of Whitefield's early childhood is on record. When he was about four years of age he had the measles, and through the ignorance or neglect of his nurse the disease left one of his eyes—dark blue they were, and lively—with a squint, which, however, is said not to have marred the extreme sweetness of his countenance, nor diminished the charm of his glance. That defective eye obtained for him in later years among scoffers and railers the nickname of 'Dr. Squintum.'

Circumstances were not very favourable to the formation of a noble character in the boy. He says that he 'soon gave pregnant proofs of an impudent temper.' He fell into some of the worst of juvenile sins; occasionally he transgressed in a more marked way. As Augustine deceived his tutor, masters, and parents with falsehoods, so that he might get off to shows and plays, and also committed thefts from his parents' cellar and table, so Whitefield stained his childhood with lying, evil-speaking, and petty thefts, which he perpetrated on his mother by taking money out of her pocket before she was up; this he thought, at the time, was no theft at all. He also says that he spent much money 'in plays, and in the common entertainments of the age.' Playing at cards and reading romances were his 'heart's delight.' Sabbath-breaking was a common sin, and he generally behaved irreverently at public worship, when he was present. As might be expected, he was fond of playing wild, roguish tricks, such as running into the Dissenting meeting-house, and shouting the name of the learned and devoted minister—'Old Cole! old Cole! old Cole!' Being asked, one day, by one of Cole's congregation, of what business he meant to be, he replied, 'A minister; but I would take

good care never to tell stories in the pulpit like the old Cole.'
A wild, merry lad he was, with no restraint upon him, excepting a wise regulation of his mother, by which he was not
allowed to take any part in the business, although he did
sometimes sell odd quantities over the counter and wrongfully
keep the money; overflowing with animal spirits, which often
led him into mischief, in the execution of which his power of
concealment so signally failed him that he was always detected.
'It would be endless,' he says, 'to recount the sins and offences
of my younger days.' But why he should, in later years, have
classed his 'roguish tricks' with graver faults is not clear.
They may really have been worse than simple fun, or his
conscience may have become morbidly sensitive and in-
tolerant, even of play, probably the latter. But there were
other forces working in his impetuous, fiery spirit. Good
thoughts struggled with sinful ones; conscience failed not to
rebuke him for his faults, and smite him with heavy blows.
A grotesque caricature of a saint sprung out of the contention.
He would not be bad, neither would he be thoroughly good.
He compromised; he tried to blend light and darkness; he
feared God, and loved sin. Some of the money stolen from
his mother was devoted to higher ends than buying tarts and
fruits—it was given to the poor! His thefts were not confined
to raids upon his mother's pocket and till, but extended to
property outside the Bell Inn; but then he stole books—
afterwards restored fourfold—and they were books of devotion!
The Bible was not unknown to him, any more than a romance;
but it was as much the book of his curses as of his prayers.
His quick temper—he was hasty tempered to the last—sought
expression for itself in the imprecatory Psalms, as well as in
vulgar cursing. The burden of the 118th Psalm was familiar to
him; and once, when he had been teased by some persons who
took a constant pleasure in exasperating him, he immediately

retired to his room, and, kneeling down, with many tears, prayed the whole Psalm over, finding relief to his feelings in the terrible refrain of the tenth, eleventh, and twelfth verses— 'But in the name of the Lord, I will destroy them.' Church might be a place for irreverence, and the service a thing to be mocked at; yet he was always fond of being a clergyman, and frequently imitated the minister's reading prayers.

All the man can be traced in the boy—delight in the emotional and exciting, a ready power of appropriating and applying to himself and to his enemies the words of Scripture, fondness for using his elocution, and aptness of imitation. And a strange contrast, as well as resemblance, is there between the man and the boy, when they are placed side by side in St. Mary de Crypt, Gloucester. In the church where the infant was baptized and the boy often mocked, the deacon of twenty-one preached his first sermon to a crowded audience.

When he was ten years old his mother married a second time, her husband being Mr. Longden, an ironmonger of Gloucester. Whitefield says that it was 'an unhappy match as for temporals, but God overruled it for good. It set my brethren upon thinking more than otherwise they would have done, and made an uncommon impression upon my own heart in particular.'

At the age of twelve he was placed at the school of St. Mary de Crypt, 'the last grammar school,' he says, 'I ever went to;' from which we may suppose that he had tried not a few schools before. The last school changed him not a whit in his earliest characteristics. Plays still fascinated him; and, if he did not read them in school, when he was there— and it is very probable that he did—he spent whole days away from school studying them, and preparing to act them. His enthusiasm for acting spread to his schoolfellows; and the master, either because he sympathised with his scholars' tastes, or thought it useless to resist them, not only composed plays for the school, but had a theatrical entertainment for the corporation on their annual visitation, young Whitefield being, on one occasion, dressed in girls' clothes to act before them. The annual oration before these visitors was also commonly entrusted to the boy from 'the Bell'; and his good memory and fine elocution won him much notice. A lively school must St. Mary de Crypt have been while this vivacious scholar sat on its benches—the master writing plays, the boys learning them, and the worthy city aldermen seeing them acted.

Whitefield has given an opinion upon his education. He says :—

' I cannot but observe, with much concern of mind, how this training up of youth has a natural tendency to debauch the mind, to raise ill passions, and to stuff the memory with things as contrary to the gospel of Jesus Christ as light to darkness, heaven to hell. However, though the first thing I had to repent of was my education in general, yet I must always acknowledge that my particular thanks are due to my master for the great pains he took with me and his other scholars in teaching us to write and speak correctly.'

The future saint and preacher was still indicated amid all this mirth. Part of the money received for his good acting and reciting was spent upon 'Ken's Manual for Winchester Scholars,' a book which had affected him much when his brother used to read it in his mother's troubles, and which, for some time after he bought it, ' was of great use to his soul.'

Before he was fifteen he longed to be free even from the mild discipline of his last grammar school; and by pressing his mother with the sage argument that, since she could not send him to the University, and as more learning might spoil him for a tradesman, it would be best for him to halt at his present attainments, he got his own way on all points but one —he must go to school every day for a writing lesson.

Adverse circumstances soon compelled the discontinuance of
the solitary lesson, and the lad of fifteen had to take—on his
part, apparently, with some little regret, but with commendable industry—to the dress and work of a common drawer in
his mother's inn.   She who had hitherto been so jealous over
her son's associations must have been hard pressed with
poverty before consenting to such a step.   Nor was the boy
unaffected by the family misfortune.   His honour prompted
him to be of use, and to shun the greater contempt of being a
burden, by enduring the lesser shame of wearing a blue apron
and washing mops and cleaning rooms.   His religious ten-
dencies were strengthened by frequent reading of the Bible
at the close of his day's work; indeed, he would sit up to read
it.   Sometimes the care of the whole house came upon him;
but still he found time to compose two or three sermons, one
of which he dedicated to his elder brother.   The first lessons
of experience were being wrought into the heart of a quick
learner, whose waywardness was receiving its first stern rebuke.
The work of the inn made him long for school again, but his
sense of filial duty never suffered him to be idle, even in a
calling which he disliked.   The sight of the boys going to
school often cut him to the heart; and to a companion, who
frequently came entreating him to go to Oxford, his general
answer was, ' I wish I could.'

A year later his mother was obliged to leave the inn; then
a married brother, 'who had been bred up to the business,'
took it; and to him George became an assistant.   The
brothers agreed well enough.   Not so the brother-in-law and
sister-in-law.   For three weeks together George would not
speak a word to her.   He was wretched, and much to blame;
and at length, thinking that his absence would make all
things easy, and being advised so by his mother and brother,
he went to Bristol to see one of his brothers.   This, he

thinks, was God's way of 'forcing him out of the public business, and calling him from drawing wine for drunkards to
draw water out of the wells of salvation for the refreshment of
His spiritual Israel.'

At Bristol he experienced the first of those rapturous feelings with which, a few years later, his soul became absolutely
penetrated and possessed, then refined and gloriously illumi-
nated, and in which it was finally sacrificed to God his
Saviour. From the first it was no weakness of his to feel
with half his heart: 'with all thy soul and mind and strength'
was to him an easy condition of religious feeling and activity.
He now had much sensible devotion, and was filled with
'unspeakable raptures,' sometimes 'carried out beyond himself.' He longed after the sacrament ; he pondered the
'Imitation of Christ,' and delighted in it; he was all impatience to hear the church bell calling him to worship ; his
former employment dissatisfied him, and he often wrote to his
mother, telling her he would never return to it. Yet with all
his fervour his heart knew not 'the peace of God which
passeth all understanding ;' something secretly whispered,
'this will not last;' and it is not from this time that he dates
his conversion. He admits that God was in the tumult of
devotion, but not as he afterwards knew Him—the God of
peace and rest and love.

Two short months sufficed to end the spiritual fever. Probably it would have left him had he continued at Bristol, but
its decline he ascribes to his return home. Once among his
old associations his delight in churchgoing and in prayer
ceased ; the only remnant of good he retained was his resolution not to live in the inn, and no doubt his firmness on this
point was mainly due to his antipathy to his sister-in-law and
to his love for his mother, who, with true motherly affection,
welcomed him to the best she could give him—her own fare

and a bed upon the floor. His old love for play-reading revived again ; his vanity made him more careful to ' adorn his body than deck and beautify his soul'; his former school-fellows, whom he had done his share in misleading, now did theirs in misleading him.

'But God,' he says, speaking in harmony with those Cal-vinistic views which he afterwards adopted, 'whose gifts and callings are without repentance, would let nothing pluck me out of His hands, though I was continually doing despite to the Spirit of grace. He saw me with pity and compassion, when lying in my blood. He passed by me; He said unto me, " Live," and even gave me some foresight of His providing for me. One morning, as I was reading a play to my sister, said I, " Sister, God intends something for me that we know not of. As I have been diligent in business I believe many would gladly have me for an apprentice ; but every way seems to be barred up, so that I think God will provide for me some way or other that we cannot apprehend."'

The deterioration of character which must have resulted from his being without employment, and without any purposes for the future, was happily averted by an accidental visit paid to his mother by one of his former schoolfellows, now a ser-vitor at Pembroke College, Oxford. When it was incidentally mentioned in the conversation that the visitor had paid his last quarter's expenses and received a penny, Mrs. Whitefield eagerly caught at the news, and cried out, ' This will do for my son ;' and turning to George she said, ' Will you go to Oxford, George?' He replied, 'With all my heart.' Appli-cation was at once made for the help of the kind friends who had aided their visitor, and mother and son were soon rejoiced to know that interest would be used to secure George a servitor's place in Pembroke College.

His learning, such as it was, had not been kept bright

during his service in the inn, his visit to Bristol, and his idle time under his mother's roof, and so the genial schoolmaster had to be applied to again to take back his former pupil. He gladly consented, and this time the pupil, animated by the hope of gaining an honourable object, worked diligently and successfully. At first his morality and religion were not improved equally with his learning. A knot of debauched and atheistical youths—their atheism probably founded on their immorality which did not like to retain the knowledge of God— succeeded in inveigling him. His thoughts about religion grew more and more like theirs ; he reasoned that if God had given him passions, it must be to gratify them. He affected to look rakish, and when he went to public service it was only to sport and walk about. Twice or thrice he got drunk.

Then a reforming impulse came upon him, and upon infor- mation given by him to his master of the principles and practices of his companions, their proceedings were stopped. Efforts after a better life, relapses into sin, meditations upon serious books, particularly Drelincourt's 'The Christian's Defence against the Fears of Death,' dutiful service done for his mother, and, finally, a firm resolution to prepare for taking the sacrament on his seventeenth birthday, marked his moral history at school for the first twelve months.

Strange fancies now began to flit through his mind. Once he dreamed that he was to see God on Mount Sinai, and was afraid to meet Him—a circumstance which impressed him deeply ; and when he told it to a 'gentlewoman,' she said, ' George, this is a call from God.' He grew more serious, and his looks—such, he says, was his 'hypocrisy'—were more grave than the feelings behind them. The gentlewoman's words also helped to increase his impressionableness, and it is not surprising to learn that ' one night, as he was going on an errand for his mother, an unaccountable but very strong impression was made upon his heart that he should preach quickly.' It is as little surprising that his mother, upon hearing from him what had come into his mind, should have turned short upon him, crying out, 'What does the boy mean? Prithee, hold thy tongue.'

He resumed, though in a much more sober way, the religious practices of his Bristol life. A rebuke administered to him by one of his brothers, who had begun to regard his alternations from saint to sinner and sinner to saint as painfully regular, did him much good, by checking his spiritual pride and by increasing his self-distrust and watchfulness. His brother told him plainly—the Whitefields were an outspoken family—that he feared the new zeal would not last long, not through the temptations of Oxford. Perhaps his prophecy might have been fulfilled had he not spoken it.

Whitefield went to Oxford in 1732, when he was nearly eighteen years old. Some of his friends, as promised, used their influence with the master of Pembroke College; another friend lent him ten pounds upon a bond, to defray the expense of entering; while the master admitted him as a servitor immediately. Once within the college walls he was not the lad to play with his chance of success. His humble station had no thorns for his pride. To be a servitor was no new thing; perhaps he felt himself advanced by having his fellow-students to wait upon, instead of boors and drunkards. Pembroke College was far before the Bell Inn, both for reputation and society; and then, was there not before the eye of the young student the prospect of an honourable and useful station in life? Might he not, at the least, become an ordinary clergyman in his Church? Might he not pass beyond that, and attain to the dignity of a very reverend, or perhaps of a right reverend? There might be present indignity in his position, as there certainly was nothing ennobling in it, yet he would not impatiently and with silly haughtiness throw away future honour by discarding humble work. He may have been rather too destitute of that high-spiritedness which made Johnson, not many weeks before Whitefield's coming to Pembroke, throw away a pair of shoes which gentle kindness had placed at his door ; indeed, an equal division of their respective qualities of pride and humbleness between the two students might have been an advantage to both.

The young servitor lightened the burden of friends who stood as his money securities, toiled at his classics, adhered to his late religious practices at the grammar school, and thus laid a good foundation for a manly life. Law's 'Serious Call to a Devout Life,' which had already 'overmatched' Johnson and made him 'think in earnest of religion,' and his treatise on 'Christian Perfection,' were the means of stirring still more profoundly the already excited mind of Whitefield. Standing aloof from the general body of students, resisting the solicitations of many who lay in the same room with him, and who 'would have drawn him into excess of riot,' and practising daily devotions with the regularity of a monk, what wonder that he was soon thrown amongst the ' Methodists,' who were beginning their new life, and whom he had always defended, even before he came to Oxford, or knew them? If there was spiritual life in the University, how could one who had so strangely, though ofttimes so inconsistently, followed prayer, meditation, sermon-writing, almsgiving, and public worship, fail to feel its touch and answer to its call? It was inevitable that the servitor, who had come to be looked upon as a 'singular, odd fellow,' notwithstanding all his merits, should turn Methodist ; and accordingly he joined the band of devout young men some time between his nineteenth and twentieth year, after his 'soul had longed for above a twelvemonth to be acquainted with them.'

The first Methodists were John and Charles Wesley, Mr. Morgan, commoner of Christ Church, and Mr. Kirkham, of Merton College; but the nickname was fastened on the little company while John was in Lincolnshire, assisting his father, the rector of Epworth. When he returned to Oxford in 1730 he took his brother Charles's place at the head of the band, and became for ever after the chief figure of Methodism. University wits called him the 'Father of the Holy Club.' When Whitefield joined the Methodists, which was about the end of 1734 or early in 1735, they were fifteen in number, and included Mr. Benjamin Ingham, of Queen's College; Mr. T. Broughton, of Exeter; and Mr. James Hervey, of Lincoln College; and it was in this wise he joined them. Wesley and his associates were marked men. Their austerities, their devoutness, and their charitable labours among the poor, attracted general attention; and on their way to St. Mary's every week to receive the sacrament they had to pass through a crowd of ridiculing students, congregated to insult them. The sight of this shameful insolence awakened his sympathy, moved his courage, and prepared him to take up his cross. He often saw the persecution endured by the few, and never without wishing to follow their brave example. An opportunity of becoming acquainted with them offered itself. A poor woman in one of the workhouses made an unsuccessful attempt to commit suicide; and Whitefield, aware of Charles Wesley's readiness for every good work, sent a message to him by an apple woman of Pembroke, asking him to visit her. The messenger was, for some unaccountable reason, charged not to tell Wesley who had sent her. That charge she broke; and Wesley, who had often met Whitefield walking by himself, pondering the deep things of God, and was aware of his pious habits, sent him an invitation to come and breakfast with him the next morning. Whitefield gladly went, and that morning the two students formed a life-long, honourable friendship. Forty years afterwards Charles wrote of their meeting with much tenderness and warmth—

> 'Can I the memorable day forget,
> When first we by Divine appointment met?
> Where undisturbed the thoughtful student roves,
> In search of truth, through academic groves;
> A modest, pensive youth, who mused alone,
> Industrious the frequented path to shun,
> An Israelite, without disguise or art,
> I saw, I loved, and clasped him to my heart,
> A stranger as my bosom friend caressed,
> And unawares received an angel-guest.'

Charles Wesley put into the hands of his guest Professor Francke's treatise against the 'Fear of Man,' and the 'Country Parson's Advice to his Parishioners.' Whitefield then took his departure.

The most interesting part of the spiritual life of Whitefield begins at this point, up to which there has been an uncertain, varying war carried on against sin, coupled with many defeated attempts to attain to a severe form of external piety. After the period just to be opened to our view he never becomes entangled in doubts concerning the Divine method of saving sinners, and never hesitates between rival plans of practical living. He tried all the three great plans of being a Christian and of serving God which have gained favour with large sections of mankind; and finding satisfaction in the one which he ultimately adopted, he felt no temptation ever afterwards to leave it. Already, as we have seen, he has had large experience of the effects upon conscience and heart of the method which theologians call 'salvation by works;' and yet he is neither at peace with God, nor established in a godly life. He is more satisfied that he is on the right track, and his resolutions to be outwardly holy have stood a good trial; but he is still asking and seeking.

While in this state of mind Charles Wesley both helped and hindered him—helped him with his books, and hindered him by his example, which was that of an honest, anxious mind, ignorant of the salvation which comes by faith in the Son of God. The great Methodist, his 'never-to-be-forgotten' friend, as Whitefield affectionately calls him, brought him within sight of the 'fulness of the blessing of the gospel of Christ,' and then led him down a by-path, which brought him to the low levels of Quietism, where he nearly perished. Charles Wesley did not conduct him thus far, and never intended to set him in that direction; it was 'the blind leading the blind.' The pupil, as we shall presently see, was the first to become a safe teacher; he knew 'the liberty of the sons of God,' while the Wesleys were struggling in chains he had broken.

Shortly after the memorable breakfast, Charles lent him a little book entitled 'The Life of God in the Soul of Man,' by the Rev. Henry Scougal, M.A., which created no small wonder within him by teaching 'that some falsely placed religion in going to church, doing hurt to no one, being constant in the duties of the closet, and now and then reaching out their hands to give alms to their poor neighbours.' The positive teaching of the book filled him with unspeakable joy. When he read 'that true religion is a union of the soul with God, or Christ formed within us, a ray of Divine light instantaneously darted in upon his soul, and from that moment, but not till then, did he know that he must be a new creature.' The doctrine of the new birth, a birth which he had now experienced in his own soul, became one of the main themes of his preaching to the end of his life.

Charles Wesley now introduced him 'by degrees to the rest of the Methodists,' and the introduction led him to adopt the

whole of their plan of living. To live by rule was the funda-
mental principle of their theology, for as yet they knew
nothing of the mighty power of joy and peace which come
through believing upon the name of Jesus. Thus Whitefield
was led astray from the scriptural truth which had poured light
into his understanding, and gladness into his heart, and once
more tried, though this time more inflexibly and more
thoroughly, his old scheme of salvation by works. It seemed
as if, like Luther, he must know all that he could do and all
that he could not do before he could 'count all things but
loss for the excellency of the knowledge of Christ Jesus.' The
redemption of time became a primary virtue, and he hoarded
his moments as if they were years. Whether he ate, or drank,
or whatever he did, he endeavoured to do all to the glory of
God. The sacrament was received every Sunday at Christ
Church. Fasting was practised on Wednesday and Friday.
Sick persons and prisoners were visited, and poor people were
read to. An hour every day was spent in acts of charity.

His studies were soon affected by his morbid state of mind,
for such a system as he was living under allowed its faithful
disciple no room for change or diversion. Every hour
brought round a weary step of the moral treadmill, which must
be taken, or conscience would be bruised or wounded; and
Whitefield had suffered enough from conscience to feel a
quivering fear of its pains. No books would now please his
disordered taste but such as 'entered into the heart of religion
and led him directly into an experimental knowledge of Jesus
Christ and Him crucified.' How he came to write these
words, which are quoted from his journal, it would be hard to
say. When he wrote them he must have known that it was
the lack of the knowledge of Jesus which had made him a
slave.

Once fully and openly connected with the 'Holy Club,' he

had soon to share in its troubles. 'Polite students' shot
barbed words at him, mean ones withdrew their pay from him,
and brutal ones threw dirt at him.   Friends became shy.   The
master of the college rebuked him, and threatened to expel
him.   Daily contempt was poured upon him.   His tutor alone
forbore to torment him.   At first he did not accept his
reproach calmly; it shook his feeble strength.   When he
went to St. Mary's, for the first time, to receive the
sacrament publicly on a week-day — sure sign to all the
University that he had 'commenced Methodist'—'Mr. Charles
Wesley,' he says, 'whom I must always mention with the
greatest deference and respect, walked with me from the
church even to the college.   I confess to my shame I would
gladly have excused him ; and the next day, going to his
room, one of our fellows passing by, I was ashamed to be seen
to knock at his door.'   The displeasure of the master of his
college, and the master's threat to expel him if he ever visited
the poor again, surprised him, as well it might.   'Overawed,'
he says, 'by the master's authority, I spoke unadvisedly with
my lips, and said, if it displeased him, I would not.   My
conscience soon pricked me for this sinful compliance.   I
immediately repented, and visited the poor the first opportunity, and told my companions if ever I was called to a stake
for Christ's sake, I would serve my tongue as Archbishop
Cranmer served his hand, viz., make that burn first.'   His fear
of man gradually wore off, and he 'confessed the Methodists
more and more publicly every day,' walking openly with them,
and choosing rather to bear contempt with them than 'to
enjoy the applause of almost Christians for a season.'

The advantage of his trials was that they inured him to
contempt, of which he was to get a full share, and lessened
his self-love.   His inward sufferings were also of an uncommon
kind, Satan seeming to desire to sift him like wheat ; and the

reason for this, Whitefield thinks, was to prevent his future blessings from proving his ruin. All along he had an intense desire, a hungering and thirsting, after the humility of Jesus Christ. Imagining that it would be instantaneously infused into his soul, he prayed night and day to receive it. 'But as Gideon,' he says, 'taught the men of Succoth with thorns, so God—if I am yet in any measure blessed with poverty of spirit—taught it me by the exercise of true, strong temptations.' The strong temptations came in reality from his mistaken though eagerly accepted views of religion, his incessant self-inspection, his moral police regulations, his abstinence from all change in reading, and his daily persecutions, the combined influence of which brought him into a terrible condition. A horrible fearfulness and dread overwhelmed his soul. He felt 'an unusual weight and impression, attended with inward darkness,' lie upon his breast ; and the load increased until he was convinced that Satan had real possession of him, and that his body, like Job's, was given over to the power of the evil one. All power of meditating, or even thinking, was taken from him. But let him tell his own tale :—

' My memory quite failed me. My whole soul was barren and dry, and I could fancy myself to be like nothing so much as a man locked up in iron armour. Whenever I kneeled down I felt great heavings in my body, and have often prayed under the weight of them till the sweat came through me. At this time Satan used to terrify me much and threatened to punish me if I discovered his wiles. It being my duty as servitor, in my turn, to knock at the gentlemen's rooms by ten at night, to see who were in their rooms, I thought the devil would appear to me every stair I went up. And he so troubled me when I lay down to rest, that, for some weeks, I scarce slept above three hours at a time.

' God only knows how many nights I have lain upon my bed groaning under the weight I felt, and bidding Satan depart from me in the name of Jesus. Whole days and weeks have I spent in lying prostrate on the ground, and begging freedom from those proud, hellish thoughts that used to crowd in upon and distract my soul. But God made Satan drive out Satan. For these thoughts and suggestions created such a self-abhorrence within me, that I never ceased wrestling with God till He blessed me with a victory over them. Self-love, self-will, pride, and envy buffeted me in their turns, that I was resolved either to die or conquer. I wanted to see sin as it was, but feared, at the same time, lest the sight of it should terrify me to death.

'Having nobody to show me a better way, I thought to get peace and purity by outward austerities. Accordingly, by degrees, I began to leave off eating fruits and such like, and gave the money I usually spent in that way to the poor. Afterwards I always chose the worst sort of food, though my place furnished me with variety. I fasted twice a week. My apparel was mean. I thought it unbecoming a penitent to have his hair powdered. I wore woollen gloves, a patched gown, and dirty shoes, and therefore looked upon myself as very humble.'

He was exhausting what he calls 'the legal system,'— salvation by works. He felt pride creeping in, in spite of him, behind every thought, word, and action ; and he was too sincere not to admit that all his labours must prove fruitless while that remained unbroken. Here Quietism offered him its aid. Whitefield a Quietist ! As easily change a comet into a fixed star. The power was not in him to dream sweet dreams of heaven, nor to swoon away in the ecstasy of a mediæval saint, his 'soul and spirit divided asunder as by the sword of the Spirit of God.' The definitions, depths, and stages of Quietism were not what attracted him to his new system ; these were an esoteric doctrine to him. All that he wanted was some ready and satisfactory method of relieving his conscience of an intolerable burden, and of attaining to a truly religious life ; and reading one day in Castaniza's 'Spiritual Combat,' 'that he that is employed in mortifying his will is as well employed as though he were converting Indians,' he set himself rudely to the task of mortifying his will. He began as an Englishman, with a rough, unsparing hand and an honest heart. He sighed for no canonisation, he coveted no marvellous revelations. To mortify his will was all that he had to do, and how else could it be done but by mortification?

So he shut himself up in his study for five or six weeks (only attending to necessary college business), and fought his corruptions by almost incessant prayer. Extravagance was added to extravagance. The narrative of our Lord's temptation among wild beasts made him think that he ought to expose himself to the cold ; and at night, after supper, he went into Christ Church Walk, knelt under a tree, and continued in silent prayer until the great bell rang and called him to his college. Mortification next required the discontinuance of a diary which he kept, and also abstinence from the use of forms and even of audible speech in prayer, and cessation from works of mercy. Its inexorable logic next required that he should forsake all his friends, for is it not written that we are 'to leave all,' if we would follow Christ? and accordingly, instead of meeting with his beloved brethren on one of their weekly fast-days, Wednesday, he went into the fields for silent prayer. The evening meeting also was neglected, and on Thursday morning he did not make his usual appearance at Charles Wesley's breakfast-table. This made Charles call upon him to see what was the matter, and finding that it was morbid anxiety, he counselled Whitefield to seek spiritual direction from his brother John, whose skill he thoroughly trusted.

The spell of Quietism was broken ; it was not potent enough to hold such a spirit as Whitefield's long in bondage, and silence was impossible under the interrogations of a loving, anxious friend. With wonderful humility Whitefield sought the aid of John Wesley, who told him that he must resume all his external religious exercises, but not depend on them— advice which might have driven him mad, not a ray of comfort in it, not a drop of the love of God. And still the bewildered inquirer, burdened with his great sorrow which no man could remove, attended diligently upon his teacher ; and the teacher, as was natural to him, confidently undertook to guide him. As they stand here before our eye, one side of each character, unconsciously displayed by that luminous sincerity which distinguished equally both these remarkable men, comes clearly and boldly into relief. The elder, while abounding in some of the divinest gifts which can adorn humanity— readiness to forgive, patience, justice—is confident, assuming, and gratified in being above his fellows; the younger, while restless with impetuosity, impatient, quick to engage in conflict if not first to provoke it, is teachable, reverent, and generous to rivals. The thought of rivalry between them is yet unborn; the 'Father of the Holy Club' is instructing its youngest member.

Wesley meant to do Whitefield good service, and partially succeeded when he urged him to return to 'externals,' as Methodists called acts of devotion and charity. Only a few days after returning to his duty amongst the poor, Whitefield added to the one convert, James Hervey, whom he had won, two more, a prisoner and his wife, while his own soul was tormented and afflicted.

Lent soon came, and its fastings and hardships brought Whitefield's spiritual conflicts to their fiercest vigour, and then to their joyful cessation. The externals of the Methodist rule for this season were duly observed. No meat was eaten by the brethren except on the Saturday and the Sunday; but Whitefield surpassed them, and often abstained on the Saturday; and on other days, Sunday alone excepted, he lived on sage tea, without sugar, and coarse bread. In the cold mornings, the biting east wind blowing, he walked out until part of one of his hands became quite black. When Passion Week came he could scarce creep upstairs for weakness, and it then seemed to be time to send for his tutor, a kind, considerate man, who immediately took the common-sense plan of calling in a doctor.

'Salvation by works' had nearly killed him ; Quietism had nearly driven him mad. Was there not another way, which, combining the excellences of the two plans, might bring him out of darkness into God's marvellous light? Might he not render his soul into the hands of God as into 'the hands of a faithful Creator,' and still devote himself with diligence to 'every good word and work,' thus getting the repose combined with the activity which his nature in a special degree needed? Both sides of the spiritual life of man are fully recognised in Holy Scripture. 'The life of God' was undoubtedly in his soul, and would have expanded rapidly, imparting to him daily joy, had he not been told that it must grow in certain stunted forms, or it was not of God at all; and the attempt to cripple it produced an inevitable agony. No life, least of all the divine life of the soul, will quietly suffer its laws to be violated. The poor servitor was taught that truth in a way never to be forgotten. Ever afterwards he was careful to go whither the Spirit might lead him, and hence his career was free from the deformities of a forced asceticism and the vagaries of a wild spiritualism. Not that he did not sternly, sometimes almost cruelly, deny his body rest and comfort, and urge it on to work ; not that he was without 'experiences' of spiritual things so rapturous, so excited, so absorbing, that, compared with them, the feelings and devotional exercises of most saints appear tame and flat; but there was health, there was naturalness in it all. His abounding labours, his 'weariness and painfulness,' were always for the salvation of others, never for his own; his agonies of soul were like those which the apostle declared that he felt for his brethren—'a travailing in birth until Christ should be formed in their hearts.'

Left alone in his sick-room he felt again the blessedness of which he had tasted one memorable draught. What book he had been reading, or what devotional exercises he had been

engaged in when he felt himself free again, does not appear.
He simply says—

' About the end of the seventh week, after having undergone innumer-
able buffetings of Satan and many months' inexpressible trials by night and
day under the spirit of bondage, God was pleased at length to remove the
heavy load, to enable me to lay hold on His dear Son by a living faith,
and by giving me the spirit of adoption, to seal me, as I humbly hope, even
to the day of everlasting redemption.'

Then catching fire at the remembrance of what he had felt,
he exclaims in his journal—

' But oh, with what joy, joy unspeakable, even joy that was full of, and
big with, glory, was my soul filled when the weight of sin went off, and
an abiding sense of the pardoning love of God and a full assurance of
faith broke in upon my disconsolate soul! Surely it was the day of my
espousals, a day to be had in everlasting remembrance. At first my joys
were like a spring-tide, and, as it were, overflowed the banks. Go where
I would, I could not avoid singing of Psalms almost aloud; afterwards it
became more settled, and, blessed be God! saving a few casual intervals,
has abode and increased in my soul ever since.'

Justification by faith had become an experience; and he
henceforth preached what he had felt and tasted of this
truth.

Oxford had by this time become a 'sweet retirement,' and it
was with much reluctance that, on a partial recovery, he yielded
to the advice of his physician to go to Gloucester till he should
be quite restored. Oxford was associated with his better life;
Gloucester with his baser life. However, he determined either
' to make or find a friend,' a person of like mind with himself;
and as soon as he reached home he resolved, after impor-
tunate prayer, to go and see an acquaintance, evidently a
woman of literary tastes (to whom he had formerly read 'plays,
Spectators, Pope's Homer, and such-like books'), with the
intention of winning her for Christ. 'She received the word

gladly, and soon became a fool for Christ's sake,' is his record in his journal. One friend was not enough. Others, young persons, were brought under the power of this new teaching, and the Methodist Oxonian soon repeated the Oxford experiment, and gathered his converts into a society. All had the honour of being despised. Similar success was not attained at Bristol, to which he went for three weeks; his way was hindered by prejudices against himself, and only one young woman became 'obedient to the faith.'

At Gloucester friends were lost and won. Some who were expected to give him pecuniary help—he was still a servitor—turned their backs on him, and disappointed him; but others, whom he had accounted enemies, though he had never spoken to them, became generous friends. It was the time of his learning first lessons of trust in that Almighty Friend upon whose bountiful and loving care he cast himself throughout the whole of a poverty-stricken life, and to whom he committed many orphan children, the foundlings of his own loving heart. He was a philanthropist, made by the man Christ Jesus.

The good Oxford physician had hoped, by getting his patient away from the University, to divert him from a too intense application to religion. Vain hope! The patient simply pursued, in the spirit of joyous liberty, duties and engagements which had previously been an anxious burden. He cast aside all other books, and, on his bended knees, read and prayed over the Holy Scriptures. 'Light, life, and power' came upon him, stimulating him still to search; every search brought treasure; all fresh treasure caused fresh searching. Experience confirmed his faith in the doctrine of the Holy Spirit, who was to him a living Comforter, the Power of God. He seemed filled with the Spirit from the time he was born again.

Another of his characteristics was his capacity of deriving unfailing pleasure from one pursuit, his independence of the changes which most of us must have if we are to keep out of the grave and out of the asylum. He was utterly consecrated to Christ from the beginning. His change was in the unsearchableness of one Person. From the first effort he put forth to the last (and he laboured without respite for thirty-four years), he never flagged in his ardent attachment to the same truth, expressed in the same words, looked at from the same standpoint. His latest letters contain the self-same phrases as his earliest; and they are given with as much feeling as if they were quite new. They were newer every day. 'Grace'—the word that comes to him when his soul is comforted and strengthened, when sinners are converted, when marvellous deliverances are wrought out for him—was sweeter, richer, fuller, more glorious the more he contemplated it. The truth was the same, but it was inexhaustible, and its power over him immeasurable. His perpetual, never withering freshness of soul will often strike us as we follow him to the end. He was like 'a tree planted by the rivers of water, whose leaf never withered, and whatsoever he did prospered.'

CHAPTER II

1736

HIS ORDINATION AS DEACON—ESSAYS IN PREACHING

IT was time for the irregular soldier to become a captain of the Lord's host. The homes of the poor and the gaols of Oxford and Gloucester had been, along with the halls of Oxford, the finest training schools for the coming leader. What progress he had made in learning does not appear; all other considerations were lost in his supreme pleasure in religion. All learning was nothing in comparison of the knowledge of God and of His Son Jesus Christ, and in that knowledge he was well instructed; nor was he ignorant of his own heart, of its weakness and sinfulness. What natural fitness he had for speaking none could fail to perceive, when once they had heard his rich, sweet voice, and saw the artless grace of all his movements. He had not waited for a bishop's ordination and licence to preach the gospel to the poor; but a licence was ready so soon as he found 'peace with God through our Lord Jesus Christ.'

Whitefield did not lightly take on him the vows of the ministry. He was well pleased to toil among the lowest, and only at the suggestion of friends did the question of his receiving orders come into his mind. It immediately recalled to him the solemn words of St. Paul to Timothy : 'Not a novice, lest, being puffed up with pride, he fall into the condemnation of the devil.' A question which he must answer on ordination-day, 'Do you trust that you are inwardly moved by the Holy Ghost to take upon you this office and administration?' filled him with trembling. With strong crying and tears, he often said, 'Lord, I am a youth of uncircumcised lips; Lord, send me not into the vineyard yet.' He even went so far as to ask the prayers of his Oxford friends, that God would confound the prayers of his Gloucester friends to have him at once in orders; but they, as might have been expected, replied, 'Pray we the Lord of the harvest to send thee and many more labourers into His harvest.' Timidity still held its ground; he continued to pray against becoming a keeper of souls so soon.

As he had longed to be with the Methodists when he saw them insulted, but was staggered when the first experience of their daily shame came to his lot, so he was desiring 'the office of a bishop' while fearing to enter upon it. His sensitive nature was quick to feel the presence of difficulties, and frank to acknowledge them; and hence his course was fashioned, not by blindness to objections and insensibility to criticism, but by the commanding influence of 'the things of God.' Wesley said of him, that—

'In whatever concerned himself, he was pliant and flexible; in this case he was easy to be entreated, easy to be either convinced or persuaded; but he was immovable in the things of God, or wherever his conscience was concerned. None could persuade, any more than affright, him to vary in the least point from that integrity which was inseparable from his whole character, and regulated all his words and actions.'

When friends were urging him to be ordained, he was pleasing himself with the persuasion that he could not enter holy orders for two more years, because Bishop Benson had expressed his resolution not to lay hands on any one who was under twenty-three years of age. That he strongly desired to do what yet he would not do, because his judgment and his conscience were not fully convinced, is evident from the way in which his mind ran in his dreams; for though he calls the dream spoken of in the next sentence 'a notice from God,' it was undoubtedly the consequence of his state of mind about the ministry. He says—

'Long ere I had the least prospect of being called before the bishop, I dreamed one night I was talking with him in his palace, and that he gave me some gold, which seemed to sound again in my hand. Afterward this dream would often come into my mind; and, whenever I saw the bishop at church, a strong persuasion would rise in my mind that I should very shortly go to him. I always checked it, and prayed to God to preserve me from ever desiring that honour which cometh of man. One afternoon it happened that the bishop took a solitary walk—as I was afterwards told—to Lady Selwyn's, near Gloucester, who not long before had made me a present of a piece of gold. She, I found, recommended me to the bishop; and, a few days after, as I was coming from the cathedral prayers, thinking of no such thing, one of the vergers called after me, and said the bishop desired to speak with me. I—forgetful at that time of my dream—immediately turned back, considering what I had done to deserve his lordship's displeasure. When I came to the top of the palace stairs, the bishop took me by the hand, told me he was glad to see me, and bid me wait a little till he had put off his habit, and he would return to me again. This gave me the opportunity of praying to God for His assistance, and for His providence over me.

'At his coming again into the room, the bishop told me he had heard of my character, liked my behaviour at church, and inquiring my age, "Notwithstanding," says he, "I have declared I would not ordain any one under three-and-twenty, yet I shall think it my duty to ordain you whenever you come for holy orders." He then made me a present of five guineas, to buy a book, which, sounding again in my hand, put me in mind of my dream; whereupon my heart was filled with a sense of God's love.'

Whitefield determined to offer himself for ordination the next Ember days. That determination made, the next question was as to his place of labour; and here contending interests disturbed him. At Gloucester he had been useful, and his friends wished to have him with them. But when he went up to Oxford, his old friends there made out a still more urgent

case on behalf of his staying with them : John and Charles
Wesley had sailed to Savannah to act as chaplains to a new
colony there, and to attempt the conversion of the Creek
Indians ; the prisoners in the gaol needed some one to supply
their lack of service ; Whitefield had been as useful at Oxford
as at Gloucester ; Oxford was one of the schools of the prophets,
and every student converted was a parish gained.   To remove
any objection of a pecuniary nature which might have been
urged, application for money aid was made to Sir John Philips,
who was a great friend of Methodists, and who at once said that
Whitefield should have twenty pounds a year from him, even if
he did not stay at Oxford, but thirty pounds if he did.   Oxford
prevailed over Gloucester, but its triumph was not for long ; all
English-speaking people came and claimed their right in him ;
and his large, brave heart was not slow to respond.   Wesley
uttered the fine saying, 'The world is my parish ;' Whitefield,
the most nearly of any man, made the saying a simple statement of fact.

Meanwhile devout and conscientious preparation was made
for the approaching ordination, which was to be on Trinity
Sunday.   The preceding day was spent by Whitefield in
abstinence and prayer.

'In the evening,' he says, ' I retired to a hill near the town, and prayed
fervently for about two hours, in behalf of myself and those who were to
be ordained with me.   On Sunday morning I rose early, and prayed over
St. Paul's Epistle to Timothy, and more particularly over that precept,
" Let no one despise thy youth ;" and when the bishop laid his hands
upon my head, if my vile heart doth not deceive me, I offered up my
whole spirit, soul, and body to the service of God's sanctuary ; and afterwards sealed the good confession I had made before many witnesses, by
partaking of the holy sacrament of our Lord's most blessed body and blood.'

Elsewhere he says—

'This is a day ' (June 20, 1736) ' much to be remembered, O my soul!
for, about noon, I was solemnly admitted by good Bishop Benson, before

many witnesses, into holy orders, and was, blessed be God! kept composed both before and after imposition of hands. I endeavoured to behave with unaffected devotion, but not suitable enough to the greatness of the office I was to undertake. At the same time I trust I answered every question from the bottom of my heart, and heartily prayed that God might say Amen. *I hope the good of souls will be my only principle of action.* Let come what will, life or death, depth or height, I shall henceforward live like one who this day, in the presence of men and angels, took the holy sacrament, upon the profession of being inwardly moved by the Holy Ghost to take upon me that ministration in the Church. This I began with reading prayers to the prisoners in the county gaol. Whether I myself shall ever have the honour of styling myself a prisoner of the Lord, I know not; but, indeed, I can call heaven and earth to witness, that when the bishop laid his hand upon me, I gave myself up to be a martyr for Him who hung upon the cross for me.'

The words we have italicised faithfully describe the ministry to which he was this day set apart : '*I hope the good of souls will be my only principle of action.*'

Many of Whitefield's friends pressed him to preach in the afternoon after his ordination, but he could not. He had been in Gloucester a fortnight, partly with the intention of composing some sermons. He wanted 'a hundred at least,' so that he might not be altogether without ministerial resources, compelled always to go from the study to the pulpit with a newly forged weapon; but, alas! he found, like many other beginners who have attempted the same thing, that sermons cannot easily be made without the helping excitement of expected and appointed work. He had matter enough in his heart, but nothing would flow from his pen. He strove and prayed, but all to no purpose. He mentioned his case to a clergyman; but that gentleman showed his refinement of feeling and his sympathy with a young man's anxiety and fear on the threshold of public life, by telling Whitefield that he was an enthusiast. He wrote to another, and this time the response was kind, assuring him of the writer's prayers, and explaining to him why God might be dealing with him in this manner. At last he thought he found the cause of his inability explained by these words : ' We essayed to go into Bithynia, but the Spirit suffered us not ; ' and by the words spoken to Ezekiel—' Thou shalt be dumb ; but when I speak unto thee, then shalt thou speak.' This made him quite easy ; he did ' not doubt but that He who increased a little lad's loaves and fishes for the feeding of a great multitude would, from time to time, supply him with spiritual food for whatever congregation he should be called to.' The morning after his ordination, while he was praying, came these words into his mind—' Speak out.' How he used that permission, and how his one sermon grew until he had preached more than eighteen thousand times, or more than ten times a week for four-and-thirty years—considerably more, if allowance be made for illnesses and long voyages—and fed multitudes beyond computation, it will be our next duty to trace.

On the Sunday after his ordination, that is, on June 27, 1736, Whitefield preached his first sermon. It was delivered in the old familiar church to a large congregation, which had assembled out of curiosity to hear a townsman ; its subject was ' The Necessity and Benefit of Religious Society. A feeling of awe crept over him as he looked upon the crowd of faces, many of which had been familiar to him from his infancy. Former efforts in public speaking when a boy, and his labours in exhorting the poor, proved of immense service to him, removing—what has often overwhelmed bold and capable speakers on their first appearance—the sense of utter strangeness to the work ; his soul was comforted with the presence of the Almighty ; and as he proceeded, the fire kindled, fear forsook him, and he spoke with ' gospel authority.' A few mocked ; but there could be no doubt about the power of the new preacher. A complaint was soon made to the bishop that fifteen persons had been driven mad by his sermon. The bishop only replied, that he hoped the madness might not be forgotten before another Sunday. Nor is that first sermon without another touch of interest. It was not prepared, in the first instance, for St. Mary de Crypt, but for ' a small Christian society '—a fact which accounts for its being on such an unusual topic for beginners, and for the thoroughly Methodistical thoughts found at its close. Just as it had been preached to the society was it sent by its author to a neighbouring clergyman, to show him how unfit the author was to preach. He kept it a fortnight, and then sent it back with a guinea for the loan of it, saying that he had divided it into two, and preached it to his people morning and evening.

On Tuesday he preached again, and repeated his attacks on polite sinners. Before he returned to Oxford on the Wednesday, Bishop Benson added to all his past kindnesses one more—a present of five guineas, which, with a quarter's allowance now due from Sir John Philips, enabled him to pay his ordination expenses and take his bachelor's degree.

For another week he wore the servitor's habit, and then assumed the gown of a bachelor of arts. The Methodists, who had received him with great joy on his return to Oxford, installed him as their chief, and committed to his charge the religious oversight of their work, and the charity-money which they collected and used for poor prisoners. A sweet repose rests upon this part of his life. Heart and mind were at peace ; studies were pursued with satisfaction ; intercourse with religious friends was free and congenial ; private Christian duties, prayer, praise, and meditation, charmed him to his room ; work was to be done for the defence and spread of truth. Our last glimpse of him in his ' sweet retirement '

sees him poring over Matthew Henry's Commentary, and
then writing to a friend down at Gloucester—

'Herewith I have sent you seven pounds to pay for Mr. Henry's Commentary.   Dear Squire Thorold lately made me a present of ten guineas,
so that now (for ever blessed be the Divine goodness !) I can send you
more than I thought for.   In time I hope to pay the apothecary's bill.   If
I forget your favours, I shall also forget my God.   Say nothing of your
receiving this money ; only give thanks, give hearty thanks to our good
and gracious God for His infinite, unmerited mercy to me, the vilest of
the sons of men.'

A trivial circumstance called him forth from his study
before he was twenty-two years old.   The curate of the Tower
Chapel, London, who was an intimate friend, having to go
into Hampshire to officiate there for a short time, asked him
to fill his place during his absence from home.   Whitefield
complied with the request, and took coach for London on
Wednesday, August 4, 1736, with much fear and trembling.
His first sermon in the metropolis was preached on the following Sunday afternoon, August 8th, in Bishopsgate Church.
His youthful appearance as he went up the pulpit stairs
provoked, as he in his sensitive state of mind thought, a
general sneer, which, however, was exchanged for solemn
seriousness when he got into his sermon.   He again conquered himself and his congregation ; and the people, on his
coming down from the pulpit, showed him every respect, and
blessed him as he passed along.   No one could answer the
question which was now on every one's lips—' Who was the
preacher to-day ?'   Attention had been gained, and the two
short months of the London visit were quite long enough to
secure a crowded chapel at the Tower every Sunday.   Any
ordinary man might have been sure of perfect quietness in
such a place, and of returning home as unknown as when he
entered the city ; and no doubt such would have been White-

field's case but for his wonderful powers and for that blessing
from above which went whithersoever he went. The usual
wearisome time which ability and worth spend in self-culture,
in striving with self till it is well mastered, in grappling with
prejudices, and, not improbably, with positive injustice, was a
time never known to Whitefield. He came to manhood in
youth, his sun rose to its zenith at early morn. For him to
preach was at once to spread excitement, and draw together
masses of people; and when they came he never lost his
hold upon them. His manner always charmed, never
offended; whereas the utmost mental power and personal
worth of many preachers can hardly sustain the patience of
their hearers through a half-hour's sermon. His thought was
always marked by good sense; no one could be disgusted
with inanity. His emotion was always fresh, streaming from
his heart as from a perennial fountain; and, unless the hearer
could not feel, could not be touched by tenderness or awe, he
was sure to find his soul made more sensitive. The hearts of
most were melted in the intense heat of the preacher's fervour
like silver in a refiner's furnace.

During his stay at the Tower he preached and catechised
once a week, and visited the soldiers in the barracks and in
the infirmary daily; every morning and evening he read
prayers at Wapping Chapel; and on Tuesday he preached at
Ludgate prison. 'Religious friends from divers parts of the
town,' he says, 'attended the word, and several young men
came on Lord's Day morning under serious impressions, to
hear me discourse about the new birth. The chapel was
crowded on Lord's Days.'

Here a letter reached him from his old friends the Wesleys
which told all that they were doing in Georgia, and made him
long to go and join them. But difficulties stood in the way.
He had no 'outward call,' and his health was supposed to be

unequal to a sea-voyage. He strove to throw off the new thoughts and feelings, prayed that the Lord would not suffer him to be deluded, and asked counsel of his friends. His friends were not less sensible in advising than he had been in asking for advice. They, too, laid emphasis on the absence of a definite call from abroad ; they urged the need of labourers at home, and begged their friend to avoid rashness and wait further for an intimation of the will of God. Their counsel was received with all respect, and Whitefield, agreeing that it was best to do so, bánished Georgia from his mind for the present, and went on heartily with his preaching and visiting until the return of his friend from the country.

Then he went back to his delightful life at Oxford for a few weeks more, and for the last time his quiet duties were resumed. His state of mind seemed to presage the wonders of his ministry ; his heart burned with even more than its former fervour ; and other students having received a similar impulse to their spiritual life, Whitefield's room was daily the scene of such religious services as distinguished the Church immediately after the descent of the Holy Ghost at Pentecost, when little bands of devout disciples met to pray and to encourage each other in the profession of the name of Jesus Christ.

Kindness waited on him during these few weeks, as it did during the rest of his life. His power to win the hearts of rich and poor, which, as Dr. Johnson would have said, always kept his friendships in repair, had constrained the heart of a gentleman in London who, without the least solicitation, sent him money for the poor, and also as much for himself as sufficed to discharge a small debt contracted for books before he took his degree. Lady Betty Hastings, sister of the Earl of Huntingdon, also assisted both him and some of his Methodist friends, thus beginning an intimacy between him and her family which lasted as long as he lived, and grew deeper towards the end.

Things were beginning to give promise of the future ; the dim outline of his career was distinguishable. College quietness had been broken ; a first attempt at public work had been successfully made. Georgia had come before his mind, and although banished for a while it was soon to return, and the next time with an imperative message.

In November another call to preach came to him, sent upon a principle which has been extensively put in practice by a large section of clergymen in the Church of England. The early Methodist preachers, who were the true predecessors, in a spiritual line, of the later 'Evangelical School' of the Church of England, were the first to set the example, which the evangelicals have largely copied, of always seeking men of their own religious views to fill their pulpits when they had occasion to be from home. Thus it was that the Methodist clergyman of Dummer, in Hampshire, 'being likely to be chosen Dean of Corpus Christi College,' sent for the Methodist deacon of Pembroke to preach for him, while he himself went to Oxford to attend to the pending promotion. The young deacon asked, as usual, the advice of his friends, and the two exchanged places.

Trouble now arose from an unexpected quarter.. He who had felt himself to be the vilest of men could not 'brook' having intercourse with the poor, illiterate people of the future Dean of Corpus Christi ! Amidst the moral and intellectual barrenness of his new charge, Whitefield would have given all the world for one of his Oxford friends, and 'mourned for lack of them like a dove.' To overcome his unholy aversion he gave himself to prayer and to the study of a fictitious character, 'Ourania,' which William Law has sketched in his 'Serious Call to a Devout Life,' as a pattern of humility The unlovely rustics became more pleasant to his eye, and he found, what everybody finds who goes among the poor with a warm heart, that their conversation, artless, honest, and fresh, was full of instruction and stimulus ; his new friends successfully contended for his heart against the old ones. It became no unpalatable duty to go and visit them, seeing they often taught him as much in an afternoon as he could learn by a week's private study. He imbibed the spirit of the apostle, who was ready 'to become all things to all men, if by any means he might save some ;' the spirit, too, of a greater than St. Paul, whom 'the common people heard gladly.'

His friend had also set him a good example of method in his work, which he wisely followed. Public prayers were read twice a day—in the morning before the people went out to work, and in the evening after they returned ; children were also catechised daily, and the people visited from house to house. His day was divided into three parts ; eight hours for study and retirement, eight for sleep and meals, and eight for reading prayers, catechising, and visiting the parish.

During this visit he had an invitation to a profitable curacy in London, no doubt through his London labours, but it was declined. A more attractive, because a more difficult and more trying, sphere of labour, was Georgia, to which he was now called in a way earnest enough to arouse all the enthusiasm of his ardent soul, and plain enough to leave him without a doubt that God willed that he should go. A predisposition in favour of the new colony was in process of formation when, in December, news came of the return of Charles Wesley. Next there came a letter from his old friend, stating that he had come over for labourers, but adding, with reference to White-field, 'I dare not prevent God's nomination.' A few days elapsed, and a letter came from John, couched in stronger and less diffident language than Charles had used. So strange and

unexpected are the changes which come over the course of
events in life that Wesley, who was shortly to leave America
and never again visit it, could write in this urgent and confident
way : 'Only Mr. Delamotte is with me, till God shall stir up
the hearts of some of His servants, who, putting their lives in
their hands, shall come over and help us, where the harvest is
so great and the labourers so few. What if thou art the man,
Mr. Whitefield ?' Another of his letters, by presenting to
Whitefield's mind nothing but heavenly rewards, was still
better calculated to secure his co-operation. 'Do you ask
me,' he says, 'what you shall have? Food to eat and raiment
to put on, a house to lay your head in such as your Master had
not, and a crown of glory that fadeth not away.' As Whitefield read, his heart leaped within him, and echoed to the call.
The call was heaven-sent, if any call has ever been.

The United States, then a line of English colonies on the
Atlantic coast, were to share largely in Whitefield's labours,
and he as largely in their kindness and generosity ; and that
hand which was beckoning him to their shore was quietly and
effectually undoing the ties which held him to England.   Mr.
Kinchin obtained the appointment of Dean of Corpus Christi,
and could take Whitefield's place as the leader of Methodism
at Oxford. Mr. Hervey was ready to serve the cure of
Dummer. No place would suffer from Whitefield's departure,
and there seemed to be a necessity for him to help Georgia,
which was a young, increasing colony, enjoying much favour
from the home government. Besides, there were many Indians
near the colony, and Whitefield felt the stirrings of a missionary spirit. The decision was given in favour of Georgia,
and in a way that made alteration almost out of the question.
Neither Oxford friends nor Gloucester relations were this time
consulted, but a firm, personal resolution was made which
nothing was to be allowed to assail. Relations were informed

of his intentions ; but told that he would not so much as come
to bid them farewell, unless they promised not to dissuade
him ; for he said that he knew his own weakness.

However, his weakness so far gained upon him as to send
him down to Gloucester on New Year's Day, 1736–37, after he
had said goodbye to his friends at Oxford; and his strength
had so much increased that he succeeded in abiding by his
purpose.   Bishop Benson welcomed him as a father, approved
of his design, wished him success, and said, ' I do not doubt
that God will bless you, and that you will do much good
abroad.'   But his ' own relations at first were not so passive.
His mother wept sore,' which was both to his credit and hers.
Others tempted him with base words, which must have
buttressed his citadel instead of undermining it ; they ' urged
what pretty preferments he might have if he would stay at
home.'   He showed no wavering, and the opposition ceased.

This farewell visit was marked by that constant industry
which distinguished him to the last.   He preached often
enough ' to grow a little popular,' and to gather large congregations, which were moved by the word of God.   In three
weeks he went to Bristol to take leave of his friends there, and
again he preached, undertaking duty this time in an unexpected
way.   It being his custom, go where he might, to attend the
daily services of the Church, he went to St. John's to hear a
sermon.   When prayers were over, and the psalm was being
sung, the minister came to him and asked him to preach.
' Having his notes about him, he complied.'   The next day
the same thing was repeated at St. Stephen's, but this time the
' alarm ' excited by his preaching was so widespread, that, on
the following Sunday, crowds of people, of all denominations,
' Quakers, Baptists, Presbyterians, &c.,' flocked to the churches
where he had to officiate, and many were unable to find
admission.   The civic authorities paid him respect, the mayor

appointing him to preach before himself and the corporation. 'For some time following he preached all the lectures on week-days, and twice on Sundays, besides visiting the religious societies.' As always, so now, he preached with power and with the Holy Ghost; and the new doctrines—new as compared with the prevalent teachings of the times—of justification by faith and the new birth, 'made their way like lightning into the hearers' consciences.' It is touching to mark the holy jealousy with which, amid the city's excitement and eagerness to hear him, he entreated a friend, 'Oh! pray, dear Mr. H——, that God would always keep me humble, and fully convinced that I am nothing without Him, and that all the good which is done upon earth, God doth it Himself.'

CHAPTER III

March, 1737—March, 1738

APPOINTED CHAPLAIN TO THE GEORGIAN COLONY — EARLY
POPULARITY—FIRST VOYAGE

GEORGIA, the last colony founded in America by England,
was named in honour of George II., and held a charter
dated June 9, 1732. It was an outpost, to keep in check the
Spaniards and the French. Its first settlers were poor English,
debtors out of gaols and dwellers in London 'slums,' Jews,
and convicts from Jamaica. Then came English, Scotch,
and Moravians—a company of a higher type; there were
also Saltzburgers from Germany, driven from their homes
by Roman Catholic cruelty to a colony where Catholics
were not permitted to come. The government was in
the hands of twenty-one Trustees, many of whom
were Presbyterians. General Oglethorpe, the romantic and
active philanthropist, was the first governor of this semi-
political, semi-philanthropical settlement. Ardent spirits were
prohibited, and no one might hold slaves. 'The Trustees
refused to make a law permitting such a horrid crime as
slavery,' says the Governor. Close to the white men were
25,000 Creek Indians, whose rights were respected and their
goodwill conciliated. The Trustees honestly aimed at con-
stituting a colony morally sound and useful.

To keep the sanctions of religion before the minds of the settlers, a chaplain, by name Bosomworth, was sent out with the first company ; but unfortunately he was a hypocrite, and, taking to himself a native woman as wife, through her he raised an armed opposition among the Indians, and unsuccessfully sought to destroy the whites. The moral condition of the colony, not over good to begin with, rapidly deteriorated, and a native chief, when urged to embrace Christianity, refused, saying : 'Why, these are Christians at Savannah ! these are Christians at Frederica ! Christian much drunk !' ('Christian' had smuggled drink in). 'Christian beat men ! Christian tell lies ! Devil Christian ! Me no Christian !' To this strange mixture of men and women came John and Charles Wesley on February 5, 1736. With the best of intentions they both signally failed—John at Savannah, Charles at Frederica. Neither of them knew the liberty which is in Christ Jesus, and that same pitiless legalism, or 'methodism,' which they applied to themselves, they strove to enforce on the colonists, with the result that they were hated, abused, resisted, and persecuted. John says that after having preached there, not as he ought, but as he was able, one year and nine months, he shook off the dust of his feet and left Georgia. Charles had been glad to sail again even sooner than John. Thus the colony was without a chaplain, and the experience of the Trustees might have made them decide to meddle no more with spiritual guides.

Yet ' James Oglethorpe, Esq., and the Honourable Trustees' received the young preacher, George Whitefield, with kindness, when he appeared before them early in March, 1737, desiring an appointment in their colony of Georgia. The Archbishop of Canterbury and the Bishop of London both approved of Whitefield's design; the former prelate, however, expressing himself in these ungracious words : 'I shall take

particular notice of such as go to Georgia, if they do not go
out of any sinister view.'   On which Whitefield remarks :
'This put me upon inquiry what were my motives in going;
and, after the strictest examination, my conscience answered—
Not to please any man living upon earth, nor out of any
sinister view; but simply to comply with what I believe to
be Thy will, O God, and to promote Thy glory, Thou great
Shepherd and Bishop of souls.'

It was not an easy thing to sail to a distant land a hundred
and sixty years ago. A prolonged stay, enforced by the slow
despatch of business, or by the absence of favourable winds,
often gave the traveller more than one opportunity of saying
farewell to his friends ; and, even when embarkation fairly
took place, it was no guarantee that he was finally gone.   A
calm might land him at any port on the British shores, and
from thence he was sure to communicate with his friends.
Thus it happened that Whitefield, after his appointment, continued three weeks in London, waiting for Mr. Oglethorpe,
who was expecting to sail every day ; and then, at last, quietly
betook himself to Stonehouse, in Gloucestershire, to supply the
place of a clerical friend, who went to London on business.
Of course the time spent in the metropolis was devoted to
preaching, and Stonehouse was to prove a happier Dummer.
His meetings in private houses and the public services
in the church were both attended by overflowing congregations.   It was a time of much spiritual gladness with him.

'I found,' he says, 'uncommon manifestations granted me from above.
Early in the morning, at noonday, evening, and midnight, nay, all the day
long, did the blessed Jesus visit and refresh my heart.   Could the trees of
a certain wood near Stonehouse speak, they would tell what sweet communion I and some dear souls enjoyed with the ever-blessed God there.
Sometimes, as I have been walking, my soul would make such sallies
that I thought it would go out of the body.   At other times I would be so
overpowered with a sense of God's infinite majesty, that I would be con-

strained to throw myself prostrate on the ground, and offer my soul as a blank in His hands, to write on it what He pleased. One night was a time never to be forgotten. It happened to lighten exceedingly. I had been expounding to many people, and some being afraid to go home, I thought it my duty to accompany them, and improve the occasion, to stir them up to prepare for the second coming of the Son of man; but oh! what did my soul feel? On my return to the parsonage-house, whilst others were rising from their beds, and frightened almost to death, to see the lightning run upon the ground, and shine from one part of the heaven to another, I and another, a poor but pious countryman, were in the field praising, praying to, and exulting, in our God, and longing for that time when Jesus shall be revealed from heaven in a flame of fire! O that my soul may be in a like frame when He shall actually come to call me!'

The gentleness and sweetness of spring also had their attractions for him; it was early in May, and the country, he says, 'looked to me like a second paradise, the pleasantest place I ever was in through all my life.' The thought of leaving Stonehouse people, with whom he 'agreed better and better,' touched his affectionate heart not a little, and he wrote to a friend: 'I believe we shall part weeping.' There had been but a month's short intercourse with them, and they were the flock of another pastor; but it was Whitefield's way to love people and to labour for them as if he had known them a lifetime, never jealous of any one, nor dreaming that any one could be jealous of him; and when he took his leave on Ascension Day, 'the sighs and tears,' he says, 'almost broke my heart.'

The guest whom Stonehouse was sorry to part with, Bristol was glad to receive; indeed the people there, gratefully remembering Whitefield's visit to them in February, insisted upon his coming to see them again. The account of their enthusiastic reception of him reads more like an extract from the journal of a conquering general, or from that of a prince on a progress through his provinces, than that of a young clergyman, twenty-two years old. Multitudes on foot and many in coaches met him a mile outside the city gates; and as he passed along the streets in the midst of his friends, almost every one saluted and blessed him. The general joy was deepened when, to his own regret, Mr. Oglethorpe sent him word that their departure for America would be delayed two months longer. Bristol was completely under the spell of its visitor, or rather of him and the doctrines he preached. The rich forsook their comforts and pleasures, to jostle and push among the crowd which five times every week besieged the church where Whitefield was to preach. The quiet Quaker left the unimpassioned talk of his meeting-house to feel the thrill of oratory. The uncompromising Nonconformist left his chapel for the church, where he had too often failed to find the heart-searching preaching which alone could satisfy his wants, but where he was now pierced as with arrows, and healed as with the balm of Gilead. The idle worldling, who seldom made an effort to be interested in anything, shook off his supineness at least to go and hear what the stranger had to say. The vicious and depraved strove for a place where they might hear the love of God toward sinners, the greatness and preciousness of the work of His Son Jesus, and the mighty help of the Holy Ghost in the hearts of all who would live a holy life, spoken of with a tenderness and an earnestness befitting themes so dear to them in their abject condition. The broken-hearted rejoiced in the sympathetic feeling of a teacher who knew all their sorrow. The mixed mass of hearers filled the pews, choked the aisles, swarmed into every nook and corner, hung upon the rails of the organ-loft, climbed upon the leads of the church. As many had to turn away disappointed as had gained admission. And the preacher's words were more than a pleasant sound, much enjoyed while it lasted, and soon forgotten when it ceased ; they struck into heart and conscience, turning the wicked man from his wickedness, that he might save his soul alive, and awakening the generous emotions of all.

Whitefield began with his congregations as he continued and ended with them. He made a practical, benevolent use of them ; for he felt that our profession of love to God is but a mockery, unless it be connected with love to one another, and 'love which is not in word, but in deed and in truth.' He did not preach to please his hearers, and they must not come to be pleased. They must come to know their duty, as well as their privilege in the Gospel ; and so, twice or thrice every week, he appealed to them on behalf of the prisoners in Newgate, and made collections. Howard had not yet begun his holy work in our gaols; but the temporal and spiritual wants of prisoners never failed to move the sympathy of Whitefield and the early Methodists. The first band of Methodists had a special fund for the prisoners in Oxford gaol, and when Whitefield left the University he had the disposing of it and the chief charge of the prisoners. In London and in Gloucester he was a regular visitor at Newgate ; and in Bristol he pursued the same charitable plan. The author of the 'Life and Adventures of Oliver Goldsmith' imagines that Dr. Primrose was the character which suggested prison philanthropy ; but Goldsmith much more likely got the suggestion from the Methodists, who had been already at work in prisons some thirty years. Joseph Alleine, an intimate friend of Wesley's grandfather, preached to prisoners a hundred years before the 'Vicar of Wakefield' was written.

The same comprehensive charity was displayed towards the poor of Georgia, whose faces Whitefield had not yet seen. During his stay at Bristol he paid a visit to Bath, where his preaching produced as deep an impression as in the sister city, and where some rich ladies gave him more than a hundred and sixty pounds for the poor of his future flock.

If parting from the simple peasants of Stonehouse was hard,

it could not be easy to tear himself away from Bristol, which
offered him both ample means and affectionate regard, if he
would continue to minister in its churches.   For the money he
cared nothing ; for love he cared everything.

' June 21st,' he says, ' I took my last farewell of Bristol.   But when I
came to tell them it might be that they would " see my face no more,"
high and low, young and old burst into such a flood of tears as I have
never seen before ; drops fell from their eyes like rain, or rather gushed out
like water.   Multitudes, after sermon, followed me home weeping ; and
the next day I was employed from seven in the morning till midnight, in
talking and giving spiritual advice to awakened souls.'

As he had heard that a great company intended to see him
out of town he departed early in the morning for Gloucester,
then he went to Oxford, and forward to London.   Thus he
had two or three leave-takings at various places.

This popularity inevitably brought trouble.   His doctrine
was not approved of by all ;. and thus, under the pressure of
aspersions from enemies and entreaties from friends, he was
induced to publish his sermon on ' Regeneration.'   It contains
a statement of the ordinary evangelical views upon that
subject, given in very ordinary language ; only two sentences
would be likely to catch the eye of any one who might read the
sermon with a previous understanding of the preacher's views.
Once he makes a side-hit at metaphorical interpreters : ' It will
be well if they do not interpret themselves out of their salvation.'   In another sentence he states a view which he and his
contemporary Methodist friends—to their honour be it said—
always carried into practice, as well as urged in their preaching ; he says : ' The sum of the matter is this : Christianity
includes morality, as grace does reason.'   Elsewhere he defines
true religion in these strikingly noble words : ' A universal
morality founded upon the love of God and faith in the Lord
Jesus Christ.'   ' The only Methodism,' he exclaims, ' I desire

to know is a holy method of dying to ourselves, and of living to God.'

The prophets themselves, to whom, in ancient time, was committed, among other exalted duties, the task of guarding the morality of the Hebrew nation, of protesting against every use of the ceremonial law and of the temple service which would degrade religion into a superstition, and the apostles, who never failed to link the plainest and humblest of duties with the loftiest doctrines they taught, were not more jealous that religion and morality should not be divorced from each other, than were Whitefield and the Wesleys. The ground of the moderns was taken up clearly and boldly by Whitefield in his sermon just referred to, and throughout his whole life was never for a moment forsaken. The great strength of the new movement lay, not in the advocacy of any peculiar doctrine, but in the union of doctrine and precept, of privilege and responsibility. It was a true expression of the apostle's argument to the Church at Rome—the doctrine of grace united with purity of life. So far from its resting alone or principally upon a particular doctrine, Whitefield and Wesley were divided upon doctrine, the one holding with Arminius, the other with Calvin; yet their work, even after the rupture between them, was not hindered or destroyed, but carried forward with as much vigour and as much to the profit of mankind as ever. Some would have morality without religion, but these men proclaimed everywhere that religion is the root of morality; that every man needs the renewing power of the Spirit of God in his heart; and that the 'fruit of the Spirit is love, joy, peace, long-suffering, gentleness, goodness, faith, meekness, temperance.'

Whether friends and enemies did Whitefield a service by forcing him to publish, has been much questioned; indeed, nearly every one has condemned the step. Franklin thought that he did himself an abiding injustice, because his power lay

not in the pen, but in the tongue ; and that it would have been
better for his reputation had he allowed only the reports of his
genius and of his triumphs to be kept as his memorial for
succeeding generations.   As to the sermons, perhaps Franklin
was right; but Whitefield would have been no more than an
idle name had we been without some of his writings, without
his journal, pamphlets, and some of his letters.   With him it
was no consideration what might be thought of his powers.
During his life he never gave a moment to recollect whether he
had any literary reputation or not ; and least of all did he
hunger after posthumous fame.   He published in the first
instance, because he wanted to clear himself of aspersions, and
his friends wished to have his sermons ; and in the second
instance, because he found that his sermons were often as useful
when read as when heard.   Many weeping eyes, in England, in.
Scotland, in America, in the hut of the emigrant, in the cottage
of the peasant, in the hall of the nobleman, once eagerly
searched for consolation and hope, and found them in those
pages which few now care to read, excepting curious orators, who
want to find out the secret of Whitefield's power.   The two old
volumes have a touching interest when their history is remembered.   They speak of broken-hearted penitents and of
rejoicing believers ; and this alone suffices to lend them an air
of sanctity.   But they are not without passion and directness.
Intellectual they are not ; their feebleness becomes their
wonder.   It would be a profound satisfaction to the humble
spirit of their author to know that men regard them as 'weak
things'; for, remembering how they once prevailed over irre-
ligion and vice, and over cultivated, thoughtful minds, he
would simply say, 'Then hath God chosen the weak things
of the world to confound the mighty.'   And God still uses
them unto salvation.

The sermons which had aroused Bristol and Bath were next

preached in London, whither Whitefield went about the end of
August. If his life in Bristol had been busy and excited
enough, what shall be said of the 'torrent of popularity and
contempt,' as he calls it, that swept through the metropolis?
His intention was to remain in perfect retirement and devote
himself, until the time of his departure for Georgia, to his much-
loved employment of reading and praying over the word of
God upon his knees; but his soul had not long tasted the
sweetness of this repose when invitations to preach poured in
amain. The stewards and members of the religious societies
(societies which did religious, moral, and social work) were
remarkably fond of hearing him, and for a good reason—he
attracted large congregations, and got large collections.
Friendly clergymen—only too soon to forget their admiration—
wanted help in their services, and sought it from this willing
worker. The churches could not hold the people; thousands
went away for want of room. Then the churchwardens and
managers of the charity schools, perceiving the effect of his
preaching, that is to say, its money-effect, thought that they
must have a share of the harvest, and began to plead with him
for the benefit of the children. For three months the stream
of people flowed steadily towards any church in which he
might be ministering; and sometimes constables had to be
placed both inside and outside the building, to preserve order.
Nine times a week did Whitefield engage in his delightful work
of preaching. On Sunday morning it was his habit to rise very
early, and during the day to walk many miles between the
various churches at which he was expected. These early
sacraments, which called him out before daybreak, 'were,' he
says, 'very awful. At Cripplegate, St. Anne's, and Foster Lane,
O how often have we seen Jesus Christ crucified, and evidently set forth before us! On Sunday mornings, long before
day, you might see streets filled with people going to church,

with their lanthorns in their hands, and hear them conversing
about the things of God.' The ordinary congregations, too,
which were not composed of such persons as these devout
communicants, but of all kinds, heard the word 'like people
hearing for eternity.'

Such popularity quite disturbed the usual order of things.
On sacramental occasions fresh elements had sometimes to be
consecrated twice or thrice. The stewards had larger offerings
than they could conveniently carry to the table, their collection boxes or bags not having been made for such an exceptional time. A newsagent, who heard of what was doing in
the religious world, thought that he was as much entitled to
turn an honest penny as the stewards; and one Monday
morning, when Whitefield was quietly taking breakfast with a
friend at the Tower, his eye caught sight in the newspaper of a
paragraph to the effect, that there was a young gentleman going
volunteer to Georgia; that he had preached at St. Swithin's,
and collected eight pounds, instead of ten shillings—three
pounds of which was in halfpence (which was all quite true);
and that he was to preach next Wednesday before the societies
at their general quarterly meeting. The paragraph chagrined
Whitefield very much. He was not yet inured to the annoyances of public life, and he requested the printer not to put
him in his paper again; but his only comfort was the printer's
saucy answer, 'that he was paid for doing it, and that he would
not lose two shillings for anybody,' and a full church—Bow
Church it was—on the following Wednesday.

As popularity and usefulness increased, opposition increased
proportionately. The ground which it took was extraordinary,
it being actually urged that these crowds which followed
Whitefield interfered with the attendance at church of regular
parishioners; further, that the pews were spoiled; next, that
he was a spiritual pickpocket; and finally, that he made use

of a charm to get the people's money—which was perfectly true. And the clergy—some of them, at least—who had listened and admired, grew angry and spiteful. The charmer, it was rumoured, would be silenced by the bishop, upon the complaint of the clergy; the pickpocket would be hindered from plying his thievish arts.

But Whitefield was not a man to tremble under a threat, or grow pale at a rumour. He had a native pugnacity, not yet humbled and subdued; and quickly did he show his enemies that he could fight as well as preach and pray, and that silencing him would be a difficult thing. He at once waited upon the bishop, and asked whether any complaint had been lodged against him; the bishop answered that there was none. He asked his lordship whether any objection could be made to his doctrine, and the bishop replied, 'No; for I know a clergyman who has heard you preach a plain scriptural sermon.' Whitefield then asked his lordship whether he would grant him a licence, and the answer was, 'You need none, since you are going to Georgia.' 'Then,' said Whitefield, 'you would not forbid me?' The bishop gave a satisfactory answer, and Whitefield took his leave.

Whitefield, too prone at this time to judge others, had, in part, broken with his profession. Some of them he had censured; and they had replied by shutting their churches against him. Others attempted to crush him by means of pamphlets. He was denounced for fraternising with Dissenters; one clergyman called him 'a pragmatical rascal,' and 'vehemently inveighed against him and the whole body of Dissenters together.' His intimacy with Dissenters, it is true, was great, and lasted throughout the whole of his life. The grounds of it were honourable to both parties concerned. The piety and zeal of the preacher drew the pious of other denominations to hear him; and in their houses, to which they kindly invited him, and he as kindly went, they assured him, 'that if the doctrine of the new birth and justification by faith were powerfully preached in the Church, there would be but few Dissenters in England.' Whitefield found their conversation 'savoury,' and thinking that his practice of visiting and associating with them was agreeable to Scripture, he judged that 'the best way to bring them over was not by bigotry and railing, but moderation and love, and undissembled holiness of life.'

The end of these London labours, which were only part of an interlude, came at Christmas, 1737. Anxious to get to his Georgian charge, and an opportunity offering by a transport ship, which was about to sail with a number of soldiers, he determined at once to start. His purpose wounded the hearts of thousands; prayers were offered for him; the people would embrace him in the church; wistful looks would follow him as he went home. A solemn, weeping communion celebrated the final parting.

He left the charity schools one thousand pounds richer by his labours, and he carried more than three hundred pounds with him for the poor of Georgia. He ever, from the first voyage to the thirteenth, crossed the Atlantic guarded by the prayers of thousands, and freighted with their benevolent gifts.

On December 28th Whitefield left London, and on the 30th went on board the *Whitaker* at Purfleet. His labours now were divided between the ship and the shore, the former containing the companions of his voyage, the latter having the presence of friends, who followed him from point to point, till he got out to sea, and who were always ready to engage him in some religious duties. Great kindness and prudence marked his conduct among the men of the ship from the first day he went on board. He attended them in sickness, taught them, and catechised them. To the officers, both naval and military, he showed marked deference, and allowed not his zeal to carry

him into any unwise attempts to force religion upon their attention. He was as attentive to teach a few soldiers or a few
women the catechism as he had been zealous for the crowds of
London. At night he would walk on the deck that he might
have an opportunity of speaking quietly to some officers whom
he wanted to gain over to the service of God, or go down into
the steerage where the sailors were congregated, that he might
be as one of them. He soon became a favourite. The captain
of the ship gave him the free use of his cabin, the military
captain was friendly, and so were the rest of the officers. At
length, prayers were read daily in the great cabin ; and, at the
request of the captain, Whitefield preached to the 'gentlemen.'
Until they left Deal on January 30th, he also regularly preached
on shore in a house, and the congregations became so large
that the preaching room had to be propped up. It seems that
'running' and buying 'run goods' was a 'sin that did most
easily beset the Deal people' of that day ; and though Whitefield took care to show them 'the absolute unlawfulness' of
their deeds, yet they still waited on his word.

The same morning that he sailed from Deal, John Wesley
arrived there from Georgia. On reaching shore, Wesley learned
that his friend was in a vessel in the offing, bound for Georgia.
From some cause or other, Wesley deemed it necessary to take
some steps to know whether Whitefield ought to continue his
voyage. His method of deciding the difficulty was by sortilege,
a practice which he long continued, but one which Whitefield
never followed. He even resorted to it in the dispute between
himself and Whitefield on the subjects of election and free-
grace. In a letter addressed to Wesley, in reply to Wesley's
sermon on free-grace, Whitefield said about the Deal lot—

'The morning I sailed from Deal to Gibraltar you arrived from Georgia.
Instead of giving me an opportunity to converse with you, though the ship
was not far off the shore, you drew a lot, and immediately set forwards to

London.   You left a letter behind you, in which were words to this effect :
" When I saw God, by the wind which was carrying you out brought me
in, I asked counsel of God.   His answer you have inclosed."   This was a
piece of paper, in which were written these words : " Let him return to
London."

'When I received this, I was somewhat surprised.   Here was a good
man telling me he had cast a lot, and that God would have me return to
London.   On the other hand, I knew that my call was to Georgia, and that
I had taken leave of London, and could not justly go from the soldiers who
were committed to my charge.   I betook myself with a friend to prayer.
That passage in the First Book of Kings, chapter xiii., was powerfully
impressed upon my soul, where we are told, " That the prophet was slain
by a lion, that was tempted to go back (contrary to God's express order)
upon another prophet's telling him God would have him do so."   I wrote
you word that I could not return to London.   We sailed immediately.
Some months after I received a letter from you at Georgia, wherein you
wrote words to this effect : " Though God never before gave me a wrong
lot, yet, perhaps, He suffered me to have such a lot at that time, to try
what was in your heart."   I should never have published this private
transaction to the world did not the glory of God call me to it.'

It was well, for the sake of every one, and for the sake of
religion, that Whitefield was not so superstitious as his friend,
and that he was not turned from a sober purpose by a ridiculous
chance.   His return to London would have demanded public
explanation, and what could he have said but this : 'John
Wesley drew a lot, on which were these words : "Let him
return to London;" and so I am here?'   Then all the
sensible part of his congregation would either have lost confidence in him, or have become as foolish as himself; and
enemies, who were rapidly multiplying, would have assailed
him with irresistible force.   All his prayers, resolutions, tears,
and ponderings, would have been covered with shame and
confusion, and he could never have become a leader, since
men will follow only the decided and consistent.   Wesley himself, notwithstanding his blind faith in lots, would not have
been turned from his purpose by a dozen of them drawn by a
friend, had he been so far and so openly committed as was

Whitefield. One short answer would have cut through the difficulty—' My friend may draw lots for himself, but not for me ; at this rate everybody will be trying to divine my duty, and the contradictory answers will leave me in hopeless embarrassment.'

So few are the references, in Whitefield's journal or letters, to the manners of the people among whom he stayed, or to the scenery through which he passed in his travels, that it is a pleasure to extract any that he made, as a proof that his was not a dull soul without delight in nature, without responsiveness to the soft sweetness of a southern sky, or to the wildness and majesty of a storm. The following account of his feelings as he approached Gibraltar is given in his first journal :—

'Saturday, February 18th.—Though the weather was exceedingly pleasant all the day, yet it grew more and more pleasant in the evening, and our ship sailed at the rate of nine miles an hour, and as steady as though we were sitting on shore. The night was exceedingly clear, and the moon and stars appeared in their greatest lustre ; so that, not having patience to stay below, I went upon deck with friend H—— and praised God for His wonderful lovingkindness in singing Psalms, and gave thanks for the blessings, and asked pardon for the offences, of the week, and then had a long intercession.

' It is worth coming from England to see what we have beheld this day.

' Sunday, February 19th.—Slept better to-night than I have a long while ; blessed be the Keeper of Israel ! Read prayers in the great cabin ; was enlarged in expounding both the lessons to the soldiers ; and had prayers, and preached one of the sermons God enabled me to make since I came on board, on open deck in the afternoon. All the gentlemen attended ; benches were laid for the people ; and the ship sailed smoothly, and the weather was finer than I can express, so that I know not where I have performed the service more comfortably. And, indeed, I have been so delighted these two days with our pleasant sailing and the promontories all around us, that I could not avoid thanking God for calling me abroad, and stirring up all to praise Him, " who by His strength setteth fast the mountains, and is girded about with power." '

On February 20th the *Whitaker* reached Gibraltar. Whitefield thought it was 'the world in epitome' ; he might have

added, the Church too ; for Dissenters and Churchmen, ' New
Lights' and ' Dark Lanthorns,' Jews and Roman Catholics,
were on the rock. The 'New Lights' were an interesting
company of soldiers, gathered into a society by a sergeant, who
for twelve years had been their leader. Their meetings were
first held in 'dens and mountains and caves of the rocks,' but
afterwards, on applying for leave to build a little sanctuary of
their own, the minister of the church and the governor wisely
and generously gave them the free use of the church.

A few days sufficed to make Whitefield as popular with the
soldiers as he had been with the sailors, with the townspeople
as he was with the garrison. Officers and soldiers crowded the
church when he preached ; and at the governor's table, where
he had dreaded being treated with more than sober hospitality,
'all the officers behaved with such a decent, innocent manner'
that they pleased him very much. They were studious to
oblige him, and solicitous for him to stay ; but his face was set
to go to Georgia. Many of the inhabitants pressed him to
stay with them, and for his sake treated the friends who
journeyed with him with marked kindness.

None of this popularity was won at the expense of fidelity.
While all were crowding to hear him, he eagerly embraced the
opportunity of reproving them for the sin of drunkenness, the
sin of the place, and for profane swearing. His presence and
labours created so much excitement that even the chief of the
Jews came to hear him on the latter subject. Not knowing
this, Whitefield next day attended the synagogue, and was
astonished when the presiding elder came to him and conducted him to a chief seat, as a mark of honour for his having
preached so well, according to Jewish ideas, against the sin of
profaning the Divine name. The Roman Catholic Church
was also visited ; but everything there was contrary to the
simplicity which the plain Methodist loved.

The stay at Gibraltar lasted thirteen days, and on the last day of it many came to Whitefield, weeping, to tell him what God had done for their souls, to ask for his prayers, and to promise him theirs in return. Others sent him presents of cake, wine, figs, eggs, and other necessaries for his voyage. Two hundred soldiers, women, officers, and others stood on the beach to see him go on board, and wish him 'good luck in the name of the Lord.'

The results of his work he thus summed up: 'Many that were quite stark blind have received their sight; many that had fallen back have repented and turned unto the Lord again; many that were ashamed to own Christ openly have waxen bold; and many that were saints have had their hearts filled with joy unspeakable and full of glory.' His labours on the ship also reformed the swearing captain and many of the soldiers.

In the next portion of the voyage fever broke out on the ship, and carried off two of the worst men on board; Whitefield was struck down for several days. To a friend he writes:—

'How goes time? I can scarce tell; for I have been some time past, as one would think, launching into eternity. God has been pleased to visit me with a violent fever, which He, notwithstanding, so sweetened by Divine consolations, that I was enabled to rejoice and sing in the midst of it. Indeed, I had many violent conflicts with the powers of darkness, who did all they could to disturb and distract me; and though I was once reduced to the last extremity, and all supernatural assistance seemed to be suspended for awhile, and Satan, as it were, had dominion over me, yet God suffered not my faith to fail, but came in at length to my aid, rebuked the tempter, and from that moment I grew better. Surely God is preparing me for something extraordinary; for He has now sent me such extraordinary conflicts and comforts as I never before experienced. I was, as I thought, on the brink of eternity. I had heaven within me; I thought of nothing in this world; I earnestly desired to be dissolved and go to Christ; but God was pleased to order it otherwise, and I am resigned, though I can scarce be reconciled to come back again into this vale of misery. . . . I would write more, but my strength faileth me. We hope to be at Savannah on Monday.'

Whitefield's farewell sermon to the soldiers was preached on May 6th, and caused much weeping. On the evening of the following day he reached Savannah, where he was welcomed by Mr. Delamotte, the friend whom Wesley left behind him, and some other 'pious souls,' who were rejoiced at his arrival, and joined him in thanksgiving and prayer.

CHAPTER IV

1738

ROUGH EXPERIENCES IN GEORGIA—SECOND VOYAGE

WHITEFIELD, on his arrival at Savannah, knew nothing of the circumstances under which his friend Wesley had left it. The whole story was related to him, and he wisely determined to act as if nothing of an unhappy kind had occurred; he would not even make any record of it in his journal. Full of loving anxiety to do his work well, and heartily believing that the gospel he preached could promote peace and harmony, he never gave a thought to the unhappy past, in which his friends had, though not without provocation, received harsh treatment, but began early and zealously to preach and to teach. At five o'clock on the morning after his arrival he read public prayers, and expounded the second lesson to a congregation of seventeen adults and twenty-five children. Such was the exchange for crowded churches in England !

In the afternoon of the same day, Mr. Causton, Wesley's keen enemy, sent word that he and the magistrates would wait upon Whitefield, but Whitefield chose to wait upon them, a courtesy which could hardly fail to prepare the way for kindly intercourse. The interview was marked by much 'civility' shown to the new chaplain; and the principal part of the conversation was upon the place of his settlement. The magistrates were as diplomatic as civil; for it was resolved that the place should be Frederica, where a house and tabernacle were to be built for him—then they themselves would not run the risk of any trouble with him—but that he 'should serve at Savannah, when, and as long as he pleased.' Thus they avoided raising a contention with him, by not arbitrarily sending him away from the principal place. They had evidently learned the secret of conceding for the sake of getting; but, in the present case, their caution was needless.

The ship-fever had not quite left Whitefield when, with his usual promptness, he arranged the plan of his work and made a beginning. His first week in Savannah was spent in confinement, and, on the second Sunday, his attempt to officiate broke down before he reached the second service; but on the following Tuesday he was out at his pastoral work, and made a call on Tomo Chici, the Indian king, who had refused to become a Christian, on the ground that Christians were such bad wretches. There can be no doubt, however, that he had no fitness, though much zeal, for preaching to the Indians.

For oratory there was little scope in Georgia, where a congregation of one or two hundred persons was the largest that could be mustered; but there was ample room for industry, for humility, for gentleness, and for self-denial; and Whitefield, by his assiduous cultivation of these graces, showed that he cared more for charity than for the gift of speaking 'with the tongues of men and of angels.' Oratory was nothing to him as an art; it was supremely valuable as a talent to be used for his Lord, an instrument by which hearts might be drawn to the cross. He went among the villages, like a travelling missionary in a heathen country; made himself the friend of every one in them, men, women, and children, no matter what their nation or their creed; praised their industry and success; reproved their faults; and invited them to trust in Him who could save them from their sins. He was scrupulously careful not to offend the religious or national prejudices of any, and strove to draw all by the cords of love. It is easy to believe that a chaplain whose heart was touched with the colonists' every sorrow, who entered into their difficulties, who came to cheer them at their work, and sit as one of them in their huts, where the children gathered round his knee, and the workers talked about the soil and the crops, was loved as a personal friend. As such they looked upon him. The love which won Dummer, Bristol, London, and Gibraltar was simply repeating its inevitable conquests. His dauntless and brotherly spirit, which still retained a touch of the asceticism of his Oxford days, made him resolve to endure the worst hardships of colonial life. The weather was intensely hot, sometimes burning him almost through his shoes; and 'seeing others do it who,' he says, 'were as unable, I determined to inure myself to hardiness by lying on the ground, which, by use, I found to be so far from being hardship, that afterwards it became so to lie on a bed.' With this endurance he combined the charming quality of gratitude for any kindness either to himself or his friends.

The settlers in the village had but a hard lot. Their children offered the best field for Whitefield's efforts, and he at once arranged to begin schools for them.

'I also,' he says, 'inquired into the state of their children, and found there were many who might prove useful members of the colony, if there was a proper place provided for their maintenance and education. Nothing can effect this but an orphan-house, which might easily be erected at, or near, Savannah, would some of those that are rich in this world's good contribute towards it. May God, in His due time, stir up the wills of His faithful people to be ready to distribute, and willing to communicate on this commendable occasion.'

The following extract shows the need of the flock and the tender-heartedness of the shepherd: 'Began to-day visiting from house to house, and found the people in appearance desirous of being fed with the sincere milk of the word, and solicitous for my continuance amongst them. Poor creatures! My heart ached for them, because I saw them and their children scattered abroad as sheep having no shepherd.'

The first of these extracts points to the inference that the idea of an orphan-house for the colony was Whitefield's own, and many of his friends who helped him gave him the credit of it; but he was frank in undeceiving them, and in giving the praise to Charles Wesley and the humane governor, General Oglethorpe. Before he had thought of going abroad, they had seen and felt the necessity of some provision being made for the orphans, who must inevitably be thrown upon the colony when their parents died and left them unprovided for. A scheme somewhat like the one which was ultimately adopted was devised, but, though the Wesleys made its practical accomplishment impossible, yet the idea was not abandoned. Whitefield was entreated by his friend Charles Wesley to remember the orphans; and such a call was never made in vain upon him. He 'resolved, in the strength of God, to prosecute the orphan-house design with all his might.' The Trustees, acting no doubt at the suggestion of Oglethorpe, favoured him.

When he reached his charge he found that the condition of the orphans was deplorable, all the kindness of the Trustees notwithstanding. Some were quartered here and there with such families as had promised, for a money consideration, to take them and rear them. Others were engaged in service when they ought to have been at school, and were kept at work so long and so hard, that educating them in their present position was impossible. The morals of all were corrupted by bad example; the learning of those who had learned anything at all was forgotten. There was but one feasible plan for curing the mischief: a home must be built, and the children must be lodged, fed, clothed, and taught in it. Meanwhile, until he could return to England to take priest's orders, and procure a grant of land from the Trustees, and beg money enough to build the home, and give it a start, he wisely did what he could to ameliorate the condition of them and of all other children by establishing schools in the villages.

The moral influence of the orphan-house, the establishment of which was now his fixed purpose, was to prove as great and as happy over Whitefield as over the destitute children. He was to receive as much as he gave. It was to be a standing appeal to his tenderness and test of his faith, a constant spur to his effort, and an anchor to his excitable mind, which might have spent itself upon trifles, because unable to cope with the statesmanlike work which the legislative mind of Wesley gloried in mastering. It was to become the ballast of a noble ship which had to carry high sail in dangerous seas. So far as good to himself was concerned, there was no reason why he should have been sent to his 'little foreign cure,' in which he was really happy, and where (such was his humility and carelessness about popularity) he could have cheerfully remained, excepting to undertake the charge of the orphans. Saving this, he did nothing in Georgia which he might not have done elsewhere, and done better. But it is remarkable to observe how the door of America was closed against Wesley, whose talents were most serviceable when concentrated on one place; while Whitefield received a charge which supplied a constant motive to him to range through every country where he could get a congregation to hear his message and help his work.   He was meant for more than a parish priest or founder of a denomination ; he was an evangelist of nations.

The journal of Whitefield on Wednesday, May 24th, and the journal of Wesley on the same day, present a striking contrast as well between the condition of mind as the work of these much attached friends.   It was a quiet day with Whitefield ; and doubtless could Wesley have seen him going among the people with a contented heart, welcomed and honoured, he would have been both surprised and gratified with his unexpected success.   It was a day of excitement, of anguish, and of joy with Wesley, the day of his conversion ; and could Whitefield have known what was going on in Aldersgate Street, London, it would have filled his mouth with joyful praise, though he might have been surprised that not until a time so late had his former religious teacher come to experience the same spiritual change that had taken place in himself long before.

While Whitefield, by his unceasing labours, his unfeigned humility, and his judicious conduct, was laying the foundation of an enduring affection between the whole colony and himself, he acknowledged himself to be largely indebted to his predecessors.   Delamotte was much beloved by the poor, to whom he was devoted, and his return home was an occasion of grief to them.   'The good Mr. John Wesley has done in America, under God, is inexpressible,' says Whitefield.   'His name is very precious among the people ; and he has laid such a foundation among the people that I hope neither men nor devils will ever be able to shake.   Surely I must labour most heartily, since I come after such worthy predecessors.'

It is pleasantest to see how he was welcomed in the villages ; how they of Savannah delighted in his visits, even enduring his rebukes without murmuring ; how at Frederica nearly the whole of the inhabitants—a hundred and twenty in number—came to hear him preach, and the settlement was all activity to build a preaching-room, to serve the place, *pro tempore* of a church ; how the sturdy Highlanders of Darien, settled under the pastoral care of a worthy minister named McLeod, crowded the house in which he preached to them at the end of a single day's visit ; and how the Salzburgers who were settled, after weary wanderings over land and sea, at a place which their grateful hearts called Ebenezer, received him with brotherly love. Their lands were the best cultivated in the colony, and yielded the best crops. Their differences were referred not to any court, but to the judgment of their two pastors, Boltzius and Gronau, whom they loved devotedly, and to whom they looked up as fathers. Their orphan-house, founded on the model of Professor Francke's, of Halle, was a model of the one he was purposing to build ; and at the close of his visit the seventeen orphan children—'the little lambs', he called them—came and shook hands with him.

On Sunday, August 27th, he preached his farewell sermon to his people, who, sorrowing to lose him, were comforted by his assurance that he would not delay his return to them. On the following day the chief magistrate, Mr. Causton, and the recorder, called to take their leave of him. The general demonstrations of affection for him overwhelmed him ; and he took the first opportunity of ' venting his heart by prayers and tears.'

The voyage was to prove one of the most dangerous that he performed. When they had been a month at sea they were caught by a gale from the east, which put all the sailors to their wits' end. Sails were slit and tackling rent. The sea broke over the vessel with such violence that not a dry spot was left anywhere, and Whitefield, who slept in the most secure part, wrapped in a buffalo's hide, was drenched twice

or thrice in one night. His composure and faith in God made
so deep an impression on the crew that they would say, ' How
should we have been blaming and cursing one another had not
Mr. Whitefield been amongst us ! '

The storm left the vessel sadly disabled, besides having
destroyed or washed away a large portion of the provisions.
There was the prospect of a tedious voyage and much hardship, and so it turned out. Contrary winds prevailed for a
long time ; at the end of October the passengers were allowed
a quart of water a day. Their constant food for a long time
was salt beef and water dumplings, which, says Whitefield,
' did not agree with the stomachs of all amongst us.' With a
humble, constant recognition of the working of the Almighty
in all things he held on to the close of this distressing voyage.
Three days before they sighted land, most of those in
the cabin had begun to be weak and to look hollow-eyed.
He exclaims: ' May we patiently tarry God's leisure ! Amen !
Amen ! ' On November 11th they were reduced to an ounce
or two of salt beef, a pint of muddy water, and a cake made of
flour and skimmings of the pot, as the allowance for each man.
Cold weather had also set in, and, to add to their distress,
they did not know where they were, there being only a prevalent
opinion that they were off the coast of Ireland. That day
was closed with the appropriate prayer, ' May we now learn
that man liveth not by bread alone.' And the next day,
Sunday, November 12th, opened with the grateful ascription,
' Blessed be the Lord God of Israel, who this day hath visited
a distressed people ! ' They had entered Carrickaholt Bay, in
the mouth of the Shannon, and were hospitably received and
succoured by Mr. MacMahon, whose house stood at the head
of the bay.

At Limerick and at Dublin he was kindly received by the
heads of the Episcopal Church, and at both places he preached

with great power and marked effect. His passion for the souls of men was as a hunger and a thirst that never left him. At the table of the primate an expression fell from the lips of Dr. Delaney, Dean of St. Patrick's, which he never forgot, and never failed to act upon : ' I wish, whenever I go up into a pulpit, to look upon it as the last time I shall ever preach, or the last time the people may hear.'

On December 8th he reached London, accompanied by some friends, who had gone to meet him on his way. Wesley was at Oxford; and, as soon as the news of Whitefield's arrival reached him, he hastened up to London, and ' God gave us,' he says, ' once more to take sweet counsel together.'

At the close of such a year of travel and labour, Whitefield had some reasons for winding up his journal with this emphatic verse—

> ' Give me Thy strength, O God of power !
> Then let winds blow, or thunders roar,
> Thy faithful witness will I be,
> 'Tis fixed ! I can do all through Thee !

CHAPTER V

December, 1738—April, 1739

FETTER LANE MEETINGS—ORDAINED PRIEST—EXPELLED THE
CHURCHES—OPEN-AIR PREACHING

NOTHING could have been more opportune for the
welfare of Methodism in England than the arrival of
John Wesley at Deal at the same time that Whitefield sailed
for Georgia. The newly kindled fire had no time to burn
low. Wesley at once began his labours with energy, decision,
and courage, and excited great opposition on the part of the
clergy. Then he went with Ingham to Hernhuth, to have
fellowship with the Moravians, whom he regarded with holy
envy as possessors of spiritual truth which he understood not.
On his return he experienced that conversion which has been
already spoken of. Charles had already undergone it. Thus
both his great co-workers preceded him into the kingdom of
God. The close of 1738 saw the beginning of the united
work of all the three, and for some time their lives were
closely blended together. They preached in the same rooms,
prayed and spoke in the same meetings, and presided over
the same private societies, which were formed for the nurture
of the Christian life.

The day after Whitefield's arrival in London he waited on

the Archbishop of Canterbury and the Bishop of London, and was favourably received ; but some of the clergy denied him their pulpits—five in two days. He also went to a meeting of the Methodist Society, which had been formed in Fetter Lane, and joined them in their love-feast. There were at this time other religious societies besides those which were springing out of the labours of the Methodists, and to some of them, known as the Religious Societies in the City of London, he had preached before he left for Georgia, getting them welcome collections for their works of charity. Formed in 1675, they had a wide range of activity, foiling Popish machinations, hunting down thieves, closing markets on Sundays, suppressing houses of ill-fame, proceeding against notorious swearers, relieving the sick, burying the poor, sheltering orphans, establishing schools for the education of children and putting the children out to trades, and seeking to form, through the pulpits of the city, a healthy public opinion and an earnest public spirit. They had declined much from their original warmth of religious zeal and energy of action, yet they still were the friends of charity, and to them Whitefield owed some of his first popularity in the city.

It must have been to one of these societies that he was preaching in Redcross Street, on Christmas Day, at four o'clock in the morning, when he first used extemporaneous prayer. A laborious day must that Christmas Day have been, with its first sermon at four, its second at six—when the preacher felt a ' little oppressed with drowsiness '—its sacramental, and three more sermons ; and not an unworthy anniversary of a man's baptism. Besides, Whitefield had preached twice on Christmas Eve, and expounded to two societies—one of them the society at Fetter Lane—and then continued with many other brethren in prayer, singing, and thanksgiving, until nearly four o'clock in the morning. No wonder he felt a 'little oppressed with drowsiness!' That society at Fetter Lane was at present the heart of the Methodist movement, its central fire. The engagements of Christmas Eve, 1738, were only an example of the prolonged, fervent, and, one would have thought, exhausting, but Whitefield says, refreshing and invigorating, devotions which the brethren engaged in there.

Sympathy of thought and feeling drew the band of men close together, and their souls glowed with a passion of religious zeal which must, sooner or later, break forth upon the land for good or evil, or both, while the opposition from without only fanned the flame. It was a hopeful and a dangerous time. First-fruits of the coming movement abounded in the meeting—first 'watchnight meeting' (?)—in which the leaders and a company of sixty brethren celebrated the departure of the old year and the coming of the new.

'About three in the morning,' Wesley says, 'as we were continuing instant in prayer, the power of God came mightily upon us, insomuch that many cried out for exceeding joy, and many fell to the ground. As soon as we were recovered a little from that awe and amazement at the presence of His majesty, we broke out with one voice, "We praise Thee, O God; we acknowledge Thee to be the Lord!"'

Five nights afterwards, eight 'ministers of Jesus Christ, despised Methodists, whom God in His providence brought together,' met at Islington to confer upon several things of importance, and continued in fasting and prayer until three o'clock, when they parted with 'the conviction that God was about to do great things.' The whole of the second night after that Whitefield spent at Fetter Lane in the same devout engagements, and the next day was got through with one hour's sleep. 'There was a great deal of Divine influence among us,' he says.

Amid these numerous engagements, the object of his return

to England, to receive ordination as a priest, was not lost sight
of. At the end of December he was appointed by the Trustees
to be minister of Savannah. With the fire of the Fetter Lane
meetings burning in his soul, he returned to Oxford ; and on
January 14, 1739, had the hands of good Bishop Benson laid
on him. The bishop sent Lord Huntingdon, evidently for
the benefit of Lady Huntingdon, an account of the ordination,
and added—

'I hope this will give some satisfaction to my lady, and that she will not
have occasion to find fault with your lordship's old tutor. Though mistaken on some points, I think him (Mr. Whitefield) a very pious, well-
meaning young man, with good abilities and great zeal. I find his Grace
of Canterbury thinks highly of him. I pray God grant him great success
in all his undertakings for the good of mankind, and a revival of true
religion and holiness among us in these degenerate days ; in which prayer
I am sure your lordship and my kind, good Lady Huntingdon will most
heartily join.'

A noticeable incident was his visit to Dr. Watts, now an
old man, who received him 'most cordially.' But the most
important fact of the month was the thought of preaching in
the open air, which was suggested to him by a crowd of a
thousand people having been unable to gain admission to
Bermondsey Church, where he preached one Sunday afternoon. It met with no encouragement when he mentioned it
to some of his friends ; they thought it was a 'mad notion.'
However, it would have been carried out the next Sunday at
Ironmongers' Almshouses had not the preacher been disappointed in his congregation, which was small enough to hear
him from the pulpit. He took two sermons with him—one for
within and the other for without. What were his impressions
about this untoward circumstance he nowhere says ; most
probably he had humble and self-reproachful thoughts for
having run before there seemed to be need.

Such intense and long-continued work as he rushed into

upon his return home could not fail to tell upon him, and his entry in his journal on February 6th is such as one expects to see—

'Went to St. Helen's, where all on a sudden I was taken so ill in body, and was so deserted in soul, that I would have given anything for my written notes; yet God gave me to trust in Him for strength and assistance, and before I had done I was warm in heart and strong enough in body to continue to offer Jesus Christ freely for a considerable time to all that would lay hold on Him by faith.'

At this time we hear the sound of those peculiar Amens, which have distinguished the children of Methodism down to this late day. 'Many seemed to feel what was spoken, and said hearty and loud Amens to my sentences.' The next day another keen attack struck him at Windsor. We shall see this weakness showing itself all through his life to the last; and if we keep in memory its existence, and not allow ourselves to think, as we follow him day and night through his ceaseless toils, that we are with a man who has no infirmities—who, as it has been expressed by Sir J. Stephen in his 'Essays in Ecclesiastical Biography,' 'was gifted with an incapacity of fatiguing or being fatigued'—we shall form a juster estimate of the heavenly fervour which triumphed over his own frailness, and then over every outside difficulty. He was often fatigued beyond endurance; but the sight of his congregation, the delight he had in his work, and the strength which comes from above, quickened him to speak with freedom and power. 'Freedom and power,' these were the two qualities in his preaching which he prized before all others.

A short tour in the provinces gave him his first taste of direct hostility, the mob and the Church being of one mind in openly opposing him. It also gave him his first taste of the sweets of field-preaching. There was truth in half of the

exclamation which a not devout observer uttered when Whitefield started from London: 'I believe the devil in hell is in
you all'—that was the untrue half;—'Whitefield has set the
town on fire, and now he is gone to kindle a flame in the
country'—that was the true half. There was alarm among the
powers of the Church in the cities of Bath and Bristol before
his arrival there; and his application to preach in the Abbey
Church at Bath on behalf of the orphan-house was met with
a positive refusal, although the bishop had given the Trustees
of Georgia a promise, before Whitefield sailed for Georgia,
that such a service might be held. The refusal came not,
however, from the bishop. Similar treatment at Bristol, to
which he at once withdrew, led to most important results.

Long ago, Kingswood was a royal chase near Bristol; in
Whitefield's time it had become a colliery district, inhabited
by men of a rough, ungodly type, who had no church nearer
than one, three, or four miles away. They were regarded as so
many Indians, and when Whitefield first went to Georgia it
was said to him: 'If you have a mind to convert Indians,
there are colliers enough in Kingswood.' And they were still
in their sins and misery when he returned. Even he might
have failed to undertake their evangelisation had he not been
almost compelled. When clergymen were cold, and the chancellor of the diocese captious, and churches scarce, he had
time and inducements to carry out those loving wishes towards
the colliers, which had stirred his heart for a long time; nor
was the desire to attempt open-air preaching without its weight
on the same side.

Understanding that the minister of St. Mary Redcliffe was
willing to lend his church for sermons to be preached on
behalf of the orphan-house, Whitefield applied first of all to
him, and the answer was a civil refusal; the church could not
be lent without a special order from the chancellor. To the

chancellor Whitefield went.   The reply from him was, 'that he would not give any positive leave, neither would he prohibit any one that should lend Whitefield a church; but he would advise him to withdraw to some other place till he had heard from the bishop, and not preach on that or any other occasion soon.'   Whitefield asked him his reasons.   He answered, 'Why will you press so hard upon me?   The thing has given a general dislike.'   Whitefield replied: 'Not the design of the orphan-house.   Even those that disagree with me in other particulars approve of that.   And as for the gospel, when was it preached without dislike?'   The dean, when called upon soon after the interview with the chancellor, gave the same ambiguous replies, with the same plain meaning: 'Mr. Whitefield, we would rather not say yea or nay to you; but we mean nay, and greatly wish that you would understand us so.'

The societies were still open, so was Newgate, and then there were the colliers.   These last were visited on a Saturday afternoon (February 17, 1739) for the first time, the very day after his interviews with the chancellor and the dean.   Whitefield took his stand on Hannan Mount, and spoke upon Matt. v. 1, 2, and 3, to as many as came to hear; upwards of two hundred attended.   He does not say what were his feelings in his novel situation, nor what were the impressions upon his audience.   His only remark in his journal is, 'Blessed be God that the ice is now broke, and I have now taken the field!   Some may censure me, but is there not a cause?   Pulpits are denied, and the poor colliers ready to perish for lack of knowledge.'   Now he was the owner of a pulpit that no man could take from him, and his heart rejoiced in this great gift.   He had broken through all conventionality, and gone straight to the lost sheep.   But all in Bristol was not so dark on Sunday morning as it had been on Friday night and Saturday.   Three pulpits were placed at his disposal, and from two of them he preached, one being that of St. Mary Redcliffe, where he had such a congregation as his eyes had never yet seen, and he preached with 'liberty.' But the most enjoyable part of the day was its close, which was spent with two of the societies. Monday opened the parish church of St. Philip and Jacob, and gave him a noble congregation, and a collection of eighteen pounds for his orphan-house.

Perhaps these quick, decisive movements put the chancellor on his mettle; for on the Monday a summons came from the apparitor, commanding Whitefield's appearance before the chancellor. With this document in his pocket, Whitefield spent a joyful night among his friends in Baldwin Street, and on Tuesday morning, at ten o'clock, he waited upon the chancellor, who plainly told him that he intended to stop his proceedings. 'I have sent for the register here, sir,' said he, 'to take down your answer.' The first question was, by what authority Whitefield preached in the diocese of Bristol without a licence. Whitefield replied that he thought that custom was grown obsolete. And then becoming questioner in turn, he asked the chancellor: 'And why, pray sir, did not you ask the clergyman this question who preached for you last Thursday?' He said that was nothing to Whitefield. He then read over part of the ordination office, and those canons that forbid any minister's preaching in a private house, &c.; and asked what Whitefield had to say to them. He answered, that he apprehended that those canons did not belong to professed ministers of the Church of England. The chancellor replied that they did. Again Whitefield resorted to the *ad hominem* method: 'There is also a canon, said I, sir, forbidding all clergymen to frequent taverns and play at cards; why is not that put in execution?' Said the chancellor: 'Why does not some one complain of them, and then it would?' The chancellor next

accused Whitefield of false doctrine, whereupon he received a
proper answer : ' I cannot but speak the things I know ; and I
am resolved to proceed as usual.'   ' Observe his answer, then,
Mr. Register,' said he.   Then, turning to Whitefield, he added :
' I am resolved, sir, if you preach or expound anywhere in this
diocese, till you have a licence, I will first suspend, and then
excommunicate you.   And what I do is in the name of the
clergy and laity of the city of Bristol.'   How much truth there
was in the whole statement appeared on the afternoon of the
day that it was made.   The laity of Bristol, who were said to
want the silencing of Whitefield, congregated in thousands
round St. Nicholas' Church, hoping to hear him preach ; but
the lecturer sent word that orders were given by the clergyman that he should not preach in his church.   The societies
remained. open, and the laity crowded their meetings that
night.

The second interview with the chancellor was followed by
the same action as the first, and with more encouraging results.
On the following day the journal relates : ' All the church
doors being now shut, and, if open, not able to contain half
that came to hear, at three in the afternoon I went to Kingswood among the colliers.   God highly favoured us in sending
us a fine day, and near two thousand people were assembled
on that occasion.   I preached and enlarged on John iii. 3 for
near an hour, and, I hope, to the comfort and edification of
those that heard me.'   Two days afterwards he stood upon
the same spot, and preached to a congregation of four or five
thousand with great freedom.   The bright sun overhead, and
the immense throng standing around him in awful silence,
formed a picture which filled him with ' holy admiration.'

It is important to know what were his feelings when he met
these immense field congregations, whose numbers had grown
from two hundred to twenty thousand, and what were the

effects of his preaching upon his audience. His own words
are :—

      ' Having no righteousness of their own to renounce, they were glad to
hear of a Jesus who was a friend to publicans, and came not to call the
righteous, but sinners, to repentance. The first discovery of their being
affected was, to see the white gutters made by their tears, which plentifully
fell down their black cheeks, as they came out of their coal-pits. Hundreds
and hundreds of them were soon brought under deep convictions, which (as
the event proved) happily ended in a sound and thorough conversion. The
change was visible to all, though numbers chose to impute it to anything
rather than the finger of God. As the scene was quite new, and I had
just begun to be an extempore preacher, it often occasioned many inward
conflicts. Sometimes when twenty thousand people were before me, I had
not, in my own apprehension, a word to say, either to God or them. But
I was never totally deserted, and was frequently (for to deny it would be
lying against God) so assisted, that I knew by happy experience, what our
Lord meant by saying, "Out of his belly shall flow rivers of living water."
The open firmament above me, the prospect of the adjacent fields, with the
sight of thousands and thousands, some in coaches, some on horseback, and
some in the trees, and at times all affected and drenched in tears together,
to which sometimes was added the solemnity of the approaching evening,
was almost too much for, and quite overcame, me.'

    The overpowering emotion of which he speaks, and the
tears which made white gutters on the begrimed faces of the
colliers, were the answer to his own passionate feelings.
Seldom did he preach without drenching his audience in tears,
and the effect was due quite as much to his unrestrained
manifestation of strong feeling as to his words. Especially
must this characteristic have struck the hearts of rough men,
who, after having been long uncared for, at last saw a clergyman willing to endure fatigue and shame for the sake of
preaching to them. He spoke as having nothing to keep
back from them, as having nothing to be ashamed of, least of
all of those tender yearnings of divine compassion which had
constrained him to come to them, and instead of assuming

a placid composure which he did not feel, he let his whole manner express what was in him.

'I hardly ever knew him go through a sermon without weeping more or less,' said his friend, Cornelius Winter, 'and I truly believe his were the tears of sincerity. His voice was often interrupted by his affection ; and I have heard him say in the pulpit : "You blame me for weeping, but how can I help it, when you will not weep for yourselves, though your immortal souls are upon the verge of destruction, and, for aught you know, you are hearing your last sermon, and may never more have an opportunity to have Christ offered to you?" His freedom in the use of his passions often put my pride to the trial. I could hardly bear such unreserved use of tears, and the scope he gave to his feelings, for sometimes he exceedingly wept, stamped loudly and passionately, and was frequently so overcome that for a few seconds you would suspect he never could recover ; and when he did, nature required some little time to compose herself.'

Much of his power lay in this abandon, but it was the abandon of quenchless love.

The visit to Bristol was interrupted for a few days to make an excursion into Wales ; but although this was the first appearance of a famous, avowed Methodist among the Welsh, Methodism was already amongst them, both in mode and spirit. Clergymen had gone beyond parish boundaries, preaching to large congregations in churches, in churchyards, and in fields ; religious societies, founded upon the rules which Dr. Woodward had laid down for the societies in London, were scattered here and there to the number of thirty ; the great doctrines and holy commandments of the gospel were taught with power which fell little, if at all, below that which marked the ministrations of Whitefield. The two prime movers in the work were Griffith Jones and Howel Harris. Griffith Jones, rector of Llanddowror, Cæmarthenshire, was a man of ardent piety and noble courage, and the greatest preacher in the Principality in his day. He preceded the Methodists in the work of preaching at wakes, fairs, and other riotous gatherings of the people. In some cases he would be invited by parishioners, without the consent of their clergyman, to come and preach to them; in which case the clergyman would probably make sure of the church key, and compel both his people and their favourite preacher to take their stand in the open air; next he would lodge an accusation in the Ecclesiastical Court. Griffith Jones had twenty years of litigation. By the establishment of 'Welsh Circulating Schools' he did his greatest work. His plan was to send a schoolmaster into a locality that wished for instruction, to teach reading the Bible in the Welsh tongue, psalmody, and the catechism. From one district the schoolmaster would pass to another, to do the same work. Jones testifies that in Wales not one Dissenter in ten separated from the Church of England for any other reason than 'for want of plain, practical, pressing, and zealous preaching, in a language and dialect they are able to understand.' For the same reason Methodism obtained a strong footing.

Howel Harris, born the same year as Whitefield, was not unlike the great evangelist in disposition, in gifts, in experience, and in whole-hearted consecration to the Saviour. Ignorant of all the disputed points of religion, he lived in the simple faith that God loved him, and would, for His own name's sake, love him freely to the end. Oxford having proved a disappointment to him, he returned to Wales, and began in his own home-parish, Talgarth, Brecon, to visit from house to house, and then to preach in the houses. The effects were marvellous, and, as a consequence, he had to encounter the opposition of the clergy, the magistrates, and the mob. Yet the work grew; there was a general reformation in several counties, and places of worship were everywhere crowded. When the news of Whitefield's labours in London reached him he felt his heart united to the evangelist 'in such a

manner as he had never felt the like with any one before.'
To his great joy à letter came to him from Whitefield soon
after his return from Georgia.

'LONDON, *December*, 1738.

'MY DEAR BROTHER,—Though I am unknown to you in person, yet I
have long been united to you in spirit ; and have been rejoiced to hear how
the good pleasure of the Lord prospered in your hands. Go on, go on !
He that sent you will assist, comfort, and protect you, and make you more
than conqueror through His great love. I am a living monument of this
truth. I love you, and wish you may be the spiritual father of thousands,
and shine as the sun in the kingdom of your heavenly Father. Oh, how
shall I joy to meet you at the judgment-seat ! How you would honour me
if you would send a line to your affectionate though unworthy brother,

'GEORGE WHITEFIELD.'

To this letter Harris replied the day after its reception,
assuring Whitefield of his profound love for him, telling him
some good news of the work of God in Wales, and saying:
'Were you to come to Wales it would not be labour in vain.'
This devoted young Welshman had several times offered himself for holy orders, and been refused because he preached as a
layman, and so he was shut up to this way, or to silence.

We can see from these brief sketches what was the state of
things in the Church of England in Wales, and, to some
extent, in Nonconformity. The preaching of the godly clergy
was frowned upon by their own brethren, and welcomed and
supported by Nonconformists. The Spirit of the Lord was
moving in this land, as well as in America and in Scotland
and England. We can also understand why Whitefield broke
away for a few days from the thousands of Bristol and Kingswood. His soul and the soul of Harris leaped to each other
like flames of fire.

An incident of the short passage to Wales is much too
characteristic of the times to be omitted. Contrary winds
delayed Whitefield at the New Passage, and he says : ' At

the inn there was an unhappy clergyman, who would not go over in the passage-boat because I was in it. Alas! thought I, this very temper would make heaven itself unpleasant to that man, if he saw me there. I was told that he charged me with being a Dissenter. I saw him soon after, shaking his elbows over a gaming table.' The clergyman had changed his mind and taken the boat. The image of him recalls Parson Shuffle in 'Roderick Random,' and shows, alas! that, at that time, some parsons in the north and some in the west were painfully alike in character and in uselessness.

The Welsh visit was very short, and was marked with those experiences which Whitefield was to know as common things for the rest of his life. First of all, the church at Cardiff was denied, and he had to resort to the town hall, where he preached from the judge's seat to a small audience of four hundred people. No outrage was attempted in the building, but some of the baser sort amused themselves by trailing a dead fox around it outside - a very trifling annoyance to a preacher with such lung power, and who could make himself heard in spite of the shouting and noise. Then there were melting meetings of a more private sort with the religious societies; and on the whole he had reason, as he says, to think that there was 'a most comfortable prospect of the spreading of the gospel in Wales.'

On his return to Bristol he had to suffer meaner opposition than any he had met with before. Newgate, where he had delighted to preach to the prisoners, and where, by his gifts, he had relieved much distress, was closed against him. Unwilling to lose their friend and teacher, many of the prisoners sent a petition to the mayor, praying that he might be allowed to come among them as usual; but the mayor would not grant them their request. Mr. Dagge, the keeper, a convert and friend of Whitefield, remonstrated, and urged that Whitefield preached agreeably to Scripture ; but the only answer was to appoint another clergyman to the post of chaplain—for shame forbade his denying the poor unfortunates all religious aid. This disappointment was cause for great rejoicing to the expelled Methodist, who wrote in his journal : ' Some preach Christ out of contention, and others of goodwill : however, Christ is preached.'

His persecution had ample compensation in the new power of which he had become conscious, and in the new opening for labour which he had found since his arrival in the west, the fields giving him room enough for any congregation, and the people delighting to meet him there in all weathers, even the cold and snow of March not being able to keep them away. At Bath, at Bristol, and in the neighbouring villages, he was daily engaged in preaching to thousands—in the churches if he could gain admission to them, and if not, then under the May-pole or in the fields, or in any open space where the people had a right to assemble.   Then it was that he felt the wonderful influence which pervades mighty audiences, possessed with one concern, bending their attention to one subject, and engaged in one common service.   His favourite congregation was the Kingswood one, which met on the Sunday.   The crowds standing in awful silence, and the echo of their singing running from side to side, was, he says, very solemn and striking.   Weariness and sickness often oppressed him, yet he always found strength when the task faced him.   He was already beginning to learn the curative properties of effort, and to trust for invigoration to what exhausted him.   Then, too, there was popular sympathy on his side.   He had but to take his stand anywhere, and an audience was before him. When Newgate was closed, and his sister's room, where he had been accustomed to address a congregation as early as six o'clock on Sunday morning, could not accommodate a fourth of the people who came, some gentlemen gave him the use of a bowling-green, and his first congregation in that novel church was five thousand. This was his first attempt at preaching in the open air early in the morning. Its success, and the kindness of friends who had come to his rescue, cheered and encouraged him; his heart was full to breaking of grateful emotions.

Pressed by repeated invitations, he next presented himself in a very different part of the city, where many dwelt who neither feared God nor regarded man, and preached to thousands in a yard of the glass-houses, declaring both the threatenings and the promises of the Almighty, so that none might either presume or despair.

His courage and tact were sometimes severely tried, but more at Bath than Bristol, by the scoffing which he heard as he passed through the crowd, and by the laughter which greeted him when he mounted a table for his pulpit. The merriment never lasted long; for that true love and unusual zeal which carried him to such congregations bore him strongly and patiently on with his work, and it was not in human nature to continue trifling with one so superior to the passions of his audience. Whoever came to annoy must either submit to the spell which soon caught the most of the audience, and stay, either a willing or an unwilling hearer, or go away disappointed of his sport. To the last we shall find that Whitefield was never beaten, hazardous and questionable as some of his efforts afterwards were. His convictions on the power of preaching, penned after he had hushed and awed a jeering crowd at Bath, give in part the secret of his confidence : ' Men may say what they please, but there is something in this foolishness of preaching, which, when attended with a Divine energy, will make the most stubborn heart bend or break. " Is not My word like fire, saith the Lord, and like a hammer that breaketh the rock in pieces ? ' "

The time when he must leave the city was near; and that his work might not fall to the ground, or come to a stand after his departure, he again and again requested Wesley to come from London and carry it on; but Wesley could not be sure that he ought to go. His inclination was not towards Bristol, and on resorting to his practice of bibliomancy, many passages of Scripture had a sinister meaning. This was one: ' Get thee up into this mountain, and die in the mount whither thou goest up, and be gathered unto thy people.' His journey was next proposed to the society in Fetter Lane. Charles could not bear the mention of it; but an appeal to a Bible, opened at haphazard, brought him under the power of these strong words: 'Son of man, behold I take from thee the desire of thine eyes with a stroke; yet thou shalt not mourn or weep, neither shall thy tears run down;' and thinking that they were a voice from heaven, he held his peace. Still, the brethren were not satisfied, and, to settle the difficulty, an appeal was made to the lot. This said he must go. Many wanted a Divine confirmation of this supposed Divine announcement, and the rest consenting to the suggestion, a Bible was opened thrice, and some strange passages were hit upon; one was this: 'And Ahaz slept with his fathers, and they buried him in the city, even in Jerusalem.'

The journal of Whitefield contains the following entry for Saturday, March 31st: ' I was much refreshed with the sight of my honoured friend, Mr. John Wesley, whom I desired to come hither, and whom I had now the pleasure of introducing to my friends, he having never before been at Bristol. Help him, Lord Jesus, to water what Thy own right hand hath planted, for Thy mercy's sake.' Wesley writes in his journal: 'Saturday, 31st. In the evening I reached Bristol, and met Mr. Whitefield there. I could scarce reconcile myself at first to this strange way of preaching in the fields, of which he set me an example on the Sunday; having been all my life (till very lately) so tenacious of every point relating to decency and order, that I should have thought the saving of souls almost a sin, if it had not been done in a church.' The freer and more impetuous nature of Whitefield stands out in all distinctness from the statesmanlike nature of the founder of Wesleyan Methodism, as the two friends begin the work of Sunday. Whitefield had seen, more by the instinct of his quick emotions than by the reasoning of his mind, the value of his irregular work, and already had its fruits approved it to him as acceptable to God ; and that day he went out confident and joyful, while Wesley was bewildered and half inclined to turn away. True to his cautious, practical mind, Wesley adopted field-preaching only when he had seen its worth, just as he took up the class-meeting idea from others, and only consented to lay preaching because it had been started by men more headlong than himself, and these supported by the wisdom and piety of his mother, who warned him not to hinder a work of God. Others moved, he quickly followed ; and, if it was found practicable, passed on and took the lead.

Whitefield took him the round of his work on April 1st, and any heart less bold and less devoted than Wesley's must have quailed when he saw what was expected of him. They began at the bowling-green with the usual Sunday morning service, which was attended by a larger audience than ever. They went to Hannam Mount, where the colliers and others came in unusually great numbers. They passed on to Rose Green, and here the congregation was more enlarged than either of the other two. Twenty-four coaches and many horsemen mingled with the crowd, and though the wind was not so favourable as usual, 'I was strengthened,' Whitefield says, 'to cry aloud, and take my last farewell.' Prayers, blessings, and good wishes were showered on him as they returned to the

city. At seven, Whitefield went to take his leave of one of the
societies, and found the room and the way to it so crowded
that he had to mount a ladder, and come at the door by climb-
ing over the tiling of an adjoining house.

The morning of the following day was spent in talking with
those who came to take their leave, and tears were freely shed
on both sides. Crowds were hanging about the door when he
left, and a company of twenty friends accompanied him out of
the city on horseback ; and if he was leaving no small gifts
behind, he also was carrying away a substantial gift of two
hundred pounds for his orphan-house. He travelled by way
of Kingswood, where the colliers, unknown to him, had, he
says, 'prepared an hospitable entertainment, and were very
forward for me to lay the first stone of their school. At length
I complied, and a man giving me a piece of ground, in case
Mr. C—— should refuse to grant them any, I laid a stone,
and then kneeled down, and prayed God that the gates of hell
might not prevail against our design.' This became the famous
Kingswood School, the original of the institution in which the
sons of successive generations of Wesleyan Methodist ministers
have been educated.

Whitefield had not been gone three hours from Bristol, when
his friend Wesley submitted, as he says, to make himself more
vile than he had on the preceding day, when he preached to
one of the societies, by proclaiming in the highways the glad
tidings of salvation to about three thousand people ; and on
the following Sunday he stepped fearlessly into the severe
path that Whitefield had shown him a week before. Within
three weeks of Wesley's assuming the lead of the Methodist
movement, scenes such as Whitefield's preaching had not yet
created became common : some of the hearers were seized
with fearful agony and cried out ; then they as suddenly
shouted for joy.

On April 9th Whitefield, after having paid a second visit to Wales, reached his native city. Early friends who took an interest in him and his work must have been peculiarly gratified both with his vast and extending influence and with the humble manner in which he bore his successes ; and there was also one, who had not been counted of that number, who had more joy than any of them. It was 'old Cole,' the Dissenting minister. Some one had told the good man the smart saying of the youth of thirteen about stories in the pulpit, and when he heard Whitefield tell one in one of the city pulpits, he quietly remarked : 'I find that young Whitefield can now tell stories as well as old Cole.' He used to subscribe himself Whitefield's curate, and follow him in his excursions into the country to preach after him. 'These are days of the Son of man, indeed !' he would exclaim, as he followed up the younger man's work. He had an end beautifully in keeping with his zeal and the simplicity of his character. One evening, while preaching, he was struck with death ; he then asked for a chair to lean on, till he concluded his sermon. That finished, they carried him upstairs, and he died. 'O blessed God !' exclaims Whitefield, when telling the story, 'if it be Thy holy will, may my exit be like his !' It was not unlike.

Passing through Chafford, Painswick, Stroud, Stonehouse, Cheltenham, Badsey, Evesham, and Bengeworth, and preaching in bowling-greens, in town-halls, and in fields, as he went, he came to Oxford. Here, through his going to exhort one of the societies, the vice-chancellor fell foul of him. The society had before been threatened, if they continued to meet for exhortation ; and when they were all upstairs, and on the point of bidding Whitefield goodbye before he started for London, the vice-chancellor sent for him to come down. In a passion, he demanded to know if Whitefield had his name in any book there.   'Yes, sir,' was the reply, 'but I intend to take it out soon.'   The vice-chancellor said : 'Yes ; and you had best take yourself out too, or otherwise I will lay you by the heels.   What do you mean by going about and alienating people's affections from their proper pastors?   Your works are full of vanity and nonsense ; you pretend to inspiration.   If you ever come again in this manner among these people, I will lay you first by the heels, and these shall follow.'   Then he turned his back and went away.   Whitefield turned, and having prayed with his friends, set out for London.   Letters from Savannah, containing good news, met him at Uxbridge, and made him desire an early departure to the people of his charge.

His eleven weeks' labour in the country had kindled a fire which is not extinguished to this day.

CHAPTER VI

May to August, 1739

IN MOORFIELDS—ON COMMONS—AT FAIRS AND RACES

M R. STONEHOUSE, vicar of Islington, was favourable to Methodism, but his churchwarden was of another mind. As soon as Whitefield arrived in London, the vicar gave him the use of his pulpit for a week-day service. The churchwarden would dispute Whitefield's right. In the midst of the prayers he entered the church, demanded Whitefield's licence, and forbade his preaching without one. No licence was forthcoming, nor was the preacher sorry for that, though by being in priest's orders and holding the living of Savannah, which was in the diocese of London, he felt that he had legal standing ground. For peace' sake he determined not to preach in the church. When the communion service was over he withdrew to the churchyard, and preached there, feeling assured that his Master now called him out in London as well as in Bristol. In a letter, written to a friend that day, he said that his Master had, by His providence and Spirit, compelled him to preach in the churchyard at Islington. ' To-morrow I am to repeat that mad trick, and on Sunday to go out into Moorfields. The word of the Lord runs and is glorified. People's hearts seem quite broken. God strengthens me exceedingly. I preach till I sweat through and through.' He evidently was well satisfied with being driven to adopt his country practices, or he would not have announced his intention to preach in Moorfields on the second day after his expulsion, or withdrawal, whichever it may be called, from Islington Church.

The news of his going to Moorfields soon spread through the city ; and many, on hearing it, said that if he ventured into that domain of the rabble he would never come out alive. Moorfields, which had been the first brickyard of London, next the exercise ground of the city archers, then the site of Bedlam, and afterwards the City Mall, where fashion took its daily stroll, had fallen into possession of the roughest part of the population, simply by this part's presenting itself in the presence of fashion, and desiring to share, in its peculiar way, the shade of the trees and the smoothness of the paths.　The partnership was quietly declined.　To this place and to this people Whitefield felt himself called to take his message of love and peace.　On Sunday morning, April 29th, an 'exceeding great multitude' assembled in the fields to hear him ; but to while away the time before his arrival there was a little preliminary sport in breaking to pieces a table which had been placed for his pulpit.　In due time he drove up in a coach, accompanied by some friends, and with one of them on either side, attempted to force his way to the place where the table ought to have been found.　His body-guard was soon detached from him, and he was left at the mercy of the congregation, which at once parted and made an open way for him to the middle of the fields, and thence—for there was no pulpit there —to the wall which divided the upper and lower fields, upon which he took his stand.　It was a novel sight to the preacher —that mass of London rabble—as his eye ranged over it ; it was a more novel sight to the people—that young clergyman of twenty-four, in gown, bands, and cassock, as he lifted himself up before them.　His tall, graceful figure ; his manly and

commanding bearing; his clear, blue eyes, that melted with
tenderness and kindness; his raised hand, which called for
attention—everything about him declared him a man who was
capable of ruling them; and they were willing to listen to him.
When he spoke, and they heard his strong but sweet voice,
exquisitely modulated to express the deepest, strongest passion,
or the soberest instruction, or the most indignant remonstrance,
they stood charmed and subdued. Then his message was so
solemn and so gracious, something in which every one was
interested for time and for eternity; and he delivered it as
if it were all real to him, as indeed it was; as if he believed
it and loved it, and wanted them also to accept it, as indeed
he did. No scoffer durst raise his shout, no disturber durst
meddle with his neighbour, as the thrilling text flew all around,
every one hearing it, 'Watch, therefore, for ye know neither
the day nor the hour in which the Son of man cometh'; and
as the preacher, with finger pointed upwards, cried, 'There
shall be a day in which these heavens shall be wrapped up
like a scroll—the elements melt with fervent heat—this earth
and all things therein be burnt up, and every soul of every
nation summoned to appear before the dreadful tribunal of
the righteous Judge of quick and dead, to receive rewards or
punishments according to the deeds done in their bodies.'
Quietness and attention reigned through all the host while,
for perhaps an hour and a half, he spoke of the wise and
the foolish virgins, and then—for he had a pleasant egotism,
which for a moment turned men's minds to himself only to
direct them onward to the Master—entreated them, with a last
entreaty, not to reject his message because he was young :—

'Oh! do not turn a deaf ear to me,' he begged; 'do not reject the
message on account of the meanness of the messenger! I am a child, a
youth of uncircumcised lips, but the Lord has chosen me that the glory
might be all His own. Had He sent to invite you by a learned Rabbi,
you might have been tempted to think the man had done something. But
now God has sent a child that cannot speak, that the excellency of the

power may be seen to be not of man, but of God.   Let letter-learned
Pharisees, then, despise my youth; I care not how vile I appear in the
sight of such men—I glory in it ; and I am persuaded, if any of you should
be set upon your watch by this preaching, you will have no reason to repent
that God sent a child to cry, " Behold, the Bridegroom cometh ! "   O, my
brethren ! the thought of being instrumental in bringing some of you to
glory fills me with fresh zeal.   Once more, therefore, I entreat you —
" Watch, watch and pray " ; for the Lord Jesus will receive all that call
upon Him faithfully.   Let that cry, " Behold, the Bridegroom cometh ! "
be continually sounding in your ears ; and begin now to live as though you
were assured this was the night in which you were to be summoned to go
forth to Him.'

Whitefield, it will be seen, preached up to his congregation;
he gave them the best.   Think of a theme so lofty, of a manner
so bold yet so humble, of a spirit moved with such yearning
for a crowd, hundreds of whom had come for sport, and scores
for violence and crime.   He saw in them men who had been
made in the image of God, and for whom Christ had died.   He
summoned them to their high duties and privileges ; he laid
on them their solemn responsibilities ; he pleaded with them,
and wept over them as with a mother's love; he opened
judgment and heaven and hell to their view ; he called upon
them to forsake sin and come to God ; he offered them pardon
and reconciliation and eternal life through the blood of Christ.
And the roughs were transformed into saints!

At five o'clock in the evening of the same day he met, on
Kennington Common,[1] an audience computed at twenty
thousand, and of a higher class of people than he had
addressed in the morning.   The wind, which was favourable,
carried his words to the furthest hearer ; the whole company
listened with as much decorum as a congregation in a church,
joined in the Psalm and the Lord's Prayer, and dispersed,
evidently touched and moved by what they had heard.

[1] Criminals were executed here, and in old prints the congregations are
represented as fringed with many of them hanging on the gallows.

All his time was now devoted to preparation for the voyage to Georgia, and to open-air preaching. All went well between him and the Trustees, who received him with much civility; agreed to everything he asked; and gave him a grant of five hundred acres of land, to him and his successors for ever, for the use of the orphan-house. The liberality of the Trustees was rivalled by that of the congregations at Moorfields and Kennington Common, for in nine days he collected from them almost two hundred pounds. The common was his church on Sunday evening and during the week, and at the close of the services he stood on the eminence from which he had preached, to receive the gifts of the people, who crowded to him from below. Moorfields was his church on the Sunday morning, and after his third service there he collected fifty-two pounds nineteen shillings and sixpence, more than twenty pounds of which was in half-pence. He declares that he was nearly weary of receiving their mites, and that one man could not carry the load home. The evident emotion of the people while he preached, their awe, their silence, their tears, and the generosity with which, evening after evening, they responded to his appeals for his orphan-house, showed that he had their faith and sympathy, and that his word was bringing forth fruit. Letters came telling him how useful his preaching had been to the writers; and many persons waited on him to receive further private instruction. He even says that he could mark an alteration for the better in the congregation at Kennington Common, which had from the first been exemplary. No doubt many came from anything but religious motives, as where is the congregation which is without the idle, the formal, the curious, the foolish, who do not come to be made any better, and who would be greatly startled if they were? The second congregation at Moorfields, which was composed of about twenty thousand people, most likely had many sightseers; and so, most likely, had the congregation on the common, on the evening of the same day—a congregation which was reckoned to consist of between thirty and forty thousand persons on foot besides many horsemen, and about eighty coaches.   The sight that evening was such as surprised even Whitefield, well-accustomed as he had become to look down upon vast crowds.

Quick, enterprising men, who perhaps would have had as much pleasure, if not a little more, in erecting stands on a racecourse, or stalls at a wake, saw that a sunshiny day for trade had come, and soon provided accommodation in the shape of waggons, scaffolds, and other contrivances ; and the audience gladly paid for it.   There was a pew-rent and a collection at every service ; but with this advantage, that no official brought the collecting-box round, and no hearer was compelled to occupy a stand or go without the privilege of hearing.

It is said that the singing of these congregations could be heard two miles off, and Whitefield's voice nearly a mile.

Much as Whitefield felt the importance of his work, deeply persuaded as he was that God had called him to it, and encouraging as were the sympathy and help of the people, he was not able to throw off some sense of discomfort arising from his being an outcast from the sanctuary and pulpits of his Church, and from his having to gather his money for the orphan-house in such an irregular way.   Something of this feeling manifests itself in an entry in his journal while he was in the first flush of his out-door popularity :—

'I doubt not,' he says, 'but many self-righteous bigots, when they see me spreading out my hands to offer Jesus Christ freely to all, are ready to cry out, " How glorious did the Rev. Mr. Whitefield look to-day, when, neglecting the dignity of a clergyman, he stood venting his enthusiastic ravings in a gown and cassock upon a common, and collecting mites from the poor people ! "   But if this is to be vile, Lord grant that I may be more vile. I know this foolishness of preaching is made instrumental to the conversion and edification of numbers. Ye scoffers, mock on ; I rejoice, yea, and will rejoice.'

The intenseness of his feeling while writing those words was not the calm satisfaction of one who could afford to let others scoff or praise as they might please ; it was the struggle of a man who felt acutely the disadvantages of his new position, and who was determined to accept them only because they were associated with duty and heavenly privilege ; there was a conflict between the flesh and the Spirit.

It is not an unwelcome release to get disengaged from these eager, excited congregations, to follow the preacher, and mark how he attempted to fulfil the precepts he had publicly taught. He does not appear to disadvantage when seen nearer at hand. One day he received a letter dated from Bethlehem Hospital, No. 50, signed Joseph Periam. Periam was supposed to be mad, but in a new way ; he was 'Methodically mad' ; and his tender relations, father and sister, had sent him to Bethlehem Hospital until the fits should leave him. The officials of the hospital treated him, on his reception, with the gross cruelty which one-while was practised towards all who were of weak mind. They thought he ought to have a huge dose of physic, but Periam, knowing that he was quite well, declined it, when four or five attendants 'took hold of him, cursed him most heartily, put a key into his mouth, threw him upon the bed, and said (though Whitefield had not then either seen him or heard of him), "You are one of Whitefield's gang," and so drenched him.' Orders were given that neither Whitefield, nor any of Whitefield's friends, should see him ; but Whitefield and his friend Seward were both admitted when, in answer to Periam's request, they went to the hospital. They thought him sound, both in body and mind. His sister was of a different opinion, and cited three symptoms of his madness.

First, that he fasted for near a fortnight. Secondly, that he prayed so as to be heard four storey high. Thirdly, that he had sold his clothes, and given them to the poor. The fact is, he was a literalist. In his first religious anxiety, reading one day about the young man whom our Lord commanded to sell all and give it to the poor, he thought that the words must be taken literally—so he sold his clothes, and gave the money to the poor. At length Whitefield and his friends secured Periam's release, on condition that he should be taken to Georgia. Accordingly he went with Whitefield to America ; there he married one of the orphan-house mistresses. After a few years both of them died, and two of their sons, promising boys, became inmates of the institution.

The ship *Elizabeth*, in which Whitefield had taken berths for himself and eleven others, was detained by an embargo until August, and during the odd weeks thus accidentally thrown into his hands he laboured with tremendous energy, and abundantly fulfilled the animated charge which Charles Wesley addressed to him in a poem of nine verses :—

> ' Brother in Christ, and well-beloved,
>   Attend, and add thy prayer to mine ;
> As Aaron called, yet inly moved
>   To minister in things divine.
>
> Faithful, and often owned of God,
>   Vessel of grace, by Jesus used ;
> Stir up the gift on thee bestowed,
>   The gift by hallowed hands transfused.[1]

*   *   *   *

---

[1] It is not strange to come upon so strong a statement concerning sacramental efficacy, in the poem of a man who was such a High Churchman that he made careful arrangements to be buried in consecrated ground ; but alas for human ignorance, that piece of St. Mary-le-bone churchyard in which he is laid is said to be the only piece not consecrated.

Go where the darkest tempest lowers,
Thy foes' triumphant wrestler foil ;
Thrones, principalities, and powers,
Engage, o'ercome, and take the spoil.

The weapons of thy warfare take,
With truth and meekness armed ride on ;
Mighty, through God, hell's kingdom shake,
Satan's strongholds, through God, pull down.'

*   *   *   *

Not to follow him step by step, we may still single out some experiences which will illustrate his own mode of action, the spirit that impelled him, the opposition he met with, and the encouragements that cheered him. It was at Northampton, the third place at which he stayed for preaching on one of his short excursions from London, that he met with the pious, able, and accomplished Dr. Doddridge, who was striving with unwearied industry to keep the lamps of learning and religion burning among the Dissenters. The doctor, whose attention to those 'forms of civility and complaisance which are usual among well-bred people,' is duly noted by his biographer, received Whitefield most courteously—perhaps more courteously than joyfully, for he had not always thought favourably of his visitor, and some of his brethren were not so well inclined as himself to the new sect, and in due time sent him 'several angry letters,' reproaching him for his 'civility' to the Methodist leaders. At any rate, the chapel pulpit was not offered, and Whitefield had to take his stand at the starting-post on the common.

Bedford had a clergyman, the Rev. Mr. Rogers, who had adopted Whitefield's plan of open-air preaching ; his pulpit was the steps of a windmill ; and there Whitefield preached to three thousand people. Good news came to him from Scotland. Ebenezer Erskine, the father of United Presbyterianism,

wrote to say that he had preached to fourteen thousand people.
Yet Whitefield was ill at ease, even when other ministers were
moving in the path he had chosen. The great need of the
country called for more help, and in his burning love for souls,
he prayed, 'Lord, do Thou spirit up more of my dear friends
and fellow-labourers to go out into the highways and hedges,
to compel poor sinners to come in. Amen.' His soul was
also stirred within him to testify 'against those vile teachers'
—so he calls them—'and only those, who say we are not now
to receive the Holy Ghost, and who count the doctrine of the
new birth enthusiasm. Out of your own mouths I will condemn you, you blind guides. Did you not at the time of
ordination tell the bishop that you were inwardly moved by
the Holy Ghost to take upon you the administration of the
Church? Surely, at that time, you acted the crime of Ananias
and Sapphira over again. "Surely," says Bishop Burnet, "you
lied not only unto man, but unto God."' These words might
have had reference to a pastoral letter written about this time
by the Bishop of London, on 'Lukewarmness and Enthusiasm,'
in which the people of London and Westminster were specially
warned against the enthusiast, George Whitefield; but from
the 'civil' reception the bishop gave him two days after he
penned them, we may infer that there was peace thus far.
But count Whitefield wrong, or count him right, in assailing
other clergymen, the heart warms to him as he is seen going
out, sick and weak, to preach in the rain or the sunshine; his
eyes overflowing with tears, while to his weeping congregations
he explains his favourite doctrines of the new birth and justification by faith; his heart so moved when he gets upon the
love and free grace of Jesus Christ, that, though an hour and
a half has passed by, he would fain continue till midnight. A
hint from him to the congregation at Moorfields, that he must
soon leave the country, makes it weep as for a brother, and

ejaculations and prayers for him are poured out on every side. The numbers who flocked to hear him increased, and at Kennington Common one Sunday their weeping was so loud as almost to drown his voice.

In the early part of June he preached mostly at Blendon, Bexley, and Blackheath ; and had great enjoyment in the fellowship of many friends (among whom was the vicar of Bexley), who were of the same mind as himself. It was on a Thursday evening that 'he introduced,' he says, 'his honoured and reverend friend, Mr. John Wesley, to preach at Black-heath.' Wesley says in his journal—

'I went with Mr. Whitefield to Blackheath, where were, I believe, twelve or fourteen thousand people. He a little surprised me, by desiring me to preach in his stead ; which I did (though nature recoiled) on my favourite subject, "Jesus Christ, who of God is made unto us wisdom, righteousness, sanctification, and redemption." I was greatly moved with compassion for the rich that were there, to whom I made a particular application. Some of them seemed to attend, while others drove away their coaches from so uncouth a preacher.'

Whitefield continues in his journal—

'The Lord give him ten thousand times more success than He has given me ! After sermon we spent the evening most agreeably together, with many Christian friends, at the " Green Man." About ten we admitted all to come that would. The room was soon filled. I exhorted and prayed for near an hour, and then went to bed, rejoicing that another fresh inroad was made upon Satan's territories, by Mr. Wesley's following me in field-preaching in London as well as in Bristol. Lord, speak the word, and great shall the company of such preachers be. Amen. Amen.'

Towards the end of the month his enemies devised a new scheme for hindering him. Whenever he journeyed reports were circulated that he was wounded, or killed, or had died suddenly. Coming to Blackheath one evening, after an excursion into the country, he found, not his usual twenty thousand, but one thousand, and the rest had stayed at home, because of a report that he was dead. Wherever he went he found the people much surprised and rejoiced to see him alive. Another blow fell on him at the same time. His friend, the vicar of Bexley, was forbidden to allow him his pulpit. That night he preached on Blackheath, to as large a congregation as ever, from the text, 'And they cast him out,' and recommended the people to prepare for a gathering storm.

Matters were a little threatening when he visited Tewkesbury on July 2nd. He had created great excitement at Gloucester, at Randwick, and at Hampton Common. The bailiffs of Tewkesbury had raised much opposition to his coming thither also, and had him, on his arrival at his inn, attended by four constables. These were quickly sent off by a lawyer, a friend of Whitefield, who demanded their warrant, and found that they had none. Three thousand people attended an evening service outside the liberties of the town.

The next morning he waited upon one of the bailiffs to ask his reason for sending the constables. The bailiff replied that it was the determination of the whole council, and that the people had been noisy, and reflected upon the bailiffs. 'The noise,' Whitefield answered, 'was owing to their sending the constables with their staves, to apprehend me when I should come into the town.' The bailiff retorted in anger, that a certain judge had declared his determination to take Whitefield up as a vagrant if he preached near him. 'He is very welcome,' said Whitefield, 'to do as he pleases, but I apprehend no magistrate has power to stop my preaching, even in the streets, if I think proper.' 'No, sir,' said the bailiff; 'if you preach here to-morrow, you shall have the constable to attend you.' Whitefield went away, telling him first that he thought it his duty as a minister to inform him that magistrates were intended to be a terror to evildoers, and not to those who do well ; he desired him to be as careful to appoint constables to attend at the next horse race, balls, assemblies, &c. Whitefield and his friends then left for Evesham, where he met with sympathising friends, and a threat from the magistrates, that, if he preached within their liberties, they would apprehend him. Next morning, however, he did preach ; and the magistrates were quiet. Passing on to Pershore, he was kindly welcomed by the incumbent, and, apparently, from him procured the loan of a field in Tewkesbury ; then at five in the evening he turned, with a company of a hundred and twenty horsemen, towards Tewkesbury, which he found much alarmed, people from all parts crowding the streets. He rode right through the town to the field, and preached to about six thousand hearers ; the bailiffs wisely refrained from keeping their threat, and no constable came within sight. Immediately after the sermon he took horse, and reached Gloucester near midnight. The exciting day's work had begun at seven o'clock at Evesham, and he was preaching next morning at ten, with a 'heart full of love to his dear countrymen.'

What trials he had were counterbalanced by the happy effects of his labours, visible in the places he visited. Kingswood had put on a different appearance ; the colliers, who had formerly been the terror of the neighbourhood, were to be heard singing hymns in the woods, instead of pouring out blasphemy ; the school had been carried on so successfully by Wesley, that in July, when Whitefield visited the place, the roof was ready to be put up. Methodism was yielding its firstfruits of purity, of honesty, of quietness, and of godliness, among the humbler classes. It would have been gratifying had any record been kept of particular cases, which might have served as examples of the rest. This, however, is wanting, and we are mainly guided by general statements about the spirit and behaviour of the congregations where he had preached somewhat continuously. Curious hearers were dropping off, and the vast number that remained may be fairly supposed to have had a profound interest in what they heard. The numbers were countless who came after the services to ask for counsel as to how they might leave the 'city of destruction,' which they had too long inhabited. One incident, related in the letter of a Quaker to Whitefield, may serve to show what thoughts were finding their way into humble homes throughout all the land. The old clerk at Breferton could get no rest in his spirit, after hearing Whitefield preach at Badsey; he set to work to compare what he had heard with the Church homilies and articles, and found a singular agreement between them. The landlord of 'Counter-cup,' with whom he got into conversation upon the subject, informed him that he too had found Whitefield's doctrines set forth in some old books which he possessed, the refuse of a clergyman's library. This fact was remembered when, shortly afterwards, the clerk, who was a tailor by trade, went to work at the landlord's; he borrowed the last book that was left, all the rest having been lent, and did not read above a page or two before 'the truth broke in upon his soul like lightning.' His fingers itched for the book more than for his work, and he was allowed to take it home with him. A second of the books which he borrowed so strengthened him in his new faith, that he felt as if he could die for it. Always well esteemed before, he was now threatened by his neighbours with the loss of custom and livelihood.

This wandering life which Whitefield was living, acceptable as it was to the people (who on one occasion at least rung the bells and received him 'as an angel of God') and satisfactory to his own conscience, was viewed with much displeasure by others. Even Bishop Benson sent him an affectionate admonition to exercise the authority he had received in the manner it was given him, by preaching the gospel only to the congregation to which he was lawfully appointed. Whitefield replied within four days, and denied that he was acting contrary to his commission of preaching wherever he could, or that he inveighed against the clergy. 'As for declining the work in which I am engaged,' he said, 'my blood runs chill at the very thought of it. I am as much convinced it is my duty to act as I do, as that the sun shines at noonday. I can foresee the consequences very well. They have already, in one sense, thrust us out of the synagogues. By and by they will think it is doing God service to kill us. But, my lord, if you and the rest of the bishops cast us out, our great and common Master will take us up.'

So much excitement and strong feeling had been raised, that it was not always commercially wise for inn-keepers to admit Whitefield to their houses; and at Abingdon he was 'genteelly told' by one of them, that there was no room for him and his party. Matters were worse at Basingstoke the next evening. Whitefield had just thrown himself, languid and weary, upon the bed, when—to use his own odd expression—he was 'refreshed with the news that the landlord would not let them stay under his roof.' Probably resentment was the occasion of the expulsion; for one of the landlord's children had been touched by Whitefield's preaching the last time he visited Basingstoke. He and his friends went out, amid the mockery and gibing of the crowd, to seek for another inn; and when they got one, the crowd amused itself by throwing fire rockets around the door. It was too late to preach, and Whitefield sought his own room; he had been there about an hour when the constable handed him a letter from the mayor, warning him against making a breach of the peace. Whitefield immediately wrote an answer, saying that he knew of no law against such meetings as his.

'If no law can be produced, as a clergyman, I think it my duty to inform you that you ought to protect, and not anyways discourage, or permit others to disturb, an assembly of people meeting together purely to worship God. To-morrow, I hear, there is to be an assembly of another nature; be pleased to be as careful to have the public peace preserved at that, and to prevent profane cursing and swearing, and persons breaking the sixth commandment, by bruising each other's bodies by cudgelling and wrestling; and if you do not this, I shall rise up against you at the great day, and be a swift witness against your partiality.'

Whitefield followed his letter next morning, and had an interview with the mayor, which must have endangered his gravity much more than his temper. His object was to see this prohibitory law, but the mayor broke out: 'Sir, you sneered me in the letter you sent last night; though I am a butcher, yet, sir, I——' Whitefield interposed: 'I honour you as a magistrate, and only desire to know what law could be produced against my preaching: in my opinion there is none.' 'Sir,' said the mayor, 'you ought to preach in a church.' 'And so I would, if your minister would give me leave.' The mayor said: 'Sir, I believe you have some sinister ends in view; why do you go about making a disturbance?' More of the same sort followed, and the mayor, who found himself a poor match for the ready preacher, and had a fair to attend, cut short the interview by saying that he 'had wrote' Whitefield another letter, which he would send him yet, if he pleased. Whitefield thanked him, paid him the respect due to a magistrate, and took his leave. The letter which followed was very much in the 'though-I-am-a-butcher' style.

Whitefield replied in his most serious manner, and had less success than he probably would have gained had he tried, what he could so well use when he chose—humour and geniality. But he could not keep down his tremendous earnestness, or, rather, he could not bring into action along with it the lighter qualities which have their part to play in the intercourse of life. His soul was absorbed in the one thought of winning the people for his Saviour. The crowds which were to assemble at the revel the next day were resolved to have their coarse pleasures and sins; nor do the authorities seem to have had any serious intention, except that of hindering the preacher and sheltering them. There seems reason to believe that Whitefield had purposely come on the day of the revel, and if he did, his wisdom may be questioned; for the people had time to become exasperated before his arrival, and that conquering influence which he generally threw over his audiences had no fair chance to exert itself. Landlords, showmen, cudgellers, wrestlers, and their attendant rabble were sure to be active on the side of their interests; and thus the whole town had been set against him before he entered it. However, being resolved to go on with his work, he went at eight o'clock in the morning into a field to preach. One had said that he should never come out alive, and another that the drum should beat close by him, but nothing occurred to hinder him from speaking freely against revelling. Only in going to and fro from the field did he meet with any unpleasantness; the rabble and the boys saluted him and called him 'strange names.'

He mounted to take his departure, but, he says :—

'As I passed by on horseback, I saw a stage; and as I rode further, I met divers coming to the revel which affected me so much I had no rest in my spirit. And therefore, having asked counsel of God, and perceiving an unusual warmth and power enter into my soul, though I was gone above a mile, I could not bear to see so many dear souls, for whom Christ had died, ready to perish, and no minister or magistrate interpose. Upon this I told my dear fellow-travellers that I was resolved to follow the example of Howel Harris in Wales, and to bear my testimony against such lying

vanities, let the consequences, as to my own private person, be what they
would. They immediately consenting, I rode back to town, got upon the
stage erected for the wrestlers, and began to show them the error of their
ways. Many seemed ready to hear what I had to say; but one, more
zealous than the rest for his master, and fearing conviction every time
I attempted to speak, set the boys on repeating their huzzahs.

'My soul, I perceived, was in a sweet frame, willing to be offered up,
so that I might save some of those to whom I was about to speak ; but all
in vain ! While I was on the stage, one struck me with his cudgel, which
I received with the utmost love. At last, finding the devil would not
permit them to give me audience, I got off ; and after much pushing and
thronging me, I got on my horse with unspeakable satisfaction within myself, that I had now begun to attack the devil in his strongest holds,
and had borne my testimony against the detestable diversions of this
generation.'

There had been more danger in Basingstoke than he saw,
and it was well that he went to an inn and not to a friend's
house, as had been expected. A band of twelve ruffians had
been lying in wait in that quarter of the town where he was
expected to sleep, determined to give him 'a secret blow and
prevent his making disturbances ; ' and one of them had the
audacity to confess their intentions to a Quaker friend of
Whitefield—J. Portsmouth—the day after Whitefield left the
town.

Nothing daunted by his late peril—full particulars of which
were sent after him — he, within a week, made another
experiment, almost as bold, which was more successful. He
announced that he would preach at Hackney Marsh, on the
day of a horse-race, and ten thousand gathered around him,
hardly any of whom left him for the race. Some who left
returned very quickly, and to them he addressed a few words
specially.

Before any censure for rashness or recklessness is pronounced
upon him for these efforts, it should be well understood that
he did not boast of them ; that he did not covet notoriety ;
and that he did not act without either prayer or consideration.

He both feared that his faith might fail him before he went to Hackney Marsh, and entreated a friend to pray that his zeal might be tempered with knowledge. 'It would grieve me,' he said, 'should I bring sufferings causelessly upon myself.'

It is almost needless to say a word about the state of mind in which such labours were carried on. They bear their own testimony to secret joy and peace, to a clear hope of everlasting glory, and to an unquestioning belief of the gospel; they could come only from one who had much of the mind of Him who, 'though He was rich, yet for our sakes became poor.' Yet one or two sentences from his letters well deserve to be linked to the story of his toils and sufferings. 'As for my own soul, God mightily strengthens me in the inward man, and gives me often such foretastes of His love that I am almost continually wishing to be dissolved that I may be with Christ. But I am only beginning to begin to be a Christian.' 'The harvest is very great. I am ashamed I can do no more for Him, who hath done so much for me; not by way of retaliation, but gratitude. Fain would I love my Master, and will not go from Him; His service is perfect freedom; His yoke is easy; His burden light.'

Controversy always attends deep religious movements, and, its abuses apart, it may be hailed as a blessing. It tempers the assumptions of the proud, gives clearness to the dim conceptions of both parties, and helps to hold the religious world in equipoise. Neither Whitefield nor his views were the worse for the assaults they sustained, any more than the formal party of the Church was damaged by the arousing calls which rang in their ears like the shout of the hosts of God. Methodist wildfire—for there was wildfire flashing in those strange congregations which assembled in Fetter Lane, on Kennington Common, and in Bristol—needed regulating and subduing, and bishops and clergy were soon at hand to help.

The first shaft was shot at Whitefield, soon after his arrival
from Savannah, by a brother clergyman ; but no notice was
taken of it, except in one sentence in the journal : ' Thou
shalt answer for me, O Lord.'   The Bishop of London, Dr.
Gibson, now thought it to be his duty to check him, and wrote
a pastoral letter on ' Lukewarmness and Enthusiasm.'   The
latter was evidently a greater sin in his eyes than the former ;
and but for the new enthusiasm, the old lukewarmness would
probably have been allowed its ancient comfort and ease.
The appeal addressed to it was not very arousing ; it was
dignified, proper, and paternal, after the ecclesiastical fashion.
To cope with the Methodists was more stimulating, and the
bishop braced himself for his task as one who relished it.   He
opened his ' Caution' with a definition of enthusiasm : ' A
strong persuasion on the mind of persons that they are guided,
in an extraordinary manner, by immediate impressions and
impulses of the Spirit of God.   And this is owing chiefly to
the want of distinguishing aright between the ordinary and
extraordinary operations of the Holy Spirit.'   After discussing
the subject generally, he culled from such parts of Whitefield's
journal as were then published illustrations of eight dangerous
phases of the new teaching.

' God forbid,' he says, ' that, in this profane and degenerate age, everything that has an appearance of piety and devotion should not be considered in the most favourable light that it is capable of.   But, at the same
time, it is surely very proper that men should be called upon for some
reasonable evidences of a Divine commission : I. When they tell us of
extraordinary communications they have with God, and more than ordinary
assurances of a special Presence with them.   II. When they talk in the
language of those who have a special and immediate mission from God.
III. When they profess to think and act under the immediate guidance
of a Divine inspiration.   IV. When they speak of their preaching and
expounding, and the effects of them, as the sole work of a Divine power.
V. When they boast of sudden and surprising effects as wrought by the
Holy Ghost, in consequence of their preaching.   VI. When they claim the

spirit of prophecy. VII. When they speak of themselves in the language and under the character of Apostles of Christ, and even of Christ Himself. VIII. When they profess to plant and propagate a new gospel, as unknown to the generality of ministers and people in a Christian country.'

'The Rev. Mr. Whitefield's answer,' which appeared only twelve days after the 'Pastoral Letter,' was written in two or three days in the midst of preaching engagements. It opens with some remarks on the first part of the letter, which are feeble and wide of the mark, and would have been better omitted. He is strong and effective on his own ground, and has little difficulty in defending positions which, in these days of subjective religious thought, would have been little questioned. He rejects, of course, the idea of having extraordinary operations of the Spirit in the working of miracles, or the speaking with tongues; but lays claim to the ordinary gifts and influences which still continue. He contends that he can know, by his own joy and peace and satisfaction in any particular work, whether the Holy Ghost is with him, graciously and effectually moving his heart; that a general influence or operation of the Spirit must imply a particular operation; that the Holy Ghost may direct and rule our hearts in the minutest circumstance. He claims for himself a Divine commission in his work, and forces the bishop to sit upon one of two horns of a dilemma—deny the priest's Divine commission, and thus his own Divine right and authority as bishop; or contend for his own commission, and thus admit the validity of the priest's, who is ordained by his hands. The charge of boasting that he spoke of his preaching and expounding and the effects of them, as the sole work of a Divine power, he rebuts by asking whether his lordship would have the preacher ascribe anything to himself? The fifth count against him gets an animated answer, which may well make any preacher of truth feel serious: 'Where, my lord,

is the enthusiasm of such a pretension? Has your lordship
been a preacher in the Church of England for so many years,
and have you never seen any sudden or surprising effects con-
sequent upon your lordship's preaching? Was this my case,
should I not have reason to doubt, my lord, whether I had
any more than a bare human commission?' In the sixth
count the bishop had laid his finger on a very weak place in
Whitefield's creed ; nor can Whitefield do more than appeal
to his own sincere persuasion that he is right. He had gone
so far astray as to prophesy (for it was nothing short of that)
in his journal, that there certainly would be a fulfilling of those
things which God by His Spirit had spoken to his soul ; that
he should see greater things than these ; and that there were
many promises to be fulfilled in him, many souls to be called,
and many sufferings to be endured before he should go hence.
In his answer he declares that God has in part fulfilled his
hopes of success ; that his enemies are fulfilling his expecta-
tions of sufferings ; and that some passages of Scripture are
so powerfully impressed upon his mind that he really believes
God will fulfil them in due time. Whitefield himself came
to see that he was mistaken in these views ; and he expunged
most, if not all, the obnoxious passages from his revised
journal, as well as declared his mistake frankly and fully. He
also did the same thing with the grounds of the seventh count,
which were a thoughtless use of Scriptural language. But on
the question of the last charge, which related principally to the
doctrine of justification, he not only boldly announced Soli-
fidianism, but adhered to it to the last. He was as impatient
as Luther of any mention of good works in connection with
justification. Works ought to come as the fruits and evidences
of justification ; but were not, even in the most limited sense,
to be called a condition of it.

A host of pens became busy upon the contested points,

some taking Whitefield's side, some the opposite. Their effusions add nothing to our knowledge.

In closing the journal which contains an account of his first open-air preaching, Whitefield made a tender appeal to others who might be constrained to do as he had done. He says:—

'I cannot but shut up this part of my journal with a word or two of exhortation to my dear fellow-labourers, whosoever they are, whom God shall stir up to go forth into the highways and hedges, into the lanes and streets, to compel poor sinners to come in. Great things God has already done. For it is unknown how many have come to me under strong convictions of their fallen state, desiring to be awakened to a sense of sin, and giving thanks for the benefits God has imparted to them by the ministry of His word. O my dear brethren! have compassion on our dear Lord's Church, which He has purchased with His own blood; and let them not perish for lack of knowledge. If you are found faithful you must undergo persecution. Oh, arm people against a suffering time; remind them again and again that our kingdom is not of this world, and that it does not become Christians to resist the powers that are ordained of God, but patiently to suffer for the truth's sake. Oh, let us strive together in our prayers, that we may fight the good fight of faith, that we may have that wisdom which cometh from above, and that we may never suffer for our own faults, but only for righteousness' sake: then will the spirit of Christ and of glory rest upon our souls, and being made perfect by suffering here, we shall be qualified to reign eternally with Jesus Christ hereafter. Amen! Amen!'

That appeal is as much needed to-day as ever, for the people must be sought, if they are to be found.

Conscious of the difficulty of passing through popularity and applause without moral injury—and by this time competing engravers were multiplying his portrait as fast as they could, and rival publishers were contending for his journals—anxious to subdue such pride and selfishness as still dwelt in him, longing to know himself better, and much worn down with the gigantic labours of the past seven months and a half, he went on board the *Elizabeth*, saying, 'Blessed be God! I am much rejoiced at retiring from the world.'

CHAPTER VII

August, 1739—March, 1741

THIRD VOYAGE—ITINERATING IN AMERICA—FOURTH VOYAGE
—BREACH WITH WESLEY

'MY family,' as Whitefield called the eight men, one boy, two children, and his friend Mr. William Seward, who accompanied him, had characters in it worth a passing notice—Periam, the methodical madman, whom we know; Seward, the rich layman; and Gladman, a sea captain, whom Whitefield got to know at the end of his last visit to Georgia. Seward was a gentleman of Evesham, thoroughly inspired with Methodist enthusiasm, who, to his wife's mortification, became Whitefield's companion in travel to help the good work. He was a Boswell in his admiration and fussiness, and but for his early death would have preserved many interesting facts which are now lost. Gladman was a convert who followed Whitefield from a double motive—love to the man and love to his Master. Distress brought him under Whitefield's notice. His ship had been wrecked on a sand-bank near the Gulf of Florida. After ten days spent in that situation by him and his crew, they sighted a vessel, and hoisted a signal of distress, which she answered. Gladman and part of his men pulled to her in a boat, and begged a passage for the whole number, which was promised them ; but, as soon as they put off for the sandbank the vessel made sail and left them   Thirty days more were spent in their confinement ; then they built a boat, into which he and five others stepped, with the determination to make their escape or perish ; the rest were fearful of such a frail craft and stayed behind.   Boat and crew came safe to Tybee Island, ten miles off Savannah, whither Gladman was brought, and where Whitefield invited him to breakfast.   A deliverance so great prepared him to receive the kindly counsels which were given him over the breakfast-table, and as host and guest soon afterwards returned to England in the same vessel, Gladman became, through further instruction, a Christian of deep conviction and firm faith.   Nothing would satisfy him but to return with Whitefield on his second voyage to Georgia.

The versatile preacher, who was well gifted with ability to become all things to all men, and to make himself contented in all places, had been on board ship but two days when he felt almost as forgetful of what he had passed through as if he had never been out in the world.   Present duty was the only thing that ever pressed hard upon him ; past bitterness he quickly forgot ; future troubles he left with God.   He lived one day at a time, and lived it thoroughly.   He framed regulations for his 'family,' instituted public prayer morning and evening, took to letter-writing and the reading of some very strongly flavoured divinity ; and at the same time indulged his favourite gift and passion of exhorting every one around him to follow his Lord and Master.   In this last-mentioned work he had the occasional help of a Quaker, to whom he would now and again lend his cabin.   The only grief was that the Quaker was not explicit enough upon justification by faith and upon the objective work of the Saviour.

Letter-writing was a great pastime of the Methodists, yet

none of them have written any letters worth preserving, either for their literary merit or their theological grasp.   All that was attempted was to comfort and cheer each other in the conflict with earth and hell; and hence their letters abound in 'experiences.'   Whitefield wrote sixty-five letters—none of them long, some of them mere notes—during his three months' voyage; they were addressed to converts who wanted encouragement, to backsliders who wanted reproof, to students who wanted cheering in their espousal of the cause of Christ, to ministers who wanted words of brotherly love.   This was the work of a man of only twenty-four years of age.

'Show them,' he says to Howel Harris about his congregations, 'show them in the map of the word the kingdoms of the upper world, and the transcendent glories of them; and assure them that all shall be theirs if they believe on Jesus Christ with their whole hearts.   Press on them to believe on Him immediately.   Intersperse prayers with your exhortations, and thereby call down fire from heaven, even the fire of the Holy Ghost,

> "To soften, sweeten, and refine,
>   And melt them into love."

Speak every time, my dear brother, as if it were your last; weep out, if possible, every argument, and, as it were, compel them to cry, "Behold, how he loveth us!"'

As America is approached, he begins to show that great things are shaping themselves in his mind, his world-wide work suggests itself; and with his usual promptitude he writes to a friend: 'I intend resigning the parsonage of Savannah.   The orphan-house I can take care of, supposing I should be kept at a distance; besides, when I have resigned the parish, I shall be more at liberty to take a tour round America, if God should ever call me to such a work.   However, I determine nothing: I wait on the Lord.'

The voyage was useful, both to his body and soul—to his soul, however, in a very distressing way.   His journal from

August to November is almost as dismal and painful as the early parts of Brainerd's. 'Tears were his meat day and night.' One extract will suffice to show what was his state of mind until towards the end of the voyage :—

'I underwent inexpressible agonies of soul for two or three days at the remembrance of my sins, and the bitter consequences of them. Surely my sorrows were so great that, had not God in the midst of them comforted my soul, the load would have been insupportable ! All the while I was assured God had forgiven me ; but I could not forgive myself for sinning against so much light and love. Surely I felt something of that which Adam felt when turned out of Paradise ; David, when he was convicted of his adultery ; and Peter, when with oaths and curses he had thrice denied his Master. I then, if ever, did truly smite upon my ungrateful breast and cry, God be merciful to me a sinner ! I ate but very little, and went mourning all the day long. At length my Lord looked upon me, and with that look broke my rocky heart, and floods of contrite tears gushed out before my whole family, and indeed I wept most bitterly. When in this condition I wondered not at Peter's running so slowly to the sepulchre, when loaded with the sense of his sin. Alas ! a consideration of aggravated guilt quite took off my chariot wheels, and I drove so exceeding heavily, that was I always to see myself such a sinner as I am, and as I did then, without seeing the Saviour of sinners, I should not so much as be able to look up. Lord, what is man !'

The old Puritan theology, of which he had been a student from the time of his conversion, began, during this voyage, to affect his views in a very decided way. Until this time the broad, plain statements of Scripture had sufficed for a foundation for his teaching. The calls to repentance and faith, the assurances of pardon and eternal life for as many as will turn to God, the commandments binding every man to purity of heart and life, the simple declarations of the unspeakable love wherewith the Saviour has loved us, and His power and willingness to help all who look to Him, constituted the message he had delighted to proclaim, and which, indeed, in spite of the views he was presently to embrace, he proclaimed to the last. He had been a primitive Christian. But now he must have a system of theology; he must hold with the free-grace men, or with the predestinarians; he must believe in free-will, or deny it; he must accept the dogma of imputed righteousness, or reject it. A book written by Jonathan Warn, called 'The Church of England-Man turned Dissenter, and Arminianism the Backdoor to Popery,' which contained extracts from *The Preacher*, by Dr. Edwards, of Cambridge, 'strengthened him much.' He tells Harris that, since he saw him, God has been pleased to enlighten him more in that comfortable doctrine of election, and now their principles agree, as face answers to face in the water. When he returns to Wales he will be more explicit than he had been; 'for God forbid, my dear brother, that we should shun to declare the whole counsel of God.' His Calvinism was not (as it never is in the purest hearts) a cold system of divinity, but a strong persuasion that, only by the acceptance of such dogmas and an earnest proclamation of them, could the glory and the honour be given to the God of our salvation. Whitefield was won over to Puritanism by the truth which has been the salt of that system—man must in no sense be a saviour to himself; he may watch and read and pray; he may practise good works— the more the better; he may—nay, he must—seek to perfect holiness in the fear of God, for every consideration of gratitude and love, every holy and tender tie which binds him to his Father in heaven, demands it; but he must not say a word about these being conditions for the reception of any favour from above. All is retrospective, all is of God. He provided —as the phrase is—a Saviour; He also determined who should be saved by the Saviour. He gave His people to the Redeemer, and the Redeemer to His people, in a covenant that should never be broken. But for the centering of every-thing in God, Whitefield would have cared nothing for his favourite theories.

While he was plunging into Calvinism, and determining to be more outspoken on the five points—happily he was slow at fulfilling this purpose—another mind, not less resolute, not less bold, and much more acute than his own, was as swiftly and irrevocably rushing into the opposite system of Arminianism. A separation between himself and Wesley was already inevitable if each adhered, as he was sure to do, to his own convictions. That determination ' to speak out, and hide none of the counsel of God,' was an extension of a crack already made in the foundations of Methodism, which was to grow wider and longer for many a day to come, though never so wide that divided friends could not shake hands across it.

Thankful for his voyage, and timid about facing the difficulties of public life on shore—the responsibility of preaching to large congregations, the temptations of popularity, and the opposition of such as differed from him—yet again joyful and fearless because he knew that many prayers were being offered for him, he landed at Lewis Town, about one hundred and fifty miles from Philadelphia. The ship's provisions had run out, as they used to do in those days, and the kind thoughtfulness of Whitefield's English friends, who had sent a good stock on board for him and his family, saved both crew and passengers from possible starvation, or a very lean dietary.

Whitefield, accompanied by his friend Seward, had a pleasant ride through the woods to the Quaker town, Philadelphia, which then numbered probably eleven or twelve thousand inhabitants, one third of whom were Quakers (half the inhabitants of the State of Pennsylvania were of the same faith). It was a long, straggling place, the houses pleasantly built in the midst of orchards ; the market-place unpaved ; the stocks, the pillory, and the whipping-post still standing   The last-named instrument of justice was in active operation, two

women a month being whipped at it.   Benjamin Franklin had
his printing-office opposite the market-place, and within sight
of the whipping-post.   The *Pennsylvania Gazette* was rejoicing
in great prosperity, through the shrewdness and industry of its
famous proprietor and editor.   *Poor Richard's Almanac* had
but a few years before given its wit and wisdom to the good
citizens for the sum of fivepence, and now some are willing to
give twenty dollars for a single number of it!   The people
were quiet, peace-loving, tolerant, and not so intellectual as the
Bostonians.   Vital godliness was said to be low among them.
Their desire to hear the great Methodist was intense ; for his
immense fame had reached their town before him.

Whitefield's first duty was to deliver some letters committed
to his charge, and then to go on board the *Elizabeth*, which
had arrived the night before him, to see his family.   He next
paid his respects to the proprietor and the commissary, who
received him 'very civilly.'   The day following, which was
Sunday, he preached to a large congregation, and took part in
other services.   The churchwardens treated him better than
their brethren in England had done, and the clergy of all
denominations showed him great courtesy.   Feeling was so
different from that which he had left behind him, that whereas
in England the only proper place for a sermon was thought to
be a church, in Philadelphia the people preferred hearing it
elsewhere, and asked him to gratify their taste, which he was
not slow to do.   The Quakers were very friendly, and their
fellowship cheered him not a little   The atmosphere all
around was peaceful, and balmy with brotherly love. . Aged
Mr. Tennent, who had an academy for training pious youths
for the ministry, about twenty miles from the city, and was
himself blessed with four sons of Christian reputation and
influence, three of whom were ministers, came into the city to
speak to him.   The week's stay which he made was as quiet

and agreeable as any he ever made in any place. All places of worship were open to him, all ministers favourable to him; and when he left the ordinary religious buildings to preach from the steps of the court-house to congregations no building could hold, and which listened in solemn silence while the prolonged twilight of the late autumn days filled the sky, he must have felt an unusual joy in his work. Once when the night was far advanced, and lights were shining in the windows of most of the adjoining houses, he felt as if he could preach all night; and indeed the night after, which was Saturday, the people, not feeling the pressure of a coming day's work, seemed so unwilling to go away after they had heard an hour's sermon, that he began to pray afresh, and afterwards they crowded his house to join in psalms and family prayer.

Franklin was a constant and delighted hearer. Calm and self-controlled under most circumstances, his temperament caught fire at the glowing words of Whitefield; and if he did not become a convert to his views, he became an attached and lifelong personal friend. It seems to have been during this visit that Whitefield triumphed so signally over Poor Richard's prudence. The story is well known, but too good to be omitted here. Whitefield consulted Franklin about the orphan-house, for which he was still making collections wherever money could be obtained. Franklin approved the scheme, but urged that the house should be built in Philadelphia, and not in a settlement which was thinly populated, where material and workmen were scarce, and which was not so prosperous as it had been. Whitefield did not heed this counsel, but determined to follow his own plan. This made Franklin decide not to subscribe.

' I happened soon after,' he says, ' to attend one of his sermons, in the course of which I perceived he intended to finish with a collection, and I silently resolved he should get nothing from me. I had in my pocket a handful of copper money, three or four silver dollars, and five pistoles in gold.   As he proceeded I began to soften, and concluded to give the copper.   Another stroke of his oratory made me ashamed of that, and determined me to give the silver ; and he finished so admirably, that I emptied my pocket into the collector's dish, gold and all !   At this sermon there was also one of our club who, being of my sentiments respecting the building in Georgia, and suspecting a collection might be intended, had, by precaution, emptied his pockets before he came from home.   Towards the conclusion of the discourse, however, he felt a strong inclination to give, and applied to a neighbour who stood near him to lend him some money for the purpose.   The request was made, perhaps, to the only man in the company who had the firmness not to be affected by the preacher.   His answer was : " At any other time, friend Hopkinson, I would lend thee freely ; but not now, for thee seems to me to be out of thy right senses." '

Anecdotes seldom bear dates, and we can only fit some of those which are told of Whitefield into the right part of space, the right locality, not heeding the right year of time.   Most probably it was near about the time of this visit that the observant Franklin tried to find out how far the preacher could be heard, when one night he was preaching near Franklin's shop.   He says : ' I had the curiosity to learn how far he could be heard, by retiring backward down the street towards the river, and I found his voice distinct till I came near Front Street, when some noise in that street obscured it. Imagining then a semicircle, of which my distance should be the radius, and that it was filled with auditors, to each of whom I allowed two square feet, I computed that he might well be heard by more than thirty thousand.   This reconciled me to the newspaper accounts of his having preached to twenty five thousand people in the fields, and to the history of generals haranguing whole armies, of which I had sometimes doubted.'

It has been said that Whitefield's visit ' threw a horrid gloom ' over the town, and for a time put 'a stop to the dancing schools, the assemblies, and every pleasant thing.' But if the innocent town was so oppressed by the 'terror-exciting preacher,' it showed a strange pleasure in always making him its welcome guest, and hanging upon his words. The truth is, terror was not the power he wielded, but loving, urgent, yearning tenderness, which could not endure the thought of any man's perishing in his sins. Whatever fault may be found with some of his views—and they lie exposed on every side, unguarded by argument, unmasked by sophistry—it never can be honestly charged upon him that he pictured the torments of the great condemnation in flashy colours, or with morbid pleasure; every allusion to the casting out was filled with a spirit which testified also of the joy of welcome. It is not meant that he was silent on the awful question of future punishment; for, seeing he firmly believed in it, silence would, in his case, have been mental reservation, and his nature was too frank and too transparent to keep anything back. Knowing the terror of the Lord, he persuaded men. All his beliefs had power over him, fashioning his character, and determining his ministry; but his soul lived mostly on the radiant side of his creed, and from his visions of love, and peace, and joy, he went forth to tell what he had seen. And if the people of Philadelphia walked under a cloud while Whitefield enjoyed their free and generous hospitality, it was a cloud which 'burst in blessings on their head.' That silent night, when the houses all around the preaching-stand had lights in their windows, near which sat or stood some listener, was a night of penitence for one lost soul, of a class which used often to find their way to the Man of Sorrows, but which too seldom come now to any pastor. Next morning, before it was light, she came to Whitefield's house, and desired to join in prayer; and when devotions were over, left the following letter with him:—

'Oh, what shall I say to express my thanks I owe to my good God, in and from you through Jesus Christ (for the good work) which you have been the instrument of beginning in my soul; and if you have any regard to a poor, miserable, blind, and naked wretch, that's not only dust but sin, as I am confident you have, you will in no wise reject my humble request, which is that I, even I, may lay hold of this blessed opportunity of for-saking all, in order to persevere in a virtuous course of life.'

The trembling, hoping penitent had not long been gone when the ' terror-inspiring ' man was approached by a child of seven, who came to request him to take her to Georgia, as she had heard that he was willing to take little children with him !

Three months before his arrival at Philadelphia, a letter had come from Mr. Noble, of New York, who wrote in his own name, and the name of many others, inviting him to that place ; a second letter came immediately after his arrival, repeating the request. He determined to go. Friends lent him and his party four horses, and they rode on through the woods, stopping at Burlington and Trent Town, at which places he preached with great freedom, and Brunswick, where they met with Gilbert Tennent, the eccentric Presbyterian minister of the place, who imitated the rude dress of the Baptist, and preached with terrible power. Nothing that Whitefield could say could surpass the fiery sarcasm and thundering denunciation of Tennent ; indeed, Whitefield's sermons must have been like refreshing showers after a prairie fire, when he came into the neighbourhood of Tennent's labours. The stern preacher had delivered his soul of a faithful message in the spring of this year on 'The Danger of an Unconverted Ministry,' and had printed it for an abiding testimony among the people. It was based upon the pathetic words of the Evangelist, 'And Jesus, when He came out, saw much people, and was moved with compassion toward them, because they were as sheep not having a shepherd.' This sermon was epoch-making, for it determined the evangelical character of the Presbyterian ministry in America from that day to the present.

Tennent joined Whitefield's party, and rode off with them to New York, to join in the preaching campaign, the journey being shortened by each traveller's telling the rest what God had done for his soul. Mr. Noble received them 'most affectionately,' and that night Tennent preached at the meeting-house, 'but never before,' says Whitefield, 'heard I such a searching sermon. He went to the bottom indeed, and did not daub with untempered mortar. He convinced me more and more that we can preach the gospel of Christ no further than we have experienced the power of it in our own heart. Being deeply convicted of sin, and driven from time to time off his false bottoms and dependencies by God's Holy Spirit at his first conversion, he has learned experimentally to dissect the heart of the natural man. Hypocrites must either soon be converted or enraged at his preaching. He is a son of thunder, and I find doth not fear the faces of men.'

New York was not so tolerant as Philadelphia. The Commissary denied Whitefield the use of his pulpit before it was even asked for, and angrily informed him that his assistance was not wanted. Whitefield replied, that 'if they preached the gospel he wished them good luck in the name of the Lord, and that, as the church had been denied without being asked for, he should preach in the fields, for all places were alike to him.' To the fields he went that afternoon, and though some seemed inclined to mock, they soon grew more serious. An attempt to get the town-hall was unsuccessful; but Pemberton, the Presbyterian minister, was glad to have him in his meeting-house, which was crowded night after night; and some who had been profligate learned to look upon their past lives with shame. That Whitefield, along with his fine indignation at the unfaithfulness of unworthy men, who held the sacred office of pastor and teacher, and his ardent zeal to save all men, had a touch of censoriousness, and perhaps peremptoriness, this latter quality growing upon him as he got older, while the former declined, cannot be denied ; but his spirit must also have had rare reverence for age and goodness. He was no young upstart, who, thinking himself so much more competent to guide the people, delighted to treat old men and their views with neglect ; he never looks more dignified and manly than when, with respect in his manner and diffidence in his heart, he meets some aged Samuel, like old Mr. Tennent, or old Mr. Pemberton, and takes his place as a listener and learner. After leaving New York, his sensitive mind, which cherished the memory of the least kindness with fond faithfulness, became uneasy about some fancied want of humility in the presence of Mr. Pemberton, and he sought to make amends in a letter which must have touched the good man's heart deeply.

A letter written to his mother, when he reached New York, will show his relation to the old home circle, and how constantly the one absorbing topic of salvation by Christ was on his pen and his tongue :—

' NEW YORK, *November* 16, 1739.

' HON. MOTHER,—Last night God brought me hither in health and safety. I must not omit informing you of it. Here is likely to be some opposition, and consequently a likelihood that some good will be done. New friends are raised up every day whithersoever we go ; the people of Philadelphia have used me most courteously, and many, I believe, have been pricked to the heart. God willing ! I leave this place next Monday, and in about a fortnight think to set out for Virginia by land. In about a twelvemonth I purpose returning to England ; expect then to have the happiness of seeing me suffer for my Master's sake. Oh ! that God may enable you to rejoice in it ! If you have the spirit of Christ, you will rejoice ; if not, you will be sorrowful. Oh ! my honoured mother, my soul is in distress for you ; flee, flee I beseech you, to Jesus Christ by faith. Lay hold on Him, and do not let Him go. God hath given you convictions. Arise, and never rest till they end in a sound conversion. Dare to deny yourself. My honoured mother, I beseech you by the mercies of God in Christ Jesus, dare to take up your cross and follow Christ.

' I am, honoured mother, your ever dutiful, though unworthy son,

' GEORGE WHITEFIELD.'

The return of the party from New York was a preaching tour, under the direction of Tennent, who in due time brought them to Neshamini, where his father lived, and where White- field was announced to preach. It may serve to keep alive an interest in his feelings amidst his labours, to mention that, in the early part of the service, the three thousand people who were assembled to hear him seemed unaffected, that this caused him to 'wrestle' much for them in himself, and that at night he had to withdraw for a while from the conversation of the circle of holy men, to recover in private his composure and joy. Then they talked together of what plans would be the best for promoting the kingdom of our Lord.   The best plan, however, was already in operation in that log-house which stood hard by, old Mr. Tennent's Academy, 'the College,' as it was contemptuously called by such as thought that learning could not be nursed in such rude quarters, whatever might become of any piety which sought its shelter.   Seven or eight good men had just gone forth from it to their work ; more were almost ready to follow ; and a foundation was being laid for the instruction of many others.   The minister whose soul was so hot about the ' Pharisee-teachers ' who knew nothing of the new birth, had here a work which thoroughly commanded his heart.   They all felt sure that it was right.   Out of the log-house, which the dauntless, vehement, sarcastic Tennents built in faith, rose Princeton College.

His wandering life, the excitement which his presence always caused, and the curiosity of all to see and hear him, were sure to bring to his notice some of the oddest phases of life, and some of the saddest and tenderest too.   One day he was taken to see a hermit, who had lived a solitary life for forty years— a hermit, but not a misanthrope.   The old man talked with much feeling of his inward trials, and when asked by White- field whether he had not many such in so close a retirement, he answered with pathos and beauty : 'No wonder that a single tree which stands alone is more exposed to storms than one that grows among others.' He rejoiced to hear of what was being done in England, and kissed his visitor when they parted —the old man to continue solitary, the young man to live and think and feel with the eyes of thousands on him daily. A little hitch in life might once have made the preacher the hermit; for had not he also shunned human society, neglected all ordinary comforts, and wrestled with his troubles alone, as the single tree which has no fellows to shelter it contends with the storm ?

The next day a German came to him as he was passing along the street, and said: 'Thou didst sow some good seed yesterday in German Town, and a grain of it fell into my daughter's heart. She wants to speak with thee, that she may know what she must do to keep and increase it.' The daughter, who was standing hard by, came at her father's call, and both stood weeping while Whitefield exhorted to watchfulness and prayer and closeness of fellowship with the Saviour. Wonderful gentleness and sympathy must have graced him whom repentant prodigals, little children, and women could approach without fear, and whom old men loved as a son.

The good people of Philadelphia showed their appreciation of their visitor, not only by crowding to his services, but by sending him presents for his family, which was to proceed to Savannah by sea while he went by land, preaching wherever he could get a congregation. Franklin's newspaper for November contained the intelligence that—

'On Thursday last, the Rev. Mr. Whitefield left this city, and was accompanied to Chester by about one hundred and fifty horse, and preached there to about seven thousand people. On Friday he preached twice at Willing's Town to about five thousand ; on Saturday, at Newcastle, to

about two thousand five hundred; and the same evening at Christiana
Bridge, to about three thousand; on Sunday, at White Clay Creek, he
preached twice, resting about half an hour between the sermons, to about
eight thousand, of whom about three thousand, it is computed, came on
horseback. It rained most of the time, and yet they stood in the open
air.'

Meanwhile his interest in other workers was not abated.
His heart was in England with the Wesleys, in Wales with
Harris, and in Scotland with the Erskines. A correspondence
with the Scotch brothers was preparing the way for a trip over
the border some day. He writes to Ralph—Ralph was the
gentle, sensitive, poetical brother; Ebenezer, the bold, fearless,
dignified one, who preached the truth in its majesty—

'The cordial and tender love which I bear you will not permit me to
neglect any opportunity of sending to you. I bless the Lord from my
soul for raising you and several other burning and shining lights, to appear
for Him in this midnight of the Church. . . . My only scruple at present
is, "whether you approve of taking the sword in defence of your religious
rights?" One of our English bishops, I remember, when I was with him,
called you Cameronians. They, I think, took up arms, which I think to be
contrary to the spirit of Jesus Christ and His apostles. Some few passages
in your sermon before the Presbytery, I thought, were a little suspicious of
favouring that principle.'

Another difficulty, besides the question of appealing to arms
to decide religious belief, stood in the way of a union between
the English priest and the Scotch Presbyters. The latter held
the divinity of their form of Church government and the
sacredness of their ordination in so exclusive a way as practically to excommunicate a minister of any other Church.
Whitefield refers to this in another letter to the same friend.
He says—

'I think I have but one objection against your proceedings—your
insisting only on Presbyterian government, exclusive of all other ways
of worshipping God. Will not this, dear sir, necessarily lead you (when-

ever you get the upper hand) to oppose and persecute all that differ from you in their Church government, or outward way of worshipping God ? Our dear brother and fellow-labourer, Mr. Gilbert Tennent, thinks this will be the consequence, and said he would write to you about it. As for my own part (though I profess myself a member of the Church of England). I am of a catholic spirit ; and if I see a man who loves the Lord Jesus in sincerity, I am not very solicitous to what outward communion he belongs.'

His fears about opposition, if not about persecution, proved only too true ; he himself was to get no small share of it. The denominational spirit and the spirit catholic clashed as soon as ever they met.

To get again upon his track southwards. Once away from White Clay Creek and William Tennent's hospitality, he had a ride through forest, swamp, and partially cleared country, seeing and sharing in the life of the sparse population which lay scattered along his route. Gentlemen were as glad to show kindness to travellers, where few human beings were to be seen, as travellers were to receive it ; and thus the private house—generally that of a military man—was as often the resting-place for the night as the tavern. But taverns were a welcome lodge, though noisy guests might sleep in the next room, or the bed be made in the kitchen ; for sometimes the way was dangerous enough to gratify anybody with a Robinson Crusoe nature—the evening wolves would come out and howl like a kennel of hounds round the travellers. Odd meetings with people who had some connection with the old country, and whose talk could pleasantly recall the past, now and again happened. The congregations were like everything else ; now a handful of forty, now a hundred in place of the usual twenty, now the family whose hospitality was being enjoyed, and now a stray visitor who came in nobody knew how, and in every case the Negroes of the house were got together.

The account of crossing the Potomac helps one to realise the condition of the whole land through which they were passing. ' Potomac,' Whitefield says, ' is a river which parts the two provinces, Maryland and Virginia. It is six miles broad. We attempted to go over it ; but, after we had rowed about a mile, the wind blew so violently, and night was coming on so fast, that we were obliged to go back and lie at the person's house who kept the ferry, where they brought out such things as they had.' Christmas Day was spent very pleasantly at Newborn Town ; public worship was attended, the sacrament was received, a congregation was gathered to hear the word, and heard it with tears ; the hostess provided a Christmas dinner, and would take no fare from the traveller when he offered it. New Year's Day was spent in riding ; and at sunset a tavern was reached, which stood just within South Carolina ; but another kind of visitor than a parson, and especially a Methodist parson, would have been more welcome when the house had a goodly company of neighbours who had come together for a dance ! Such a company, however, must have a word of exhortation, and he gave it both night and morning. The morning proved as delightful as the night was to prove disagreeable. For twenty miles the travellers rode along the shore of a beautiful bay, as level as a terrace walk, the porpoises that were enjoying their pastime making sport for them all the way. Whitefield's heart rejoiced to hear shore resounding to shore, across the noble expanse, the praise of Him who hath set bounds to the sea that it cannot pass. Then they rode into the forest, and had to take their chance among the roads and by-roads. As night came on the moon was too beclouded to show them where the by-paths led from the main road, and thus the path to a house where they purposed seeking lodgings was missed. There was nothing for it but to push on till some resting-place could be reached,

and they had not gone far before they saw a light. Two of
them went up towards it, and saw a hut full of Negroes, of
whom they inquired about the gentleman's house to which
they had been directed. The Negroes seemed surprised, and
said that they were but new-comers, and knew no such man.
This made one of the more timid hearts infer that these
Negroes might be some of a company which had made an
insurrection in the province, and had run away from their
masters. All the rest adopted his suspicion, and therefore
thought it best to mend their pace. Soon another great fire
was seen near the roadside, and the travellers, imagining that
there was a second nest of rebels, made a circuit into the
woods, and one of them observed Negroes dancing round the
fire. The moon now shone out clearly, and they soon found
their way again into the main road, along which they rode for
twelve miles, expecting at every step to come upon more fires
and more Negroes, when they had the good fortune to see a
large plantation, the master of which gave them lodging.
' Upon our relating the circumstances of our travels,' says
Whitefield, ' he gave us satisfaction about the Negroes,
informed us whose they were, and upon what occasion they
were in those places in which we found them.' Two short
days more and a morning carried him safe into Charles Town
(abbreviations in names had not begun at this time, and
Charleston was still called by its full name), and a ride of
seven hundred and fifty miles was over.

His absence from Charles Town had not been long, but
still sufficiently so to allow of changes. He himself was
changed into a field-preacher ; and in consequence of this,
Commissary Garden, who, on the preceding visit to America,
had promised to defend him with life and fortune, was changed
into a cold friend and then into a hot enemy, who refused the
use of the English Church. However, there were the Inde-

pendent meeting-house and the French Church, where 'very polite congregations' were as plainly addressed as the Kingswood colliers.

The rest of the distance to Savannah was performed by water, in an open canoe, steered and rowed by five Negro slaves. 'The poor slaves,' he says, 'were very civil, diligent and laborious.' The first night they slept on the water, and the second on the shore, with a large fire to keep away wild beasts. At noon on the second day they reached Savannah, and had a joyful meeting with the family, which had been there three weeks. He looks more like a settled family man during the three months after his arrival, than during any other part of his life. The huge congregations, which would not allow of five minutes' leisure with him, are left behind; so too is the anger of opponents. The poor orphans are around him, and his humane heart thinks and feels for them with unwearied tenderness, as if they were the lambs of his own home. He busies himself about them daily, and watches the progress of the work which is to make them as good a home as they can have, now that the dear old places are silent and lonely, without father or mother. On the second morning after his arrival he went to see a tract of land, consisting of five hundred acres, which Habersham, whom he had left schoolmaster of Savannah when he returned to England, had chosen as the site of the orphanage.

'The land,' he says, 'is situated on the northern part of the colony, about ten miles off Savannah, and has various kinds of soil in it ; a part of it very good. Some acres, through the diligence of my friends, are cleared. He has also stocked it with cattle and poultry. He has begun the fence, and built a hut ; all which will greatly forward the work. I choose to have it so far off the town because the children will then be more free from bad examples, and can more conveniently go upon their lands to work ; for it is my design to have each of the children taught to labour, so as to be qualified to get their own living. Lord, do Thou teach and excite them to labour also for that meat which endureth to everlasting life.   Thursday, January 24th.—Went this morning and took possession of my lot.   I hope it is cast in a fair ground, and God, in answer to our prayers, will show that He has given us a goodly heritage.   I called it Bethesda, that is, the house of mercy ; for I hope many acts of mercy will be shown there, and that many will thereby be stirred up to praise the Lord, as a God whose mercy endureth for ever.   Tuesday, January 29th.—Took in three German orphans, the most pitiful objects, I think, that I ever saw.   No new Negroes could possibly look more despicable, or require more pains to instruct them. Was all the money I have collected to be spent in freeing these three children from slavery, it would be well laid out.   I have also in my house near twenty more, who, in all probability, if not taken in, would be as ignorant of God and Christ, comparatively speaking, as the Indians. Blessed be God, they begin to live in order.   Continue this and all other blessings to them, for Thy infinite mercy's sake, O Lord, my strength and my Redeemer.   Wednesday, January 30th.—Went this day with the carpenter and surveyor, and laid out the ground whereon the orphan-house is to be built.   It is to be sixty feet long and forty wide ; a yard and garden before and behind.   The foundation is to be brick, and is to be sunk four feet within, and raised three feet above, the ground.   The house is to be two story high with a hip roof ; the first ten, the second nine feet high.   In all there will be nearly twenty commodious rooms. Behind are to be two small houses, the one for an infirmary, the other for a workhouse.   There is also to be a still-house for the apothecary ; and I trust ere my return to England, I shall see the children and family quite settled in it.   I find it will be an expensive work ; but it is for the Lord Christ.   He will take care to defray all charges.   The money that will be spent on this occasion will keep many families from leaving the colony ; there are near thirty working at the plantation already, and I would employ as many more if they were to be had.   Whatsoever is done for God ought to be done speedily, as well as with all our might.   Monday, February 4. Met, according to appointment, with all the magistrates, and the former trustee of the orphans, who heard the recorder read over the grant given me by the Trustees, and took a minute of their approbation of the same. Lord, grant that I and my friends may carefully watch over every soul that is or shall be committed to our charge ! '

Whitefield did not wait until the orphanage was ready before beginning his philanthropic work, but at once hired a large house, and took in all the orphans he could find in the colony ; and that he might get all, he went to several of the settlements and brought them home himself. He says that 'a great many also of the town's children came to school gratis ; and many poor people who could not maintain their children, upon application had leave given them to send their little ones for a month or two, or more, as they could spare them, till at length my family consisted of between sixty and seventy. Most of the orphans were in poor case, and three or four almost eaten up with lice. I likewise erected an infirmary, in which many sick people were cured and taken care of gratis. I have now by me' (he writes this six years afterwards) 'a list of upwards of a hundred and thirty persons who were under the surgeon's hands, exclusive of my private family. This surgeon I furnished with all proper drugs and utensils, which put me to no small expense.'

The foundation-brick of the 'great house,' as he calls the orphanage, was laid by himself on Tuesday, March 25, 1740, without any parade—even without a silver trowel or a mahogany mallet—but with full assurance of faith. The workmen were the spectators, and knelt down with him to offer the dedication prayer. They sang a hymn together, and he gave them a word of exhortation, bidding them remember to work heartily, knowing that they worked for God. Forty children were then under his care, and nearly a hundred mouths had to be sup-, plied with food.

But all was not at rest. His very friendships were to cause him his greatest troubles ; and the first signs of them appeared while he was busy among his family ; there a letter and a journal from John Wesley reached him. That Whitefield himself had been anxious about the respective views of Calvin and Arminius has been told already, and also that he had determined to speak out the conclusions he had come to. For once he was behind his friend, and it was an honourable slowness to contention. Wesley, while at Bristol, had been accused in a letter, apparently anonymous, of not preaching the gospel, because he did not preach up election. This led him to consult the lot as to whether he should preach and print his sermon on free-grace, and the lot he drew said 'preach and print'; and accordingly he did so; but at Whitefield's request, who was then in England, he desisted from publishing so long as his friend remained in the country.

Soon after Whitefield sailed the sermon appeared. Wesley also adopted into his creed the doctrine of perfection; that is, 'free, full, and present salvation from all the guilt, all the power, and all the in-being of sin.' His letter to Whitefield at Savannah was upon their respective doctrines of election and perfection, asking him to give up the former and embrace the latter. To this Whitefield could not consent; he answered him :—

'I could now send a particular answer to your last; but, my honoured friend and brother, for once hearken to a child, who is willing to wash your feet. I beseech you by the mercies of God in Christ Jesus our Lord, if you would have my love confirmed toward you, write no more to me about misrepresentations wherein we differ. To the best of my knowledge, at present no sin has dominion over me, yet I feel the strugglings of indwelling sin day by day. I can therefore by no means come into your interpretation of the passage mentioned in the letter, and as explained in your preface to Mr. Halyburton. The doctrine of election, and the final perseverance of those who are in Christ, I am ten thousand times more convinced of, if possible, than when I saw you last. You think otherwise; why, then, should we dispute, when there is no probability of convincing? Will it not in the end destroy brotherly love, and insensibly take from us that cordial union and sweetness of soul which, I pray God, may always subsist between us? How glad would the enemies of the Lord be to see us divided! How many would rejoice, should I join and make a party against you! And, in one word, how would the cause of our common Master every way suffer by our raising disputes about particular points of doctrine! Honoured sir, let us offer salvation freely to all by the blood of Jesus; and whatever light God has communicated to us, let us freely communicate it to others. I have lately read the life of Luther, and think it nowise to his honour, that the last part of his life was so much taken up in disputing with Zuinglius and others, who in all probability equally loved the Lord Jesus, notwithstanding they might differ from him in other points. Let this, dear sir, be a caution to us ; I hope it will be to me ; for, by the blessing of God, provoke me to it as much as you please, I do not think ever to enter the lists of controversy with you on the points wherein we differ. Only I pray to God, that the more you judge me, the more I may love you, and learn to desire no one's approbation but that of my Lord and Master Jesus Christ.'

Unfortunately he did not abide by these truly Christian purposes, neither was Wesley so forbearing as he ought to have been.

Whitefield's kind heart was busy with another good work while he was gathering the orphans to his house. That month's ride through Maryland, Virginia, and Carolina had brought him near slavery and all its revolting accessories ; and he was pained at the heart. It would not do to be silent about the wrongs of such as had no helper ; he took pen in hand, and wrote to the inhabitants of those three states, expostulating with them on their cruel treatment of their slaves. But Whitefield was absolutely blind to the wickedness of slavery as slavery ; it was only the brutal conduct of some of the masters that appeared wrong to him. At his first visit to Georgia he expressed his persuasion that the colony must always continue feeble, if the people were denied the use of rum and slaves ; and he afterwards dishonoured himself by becoming a slave-owner, and working his slaves for the good of the orphanage. There is little or nothing to be said in extenuation of his conduct ; for though it was a popular notion in his day, that slavery was permissible, it was not the notion of every one ; and he might have come to a better understanding of the subject had he pondered it. Among his Quaker and Moravian friends there were some who could have led him into the light, had he spent time in conferring with them ; but his incessant preaching gave him no opportunity for thinking and forming an independent conclusion. He had only one thought, and cared nothing for a second, because the first was paramount. It might have been impossible for him to preach, and at the same time plead for the freedom of the Negroes; but at least he might have kept his own hands clean, and have given a practical rebuke to his neighbours' sins. One sentence in his letter shows that his mind might have arrived at a just conclusion but for the hurry which called him away to other things : ' Whether it be lawful for Christians to buy slaves, and thereby encourage the nations from whence they are brought to be at perpetual war with each other, I shall not take upon me to determine.' But that was just the thing he was bound to determine ; and if his convictions on the unlawfulness of war for religious ends had any depth in them, which hardly appears to have been the case, he must have concluded that war for enslaving men who were of the same flesh as their captors and buyers, and of equal value in the sight of God, must be much less justifiable than religious wars. It may be safely affirmed that the lash was never used on the farm where the orphan-house stood ; that the children were not brutalised by the sight of cruelty ; and that the Negroes did not go home weary and sore to grind their corn for the evening meal. But slavery is still slavery, however its condition is mitigated.

On the day of the appearance of the letter to the slave-owners, Seward chronicled in his journal a story which well illustrates the quality of Negro human nature. He says : ' Heard of a drinking club that had a Negro boy attending them, who used to mimic people for their diversion. The gentlemen bid him mimic our brother Whitefield, which he was very unwilling to do ; but they insisting upon it he stood up, and said, " I speak the truth in Christ, I lie not ; unless you repent, you will all be damned." This unexpected speech broke up the club, which has not met since.'

Within six days of the ceremony at Bethesda, Whitefield was called northward by the claims of the orphans, who must be maintained ; and nothing could be found for them in Georgia. He sailed in his sloop, and no sooner got on board than he devoted his time to the writing of as strange and loveless a love-letter as ever was penned. It was addressed to an English lady at Blendon, no doubt Miss Elizabeth Delamotte, sister of Mr. Delamotte, who first welcomed him to Georgia, and was enclosed in one addressed to her parents, in which they are asked whether they think their daughter a proper person to be his helpmeet in his work, *i.e.*, be the matron of his orphanage. He declared that his heart was free from 'that foolish passion which the world calls LOVE.' His letter to Miss E—— was in the same strain ; he makes 'no great profession' to her. She, however, did not care to be wooed for a housekeeper instead of a wife ; and Whitefield stood a rejected suitor, but not a disappointed lover, for he subsequently learned that at the time of his offer the lady (in spiritual things) was in a 'seeking state' only ; besides, he was not in love.

The sloop made a quick passage to Newcastle, from whence Whitefield hastened his journey to Philadelphia by way of Willingtown. The truth had not been inactive during the absence of its eloquent preacher ; some it had conquered, others it had hardened and driven into open hostility. All around Philadelphia, as well as in the city, there was much religious excitement ; and many ministers who had been of the 'Pharisee-teacher class,' had become earnest, active labourers, and were following up Whitefield's work. The minister of Abingdon passed through a very great trial before he entered into the spiritual peace enjoyed by Whitefield ; and his honesty of conduct attests his sincerity of mind. He had been for some years a preacher of the doctrines of grace without knowing the power of what he taught, until Whitefield came and preached for him. After Whitefield's departure, he attempted to preach, but failed. Humbly confessing to his congregation the deception he had practised on himself and them, he asked those of them who could pray to make inter-cession for him. Still anxious and unsettled, he again resumed his work ; for he judged that in the way of duty he would be most likely to find light and peace ; nor was he left without the blessing he so earnestly desired. A congregation which had a pastor in such a state of mind could hardly fail to receive Whitefield's word with great emotion ; 'a great in-fluence was observable' among them when he spoke, and 'the word came with a soul-convicting and comforting power to many.'

The Commissary of Philadelphia told Whitefield that he could lend him his pulpit no more. Thanking God that the fields were open, he betook himself to Society Hill next day, and preached in the morning to six thousand, and in the even-ing to eight thousand. On the following Sunday morning, at seven o'clock, ten thousand assembled to hear him, and gave him one hundred and ten pounds for his orphans ; and yet Philadelphia itself had only about twelve thousand souls. The same day he went morning and evening to church, and had the comfort of being treated as he treated others who did not think with him. The minister preached upon justification by works, and did his best to damage Whitefield's favourite doctrine of justification by faith, though with ill success ; for many hearers who had entered church on seeing Whitefield go in, were more deeply persuaded than ever of the truth of evangelical doctrines. Besides, such attacks made him look like a persecuted man, and gave him something to answer ; hence it was no wonder that, when he went from the church to preach in the open air, fifteen thousand people came together. A second collection of eighty pounds showed that more than curiosity, or a desire to hear a reply, had moved them to come.

From Franklin to tipplers there was one subject of conversation. The tipplers, Whitefield says, 'would mutter in coffee-houses, give a curse, drink a bowl of punch, and then cry out against me for not preaching up more morality.' Franklin was amazed at the way in which people of all denominations went to hear him ; he speculated on the extraordinary influence of Whitefield's oratory on his hearers, and on their admiration and respect for him, notwithstanding they were often told they were half beasts and half devils. He wondered to see the change soon made in the manners of the inhabitants—how, from being thoughtless or indifferent about religion, it seemed as if all the world were growing religious; so that no one could walk through the town of an evening without hearing psalms sung in different families of every street.

The indiscreet zeal of Seward might, during this visit, have cost both him and Whitefield, whom he seems to have fawned upon, very serious consequences. Excited at finding that a son of Penn was one of the proprietors of the assembly rooms, he obtained the key of the rooms from the keeper, under a promise that he would take the consequences, and then locked the door, to drive out all the people to hear Whitefield. This freak cost him a good deal of abuse, a threat that he should be caned, and the maintenance of the keeper's family. Another of his follies was to trumpet Whitefield's praises in the newspapers by writing both advertisements and paragraphs. He gave his own colouring in the New York papers to his exploit with the assembly rooms, and made it appear that the rooms had been closed by some one in authority. His disingenuous paragraph was as follows :—

'We hear from Philadelphia that, since Mr. Whitefield's preaching there, the dancing-school and concert-room have been shut up as inconsistent with the doctrines of the gospel ; at which some gentlemen were so enraged that they broke open the door.   It is most extraordinary that such devilish diversions should be supported in that city, and by some of that very sect whose first principles are an utter detestation of them, as appears from William Penn's " No Cross, no Crown," in which he says, " every step in a dance is a step to hell." '

Circumstances called both Gladman and Seward away from Whitefield's side before New York was reached ; and it cannot be regretted that the latter, much as Whitefield was attached to him, never returned.¹ They were despatched to England to bring over some one to take charge of the orphanage in Whitefield's absence, to acquaint the Trustees of Georgia with the state of the colony, to procure an allowance of Negroes — that is, slaves ; also a free title to the lands, an independent magistracy, and money for building the church at Savannah. Seward died in 1741, in Wales, as the result of a blow from a rioter—a martyr, his work for Whitefield unfinished.

Sick and weary, Whitefield preached his way from Philadelphia to New York, where his friend Mr. Noble received him. A strong, healthy man might flatter himself that he had achieved marvels, could he say that he had done as much as Whitefield did there under weakness of body and much loneliness of heart.   The services were early and late, numerous, sometimes

---

¹ Here is a scene in Benjamin Franklin's shop, occasioned by this paragraph. ' May 23, 1740.—Called at Mr. Franklin's the printer's, and met Mr. P—— and several other gentlemen of the Assembly, who accosted me very roughly concerning a paragraph I had put in the papers, alleging it to be false.   They much insisted that my paragraph insinuated as if the gentlemen were convicted of their error by Mr. Whitefield's preaching, which they abhorred.   I told them I thought no one would construe it so ; but if they did, it was an honour to them, for that I myself was formerly as fond of them as they could be, but, blessed be the Lord, that I was convinced to the contrary,'—' Journal of a Voyage from Savannah to Philadelphia, &c., by William Seward, Gent., companion in travel with the Rev. Mr. George Whitefield,' 1740.

in the fields, and attended by crowds which few speakers could have made hear. Brotherly kindness was there to cheer him, and the generosity of the people, who gave him three hundred pounds, stirred all his gratitude. It was here, too, that he received the first of those childish letters from his dear orphans, which were afterwards to reach him both in England and America. He does not say what they contained, but only that in a packet of letters from Charles Town and Savannah 'were two or three letters from my little orphans.'

Still feeble and low in spirits, he preached his way back from New York to Philadelphia, and was welcomed to the house of Anthony Benezet, the friend of the Negroes; but to tell how he preached and was preached against—how he comforted the sin-stricken and cared for the Negroes, who came in large numbers to ask for his counsel, would be to repeat a tale already told. A new feature, however, was beginning to manifest itself in his congregations, though it was not very remarkable until he reached Nottingham, where the Tennents and other men of a similar spirit had been labouring with much success for some time, and to which he was invited in the strongest terms by some of the inhabitants. Thinly populated as the place was, nearly twelve thousand people were assembled, many of them having come from a great distance ; indeed, it was common for a great number to go with him as far from their homes as they conveniently could ; and on the morning when he last left Philadelphia, two boats, that plied the ferry near Derby, were employed from three o'clock in the morning until ten in ferrying passengers across who wanted to hear him as often as possible. He had not spoken long before he perceived numbers melting; as he proceeded the influence increased, till at last, both in the morning and afternoon, thousands cried out, so that they almost drowned his voice.

Oh, what strong crying and tears,' he says, ' were shed and poured
forth after the dear Lord Jesus ! Some fainted, and when they had got a
little strength, would hear and faint again. Others cried out in a manner
almost as if they were in the sharpest agonies of death. And after I had
finished my last discourse, I myself was so overpowered with a sense of
God's love, that it almost took away my life. However, at length I
revived, and having taken a little meat, was strengthened to go with
Messrs. Blair, Tennent, and some other friends, to Mr. Blair's house, about
twenty miles from Nottingham. In the way we refreshed our souls by
singing psalms and hymns. We got to our journey's end about midnight,
where, after we had taken a little food, and recommended ourselves to
God by prayer, we went to rest, and slept, I trust, in the favour as well as
under the protection of our dear Lord Jesus. Oh, Lord, was ever love like
Thine ? '

The next day, at Fog's Manor, where Blair was minister,
the congregation was as large as that at Nottingham, and as
great, Whitefield says, ' if not a greater, commotion was in the
hearts of the people. Look where I would, most were
drowned in tears. The word was sharper than a two-edged
sword, and their bitter cries and groans were enough to pierce
the hardest heart. Oh ! what different visages were there to
be seen. Some were struck pale as death, others were
wringing their hands, others lying on the ground, others
sinking into the arms of their friends, and most lifting up
their eyes towards heaven, and crying out to God for mercy !
I could think of nothing, when I looked upon them, so much
as the great day. They seemed like persons awakened by the
last trump, and coming out of their graves to judgment.'

His affectionate nature was beautifully shown in the many
thoughtful letters and messages which he addressed to all kinds
of friends during the time that the sloop waited at Newcastle
for a fair wind to take him to Savannah. But the affection he
was wont to inspire was strongest in the hearts of the orphans
and his dependent family, and on his return to Savannah with
the five hundred pounds that he had collected among the

northern Churches, each in turn hung upon his neck, kissed him, and wept over him with tears of joy.

Next day the house was a miniature Nottingham-Fog-Manor congregation. The excitement began with a man who had come with him from the scenes of his preaching triumphs, and who became much stirred up to pray for himself and others. Whitefield also went and prayed for half an hour with some of the women of the house and three girls, who seemed to be weary with the weight of their sins. At public worship young and old were all dissolved in tears. After service, several of his parishioners, all his family, and the little children, returned home crying along the street, and some could not refrain from praying aloud as they went. Weak and exhausted he lay down for a little rest, but the condition of most in the house constrained him to rise again and pray; and had he not lifted his voice very high, the groans and cries of the children would have prevented his being heard. This lasted for nearly an hour, and the concern increasing rather than abating, he wisely desired them to retire. They did so, and then began to pray in every corner of the house. A storm of thunder and lightning which burst over the town at this time added to the solemnity of the night, and reminded them the more vividly of the coming of the Son of man. All were not quiet even the next day. And no marvel, when we consider how profoundly interested every one had been in the result of Whitefield's trip to the North. His success was their home, their comfort, their life; and his failure their return to want and misery. His coming opened the fountain of all hearts, and natural gratitude rose quickly into higher religious emotions under his influence, by whom God had wrought penitence, broken-heartedness, and reformation among total strangers, among rugged sailors, and among opposers, who owed him nothing till they owed him themselves.

His return to Savannah introduces us again to the Wesley trouble. His last day on board the sloop, May 24, 1740, was partly spent in writing to friends in England, John Wesley among the number. He said :—

' Honoured sir, I cannot entertain prejudices against your principles and conduct without informing you. The more I examine the writings of the most experienced men, and the experiences of the most established Christians, the more I differ from your notion about not committing sin, and your denying the doctrines of election and the final perseverance of the saints. I dread coming to England, unless you are resolved to oppose these truths with less warmth than when I was there last. I dread your coming over to America, because the work of God is carried on here, and that in a most glorious manner, by doctrines quite opposite to those you hold. Here are thousands of God's children who will not be persuaded out of the privileges purchased for them by the blood of Jesus. Here are many worthy experienced ministers who would oppose your principles to the utmost. God direct me what to do ! Sometimes I think it best to stay here, where we all think and speak the same thing : the work goes on without divisions, and with more success, because all employed in it are of one mind. I write not this, honoured sir, from heat of spirit, but out of love. At present I think you are entirely inconsistent with yourself, and therefore do not blame me if I do not approve of all you say. God Himself, I find, teaches my friends the doctrine of election. Sister H—— hath lately been convinced of it ; and if I mistake not, dear and honoured Mr. Wesley hereafter will be convinced also. From my soul I wish you abundant success in the name of the Lord. I long to hear of your being made a spiritual father to thousands. Perhaps I may never see you again till we meet in judgment ; then, if not before, you will know that sovereign, distinguishing, irresistible grace brought you to heaven. Then you will know God loved you with an everlasting love, and therefore with loving-kindness did He draw you. Honoured sir, farewell. My prayers constantly attend both you and your labours. I neglect no opportunity of writing. My next journal will acquaint you with new and surprising wonders. The Lord fills me both in body and soul. I am supported under the prospect of present and future trials with an assurance of God's loving me to the end, yea, even to all eternity.'

The brotherly spirit is still there, but in a more decided attitude towards the disputed question and the treatment it should receive, his intercourse with the northern Presbyterians having made him change thus much. The counsel to moderation and to avoid teaching doctrines on which the Methodist leaders were divided was, notwithstanding his resolution, made during his last voyage, to speak out, honourably acted upon by himself. He wrote to a friend in London, beseeching him to 'desire dear brother Wesley, for Christ's sake, to avoid disputing with him. I think I had rather die than to see a division between us ; and yet, how can we walk together if we oppose each other?' In another letter, which was written on June 25th, he beseeches Wesley, for Christ's sake, never, if possible, to speak against election in his sermons. 'No one,' he says, ' can say that I ever mentioned it in public discourses, whatever my private sentiments may be. For Christ's sake let us not be divided among ourselves ; nothing will so much prevent a division as your being silent on this head.' Then he runs into a pleasanter strain, where his heart was most at home: 'I should have rejoiced at the sight of your journal. I long to sing a hymn of praise for what God has done for your soul. May God bless you more and more every day, and cause you to triumph in every place.'

Before these last words reached Wesley, he replied, in a very short but kindly letter, to the letter of May 24th :—

'The case is quite plain. There are bigots both for predestination and against it. God is sending a message to those on either side. But neither will receive it, unless from one of their own opinion. Therefore, for a time, you are suffered to be of one opinion, and I of another. But when His time is come, God will do what man cannot, namely, make us both of one mind. Then persecution will flame out, and it will be seen whether we count our lives dear unto ourselves, so that we may finish our course with joy.'

We look in vain, however, for any response to the entreaty not to follow a public course of hostility to his old friend.

The fashionable people of Charleston, now considerably changed in spirit and manner by the preaching of Whitefield, were anxious again to hear him before his intended visit to New England. He set sail, and came to them fresh from the excitement of Savannah, where, to use his own metaphor, 'the stately steps of our glorious Emmanuel often appeared.' Commissary Garden having denied him the use of the church, he preached in the meeting-house of his friend the Independent minister, and for this alleged irregularity the commissary cited him to appear before him. Whitefield denied the authority, and appealed home. To preach his last sermon to 'the dear people of Charleston' he went from his bed, and was carried to the chapel, the intense heat having quite exhausted him. Many of the rich people all around showed him great respect and hospitality; and on the day of his departure from Charleston he rode to the house of Colonel Bee, of Ponpon, forty miles from town, which was reached at midnight. The next morning he was too weak to offer family prayer, but at noon he rode a mile and preached under a great tree to an attentive auditory. Weakness hindered either a second sermon or any further advance that day. 'Surely,' he said, 'it cannot be long ere this earthly tabernacle will be dissolved. As the hart panteth after the water brooks, so longeth my soul after the full enjoyment of Thee, my God.' The next day he travelled and preached, but the effort almost cost him his life. Sometimes he hoped that God would set his imprisoned soul at liberty. The thoughts of his Saviour's love to him, and that the Lord was his righteousness, melted him into tears. A dear friend and companion wept over him, and seemed not unwilling to take his flight with him into 'the arms of the beloved Jesus.' The poor Negroes, who had learnt from their master that the sufferer was a friend of their race, crowded around the windows, expressing by their looks and attentions

great concern. The master sat by and wept. ' But, alas ! '
says Whitefield, who hoped his time of departure was come,
'alas ! in a short time I perceived my body grow stronger, and
I was enabled to walk about.' He got back among the
beloved orphans in a very prostrate condition, and could
hardly bear up under the joy and satisfaction which he felt.
The arrival of some Charleston friends somewhat revived him,
but again he was cast down by weakness of body and concern
of mind; and one night, just as he began family prayer, he was
struck, as he thought, with death. A few broken accents, a
soft prayer—' Lord Jesus, receive my spirit'—fell from his
lips. Yet he was still appointed to life. The next day was
Sunday, and feeble indeed must he have been to give up, as
he did, the thought of officiating. More friends, however,
had come in, and when he solicited a Baptist minister who
was among the visitors to preach for him, that gentleman
peremptorily refused, and urged (so great was his faith for
another !) that God would strengthen him if he began. And
Whitefield stood rebuked. The willing heart mustered the
body's broken powers for another effort, and hardly had his
prayer begun when one of the visitors dropped ' as if shot by
a gun.' The power of God's word, as the visitor himself
explained his conduct, had entered his heart. He soon arose,
and sat attentively to hear the sermon. The influence quickly
spread abroad, and the greatest part of the congregation was
under deep concern. When Whitefield and his friends
returned home, the Baptist minister said : ' Did I not tell you
God would strengthen you ? ' Whitefield bowed his head,
feeling that he was justly reproved, and prayed, when he
recorded the events of the day in his journal, ' Dearest Lord,
for Thy mercies' sake, never let me distrust Thee again.
O me of little faith ! "

Pressing invitations to visit New England having come to

him from the Rev. Dr. Colman and Mr. Cooper, ministers in Boston, and feeling desirous to see the descendants of the Puritans, he left his family again, and sailed first to Charleston and thence to Rhode Island, several Charleston friends accompanying him. By this time his frame had recovered something of its former vigour, through the cooler weather and the fresh sea breezes, yet he was not sanguine of recovery. He wrote to Wesley—

' Last night I had the pleasure of receiving an extract of your journal. This morning I took a walk and read it. I pray God to give it His blessing. Many things, I trust, will prove beneficial, especially the account of yourself; only give me leave with all humility to exhort you not to be strenuous in opposing the doctrines of election and final perseverance, when, by your own confession, "you have not the witness of the Spirit within yourself," and, consequently, are not a proper judge. I remember dear brother E—— told me one day that " he was convinced of the perseverance of the saints. I told him you was not. He replied, but he will be convinced when he hath got the Spirit himself. I am assured God has now for some years given me this living witness in my soul. When I have been nearest death, my evidences have been the clearest. I can say I have been on the borders of Canaan, and do every day—nay, almost every moment—long for the appearing of our Lord Jesus Christ ; not to evade sufferings, but with a single desire to see His blessed face. I feel His blessed Spirit daily filling my soul and body, as plain as I feel the air which I breathe, or the food I eat. . . . I wish I knew your principles fully. Did you write oftener and more frankly, it might have a better effect than silence and reserve.'

Whitefield was thoroughly consistent in his pleadings for peace. His complaint that Wesley was silent and reserved came from his deep dislike of having anything hidden. To 'walk with naked hearts together' was his conception of brotherliness and friendship, and his patience was taxed by the cooler temperament of his friend. Longer consideration might have led him to believe that Wesley's silence was a sign of unwillingness to dispute, but an ardent nature like his cannot understand such profound self-possession. The day after he wrote to Wesley he wrote to a friend in Bristol, and said—

> 'I hear there are divisions among you. Avoid them if possible. The doctrines of election and final perseverance I hold as well as you. But then they are not to be contended for with heat and passion. Such a proceeding will only prejudice the cause you would defend. Pray show this to your other friends. Exhort them to avoid all clamour and evil speaking, and with meekness receive the engrafted word, which is able to save your soul.'

Rhode Island was expecting its visitor. He reached Newport just after the beginning of Sunday evening service, and sat in the church undiscovered, as he thought; but friendly eyes had marked him, and, after sermon, a gentleman asked him whether his name was not Whitefield. 'Yes, it was.' Then the unknown friend would provide lodgings for him and his party. Soon a number of gentlemen, chief of them all old Mr. Clap, an aged Dissenting minister, who had held his charge for forty years, and was much esteemed for his good works, came to pay their respects to him. The minister of the Church of England consented to Whitefield's preaching in his pulpit. The Assembly one day adjourned its sitting to attend Divine worship. The same respect was shown him at Bristol; but his heart was cold in his work, and others seemed to feel little. When he had approached within four miles of Boston, he was met by the governor's son, several other gentlemen, and two ministers; the brother-in-law of Dr. Colman received him to his house; the governor of Massachusetts, Jonathan Belcher, was gratified that he had come, and gave him his special friendship, a friendship that never wavered; the commissary was polite, but declined to give him the use of the church. A famous divine, who was said to be prejudiced against him and also his enemy, when he met him in the street, remarked: 'I am sorry to see you here.' 'And so is the devil,' replied Whitefield. Once again were the meeting-houses and the fields to be his sanctuaries. But before we mingle with the crowds which thronged them, it will be necessary to pay some attention to several packets of letters which came to him at Boston immediately after his arrival.

The friends from England wrote him strange things. The Methodist camp was distracted with the cries of two sections of theologians, holding respectively the views of Wesley and Whitefield. To have his favourite doctrine of election contested and spoken against had troubled Whitefield; to see a new doctrine, that of perfection, exalted in its place, ruffled him still more; and the news which came to Boston made him offer his first word of expostulation. To Howel Harris he expressed his fears for his place in the affection of his English converts. 'Some of Fetter Lane Society, I fear, are running into sad errors; but this happens for our trial, especially mine. Those that before, I suppose, would have plucked out their eyes for me, now, I suspect, I shall see very shy, and avoiding me. My coming to England will try my fidelity to my Master.' His manner to Wesley was the impatience of an unheeded affection :—

'HONOURED SIR,' he began, 'this is sent in answer to your letter dated March 25th. I think I have for some time known what it is to have righteousness, joy, and peace in the Holy Ghost. These, I believe, are the privileges of the sons of God; but I cannot say I am free from indwelling sin. I am sorry, honoured sir, to hear by many letters that you seem to own a sinless perfection in this life attainable. I think I cannot answer you better than a venerable old minister in these parts answered a Quaker : "Bring me a man that hath really arrived to this, and I will pay his expenses, let him come from where he will." I know not what you may think ; I do not expect to say indwelling sin is finished and destroyed in me till I bow down my head and give up the ghost. Besides, dear sir, what a fond conceit it is to cry up perfection, and yet cry down the doctrine of final perseverance ! But this and many other absurdities you will run into, because you will not own election, because you cannot own it without believing the doctrine of reprobation. What, then, is there in reprobation so horrid? I see no blasphemy in holding that doctrine, if rightly explained. If God might have passed by all, He may pass by some. Judge whether it is not a greater blasphemy to say, "Christ died for souls now in hell." Surely, dear sir, you do not believe there will be a general gaol delivery of damned souls hereafter? Oh, that you would study the covenant of grace! Oh, that you were truly convinced of sin and brought to the foot of sovereign grace! Elisha Cole, on "God's Sovereignty," and "Veritas Redux," written by Dr. Edwards, are well worth your reading. But I have done. If you think so meanly of Bunyan and the Puritan writers, I do not wonder that you think me wrong. I find your sermon has had its expected success; it hath set the nation a disputing. You will have enough to do now to answer pamphlets; two I have already seen. Oh, that you would be more cautious in casting lots! Oh, that you would not be too rash and precipitant! If you go on thus, honoured sir, how can I concur with you? It is impossible; I must speak what I know.'

That 'great blasphemy,' if blasphemy it be, was not altogether avoided by Whitefield himself, who, in the most impassioned way, would call upon his hearers to tell him how he could let souls perish for whom Christ died; no phrase recurs with greater frequency in his tenderest passages. Neither need much emphasis be laid on the doctrine of reprobation, which he seemed to regard with unruffled complacency and satisfaction. It was only in his letters and in his talk, and that only for a brief period, that it got such honourable mention. His sermon on 'The Potter and the Clay,' which might fairly have been supposed to be built upon this conception of election and reprobation, rests on a far different foundation—the old foundation of all theology. Every son of man is, in the sight of God, 'only as a piece of marred clay'; being marred, he must necessarily be renewed by the Holy Ghost. 'A short word of application' winds up the whole discourse.

The Boston meeting-houses were filled to the utmost of

their large dimensions by the congregations which crowded to hear the famous clergyman. A terrible and unaccountable panic seized one of the congregations as it was awaiting his appearance. Some threw themselves out of the gallery, others leaped from the windows, and some of the strong trampled upon the weak. When he came it was a scene of wild confusion. His invincible presence of mind did not forsake him, and he announced his intention to preach on the common. Many thousands followed him through the rain into the field; but there were five dead persons left behind in the meeting-house, and others were dangerously wounded. The calamity, which weighed heavily on his spirits, in nowise damaged his popularity, because, notwithstanding the lamentable selfishness shown by some of the people in the meeting-house, there was a real desire to know the truth.

Neighbouring towns were not forgotten. One of his excursions extended over one hundred and seventy-eight miles, and had sixteen preachings, yet he returned to Boston without being in the least fatigued. The students of Cambridge had several visits from him, and his language to them was, according to his after confession, made in the most public manner both from the pulpit and the press, both harsh and uncharitable. He suffered himself to be guided too much by hearsay; and there are always plenty of alarmists who can find nothing but heresy in tutors and worldliness in students.

One of his greatest pleasures was to meet with the many aged, devout ministers who were in Boston and its neighbourhood. There was old Mr. Clap, of Rhode Island, a bachelor, who gave away all his income to the poor and needy, and stood the friend of children, servants, and slaves, through a ministry of forty years. There was also old Mr. Walters, of Roxburg, whose ministry, with that of his predecessor, Eliot, the apostle of the Indians, had lasted in the Roxburg congre-

gation one hundred and six years. There was the Rev. Mr.
Rogers, of Ipswich, a lineal descendant of Rogers the martyr,
who lived to hear three of his sons and a grandson preach
the gospel : they were all labouring in Whitefield's day. At
York was one Mr. Moody, a worthy, plain, and powerful
minister of Jesus Christ, though now much impaired by
old age, says Whitefield. Puritan habits still obtained in
New England. Whitefield relates with satisfaction that the
'Sabbath in New England begins on Saturday evening, and
perhaps is better kept by the ministers and people than in
any other place in the known (!) world.'

The generosity of Boston was not behind that of any place.
At Dr. Sewall's meeting-house an afternoon congregation gave
five hundred and fifty pounds to the orphanage ; and on the
same day, at Dr. Colman's meeting-house, a second afternoon
congregation gave four hundred and seventy pounds.[1] The
immense number of people slowly, and as if unwilling to depart
without giving, left the meeting-house. The minister said that
it was the pleasantest time he had ever enjoyed in that place
throughout the whole course of his life. There must have
been something thoroughly good in these 'Lord Brethren.'

By what power of compression Whitefield contrived to get
five different services into the Sunday when he had those
noble collections is not clear, and the perplexity is increased
on finding that three letters bear the date of that autumn day.
Well might his animal spirits be almost exhausted, and his
legs be almost ready to sink under him at night. One of the
letters, the longest, relieved the day with a good-humoured
piece of banter, sent to a brother whose weak mind had been
disturbed by Whitefield's neatness of dress ; for things were
very different from the Oxford days, when he neglected him-

---

[1] The currency in New England was so much depreciated at this time
that £100 sterling was equal to £550 Massachusetts currency.

self that he might be a good Christian. Now his dress and
everything about him was kept in scrupulous order. Not a
paper in his room was allowed to be out of its place, or put
up irregularly ; every chair and piece of furniture was properly
arranged when he and his friends retired for the night. He
thought he could not die easy if he had an impression that his
gloves were mislaid.

'I could not but smile '—he wrote to his friend—'to find you wink at
the decency of my dress. Alas ! my brother, I have known long since
what it is to be in that state you are, in my opinion, about to enter into.
I myself once thought that Christianity required me to go nasty. I
neglected myself as much as you would have me for above a twelvemonth ;
but when God gave me the spirit of adoption, I then dressed decently, as
you call it, out of principle ; and I am more and more convinced that the
Lord would have me act in that respect as I do. But I am almost ashamed
to mention any such thing.'

The second letter of that day's date informed his friend,
that so many persons came to him under convictions and for
advice, that he scarce had time to eat bread. In the third
letter he says :—

'DEAR BROTHER WESLEY,—What mean you by disputing in all your
letters? May God give you to know yourself, and then you will not plead
for absolute perfection, or call the doctrine of election a "doctrine of
devils." My dear brother, take heed ; see you are in Christ a new creature.
Beware of a false peace ; strive to enter in at the strait gate, and give
all diligence to make your calling and election sure. Remember you are
but a babe in Christ, if so much. Be humble, talk little, think and pray
much. Let God teach you, and He will lead you into all truth. I love
you heartily. I pray you may be kept from error, both in principle
and practice. Salute all the brethren. If you must dispute, stay till
you are master of the subject ; otherwise you will hurt the cause that
you defend.'

The commotion caused in Boston by his presence and
preaching was not diminished by a report which was very
current during one of his excursions, that he had died
suddenly, or had been poisoned ; the people were all the

more rejoiced to see him for their late fear that they had lost him. Everything fanned the flame of zeal, both in the people and in the preacher, and the end of the visit was more remarkable than the beginning. The touching words of a little boy, who died the day after he heard Whitefield preach, furnished the ground of one of Whitefield's strongest appeals to old and young ; immediately before he died the child said : ' I shall go to Mr. Whitefield's God.' Old people bowed their heads in grief, not in anger, when the preacher, with a tenderness that desired the salvation of all, said : ' Little children, if your parents will not come to Christ, do you come, and go to heaven without them.' The last congregation, which consisted of about twenty thousand, assembled on the common, and the myriad faces, thoughtful, eager, attentive, the great weeping, and the darkening shades of evening which, towards the close of the service, was coming on fast, recalled Blackheath scenes of a year before. His labours over, Governor Belcher, whose attentions had been most kind and uninterrupted, drove him, on the Monday morning, in his coach to Charleston Ferry, handed him into the boat, kissed him, and with tears bade him farewell. Whitefield returned with five hundred pounds for his orphans.

Whitefield's intention on leaving Boston was to proceed to Northampton to see Jonathan Edwards, whom he describes as ' a solid excellent Christian, but at present weak in body.' A great revival had taken place in Northampton some five or six years before, and Whitefield's ministrations quickened afresh all the feelings of that memorable season. In point of fact he was, through all his travels in New England, largely entering into other men's labours, and he frankly and gladly said so. Yet the two great men did not come very close together. Whitefield did not make a confidential friend of Edwards, and Edwards gave Whitefield very necessary cautions about his notions on impulses, and his habit of judging others to be unconverted. They, indeed, loved each other as servants of the same Lord, and rejoiced in each other's work. Edwards might be seen sitting weeping while his visitor preached.

From Northampton he passed on to other places. At New Haven he dined with the rector of the college, Mr. Clap. The aged governor of the town also received him with tears of joy. His preaching here was upon the subject of an unconverted ministry, and he did not altogether avoid his Cambridge fault of censuring too hastily and too severely. Riding through Milford, Stratford, Fairfield, and Newark, at each of which he preached, he came to Stanford, where his words smote with unusual effect. Many ministers hung upon his track, and at Stanford two of them confessed, with much sorrow, that they had laid hands on two young men without asking them whether they were born again of God or not. An old minister, who could not declare his heart publicly, called Whitefield and his friend Mr. Noble out, to beg, as well as his choking emotions would allow him, their prayers on his behalf. He said that although he had been a scholar, and had preached the doctrines of grace a long time, he believed that he had never felt the power of them in his own soul.

At this point Whitefield set up his 'Ebenezer' and gave God thanks for sending him to New England, of which he speaks in the highest terms. It was well settled; large towns were planted all along the east of it; meeting-houses abounded; no such thing as a pluralist or non-resident minister could be found; the colleges had trained many men of God; God was honoured in private and public life; and the Holy Spirit had often been poured out upon churches and people.

It was with but a desponding heart, and not expecting any

great movings of soul among his hearers, that he rode towards New York. His companion, Mr. Noble, tried to encourage him, by assuring him that his last visit had done good to many, and bade him look for great things from God. The first service was an earnest of things not looked for. Pemberton's meeting-house contained an anxious congregation on Friday morning, some being hardly able to refrain from crying out ; and at night the excitement was greater still. On Sunday his soul was down in the depths ; before going to evening service he could only cast himself on the ground before God, confessing himself to be a miserable sinner, and wondering that Christ would be gracious to such a wretch. On his way to the meeting-house he became weaker, and when he entered the pulpit he would rather have been silent than have spoken. The preparation for his work was such as only devoutest souls, who feel a constant need for the comfort and aid of an invisible Friend, can have ; and the effect of the sermon was marvellous. Scarcely was it begun before the whole congregation was alarmed. Loud weeping and crying arose from every corner of the building. Many were so overcome with agitation that they fell into the arms of their friends. Whitefield himself was so carried away, that he spoke until he could hardly speak any longer.

Larger congregations came the next day, and the feeling was still intense. In the evening he bade them farewell, and carrying with him a hundred and ten pounds as their gift to his orphanage, passed across to Staten Island. At Newark the scenes of New York were renewed. The word fell like a hammer and like fire. Looking pale and sick as if ready to die, one cried as he staggered to the ground, 'What must I do to be saved ? ' Whitefield's host from Charleston, who seemed to be accompanying him because of a personal affection for him, and not because of thorough religious sympathy

with him, was struck down and so overpowered that his
strength quite left him; it was with difficulty he could move all
the night after.   From that time he became an exemplary Christian, and continued such to the last.   Whitefield was now
thoroughly spent, and could only throw himself upon the bed
and listen to his friend Tennent while he recounted a
preaching excursion he had lately made.   The power of the
Divine Presence passed on with them to Baskinridge, where
weeping penitents and rejoicing believers prayed side by side.
The apathy of many was changed into deep alarm, and the
alarm passed into exultant joy.

Whitefield reached Philadelphia exactly a year after his
first visit to that city.   The season of the year, November,
was too late for comfortable open-air services, and the
Philadelphia people, having once suffered from inconvenience,
had made provision against it for the future.   Whitefield had
not been long gone when they determined to build a house
which should be at the disposal of any preacher who had
anything to say to them, but his accommodation was their first
object.   Persons were appointed to receive subscriptions;
land was bought; and the building, which was one hundred feet
long and seventy broad, begun.   When Whitefield returned,
it was well advanced, though the roof was not up.   The floor
was boarded, and a pulpit raised, and he had the satisfaction
of preaching the first sermon in it.   It afterwards became, by
common consent, an academy as well as a preaching place,
and is now the Union Methodist Episcopal Church.

This visit was similar to the previous one; only a success
and a failure were noticeable.   The failure was that once his
congregation did not cry.   The success was with Brockden,
the recorder, a man of more than threescore years, who came
under the power of Whitefield's words.   In his youth he had
had some religious thoughts, but the cares of business

banished them, and he at length sunk almost into atheism. His avowed belief, however, was deism, on behalf of which he was a very zealous advocate. At Whitefield's first visit he did not so much as care to see what his oratory was like, and at the second visit he would not have gone to hear him but for the persuasion of a deistical friend. He went at night when Whitefield was preaching from the court-house steps, upon the conference which our Lord had with Nicodemus. Not many words were spoken before his interest was awakened by the conviction that what he was hearing tended to make people good. He returned home, reaching it before his wife or any of his family. First his wife entered, and expressed her hearty wish that he had heard the sermon ; but he said nothing. Another member of the family came in, and made the same remark ; still he said nothing. A third returned, and repeated the remark again. ' Why,' said he, with tears in his eyes, ' I have been hearing him.' The old man continued steadfast in the truth, and was privileged to have spiritual joys as deep as his teacher's.

When Whitefield came to Savannah and learnt that his family had been removed to their permanent home at Bethesda, he went thither. The great house, he found, would not be finished for two months longer, in consequence of the Spaniards having captured a schooner laden with bricks intended for it, and with provisions intended for the workmen and children. He found also that a planter, who had learned of Christ at the orphanage, had sent the family rice and beef, and that the Indians had often brought in large supplies of venison when there was no food left. The work of religion, which was dearer to him than even feeding the orphan, prospered among the children, among the labourers, and among the people round about. His heart was contented with his work, although he was five hundred pounds in debt, after all his

exhausting labours and the generous gifts of his friends.   He
now appointed Mr. Barber to take care of the spiritual affairs
of the institution, and intrusted to James Habersham the
charge of its temporal affairs.   The institution anticipated,
in its cheerful tone and wise management, those well-ordered
schools which in later times have brightened childhood's years
in thousands of instances.   Religion was the great concern;
but due weight was laid upon the connection between its
emotional and its practical parts.   Praying might not exempt
from working in the fields or at some trade, and spiritual
delights might not supersede method in labour and humility
of heart.   The orphans often sang a hymn for their benefactors; daily they sang to the praise of their Redeemer;
and always before going to work they joined in a hymn
intended to teach them that they must work for their own
living.

Whitefield had carried about with him, and shown to several
New England ministers, the draft of a letter which he had
written in reply to Wesley's sermon on 'Free-Grace,' and on
Christmas Eve, 1740, he sat down at the orphan-house to
finish the letter, and send it to his friend.   The sermon was
a noble specimen of eloquence; its thrilling denunciations of
Calvinistic doctrines almost produce the persuasion that they
are as horrible and blasphemous as Wesley believed them to
be.   The headlong zeal of the preacher allows no time,
permits no disposition, to reason.   You must go with him; you
must check your questions, and listen to him.   At the end
it seems as if the hated doctrines were for ever consumed in
a flame of argument and indignation.   The letter in reply
can boast no such qualities; it never rises above the level of
commonplace.   It was headed by a short preface touching the
probable effect of its publication and expressing the persuasion
that the advocates of universal redemption would be offended;

that those on the other side would be rejoiced ; and that the lukewarm on both sides—such as were 'carried away with carnal reasoning'—would wish that the matter had never been brought under debate. The second were very properly, but very unavailingly, asked not to triumph, nor to make a party; and the first not to be too much concerned or offended. One paragraph was sadly illustrative of the keenness with which men who have enjoyed each other's confidence can strike at weaknesses.

'I know,' Whitefield says, 'you think meanly of Abraham, though he was eminently called the friend of God ; and I believe, also, of David, the man after God's own heart. No wonder, therefore, that in the letter you sent me not long since, you sho..ld tell me, " that no Baptist or Presbyterian writer whom you have read knew anything of the liberties of Christ." What ! neither Bunyan, Henry, Flavel, Halyburton, nor any of the New England and Scots divines? See, dear sir, what narrow-spiritedness and want of charity arise from your principles, and then do not cry out against election on account of its being " destructive of meekness and love." '

It was a small matter what Wesley might think of Abraham or David, but Whitefield should have abstained from alluding to opinions expressed in private. The last part of the letter was a wonderful compound of sense, love, and assumption.

'Dear, dear sir, oh be not offended ! For Christ's sake be not rash ! Give yourself to reading. Study the covenant of grace. Down with your carnal reasoning. Be a little child, and then, instead of pawning your salvation, as you have done in the late hymn-book, if the doctrine of universal redemption be not true ; instead of talking of sinless perfection, as you have done in the preface to that hymn-book, and making man's salvation to depend on his own free-will, as you have in this sermon, you will compose a hymn in praise of sovereign, distinguishing love. . . And it often fills me with pleasure to think how I shall behold you casting your crown down at the feet of the Lamb, and as it were filled with a holy blushing for opposing the Divine sovereignty in the manner you have done. But I hope the Lord will show you this before you go hence. Oh, how do I long for that day !'

The letter made a shorter passage across the Atlantic than its writer generally did; and having, in some unexplained way, fallen into the hands of the Calvinistic party in London, was instantly printed, and used for their ends without either Whitefield's or Wesley's consent. A great many copies were given to Wesley's Foundry congregation, both at the door, and in the Foundry itself. 'Having procured one of them,' says Wesley, 'I related (after preaching) the naked fact to the congregation, and told them, I will do just what I believe Mr. Whitefield would, were he here himself. Upon which I tore it in pieces before them all. Every one who had received it did the same; so that, in two minutes, there was not a whole copy left. Oh! poor Ahithophel! *"Ibi omnis effusus labor!"'*

Apprehensive of some difficulties that awaited him in England, Whitefield took ship at Charleston, along with some friends, in the middle of January. During the whole voyage he was anxious for the future. One day he was yearning for a full restoration of friendship with the Wesleys; the next he was meditating the publication of his answer to the sermon on 'Free-Grace,' and consoling himself with the thought that it was written in much love and meekness; a third day he seemed to hear the Divine voice saying to him, 'Fear not, speak out, no one shall set upon thee to hurt thee;' another day he was writing to Charles Wesley deploring the pending separation, expostulating with him and John as if they could undo the past, and declaring that he would rather stay on the sea for ever than come to England to oppose him and his brother. He knew not what to do, though he knew perfectly well what he wanted—the old friendship to be what it had once been, and every dividing thing, whether raised by him self or the brothers, done utterly away. Nor were his longings for peace stronger than those of Charles Wesley. It is painful to observe the way in which the two friends strove, with un-

availing effort, against a tide which they felt was hurrying
them into trouble and sorrow. Four months before Whitefield
wrote his reply to the sermon on 'Free-Grace,' Charles, just
recovering from a severe illness, sent him a letter, 'labouring
for peace,' in which he used the strongest and most affectionate
language; he declared that he would rather Whitefield saw
him dead at his feet than opposing him; that his soul was
set upon peace, and drawn after Whitefield by love stronger
than death. When Whitefield reached England, the meeting
between them was most touching. 'It would have melted
any heart,' says Whitefield, 'to have heard us weeping, after
prayer, that, if possible, the breach might be prevented.'
Soon afterwards, however, he submitted his letter, which he
had had printed before leaving America, to the judgment of
his friend, who returned it endorsed with these words: 'Put
up thy sword into its place.' But not so. That evil fortune
which made Wesley preach and print a sermon on one of the
profoundest subjects, under the provocation of an anonymous
letter, and at the dictation of a lot; which prevailed over
Charles' loving letter, and tempted Whitefield to pen and
print his reply, still hovered near, and soon triumphed over
the counsel of love and wisdom which was heeded only for
awhile. At first he said that he would never preach against
the brothers, whatever his private opinion might be. Then
his doctrines seemed to him to be too important to be held
back; and when he went to the Foundry, at the invitation of
Charles, to preach there, he so far forgot himself, though
Charles was sitting by him, as to preach them, according to
the testimony of John, 'in the most peremptory and offensive
manner.' When John, who had been summoned to London,
met him, he was so far from listening to compromise as to
say, that 'Wesley and he preached two different gospels, and
therefore he not only would not join with him, or give him

the right hand of fellowship, but would publicly preach against him wheresoever he preached at all.' He next ungenerously accused Wesley of having mismanaged things at Bristol, and perverted the school at Kingswood to improper uses, foreign to the intention with which it had been undertaken. It was easy for the accused to answer all that was alleged against him ; but, unfortunately, he took occasion, at the same time, to indulge in most irritating language towards Whitefield. He assumed an air of superiority, of patronage and pity, which would have ruffled many a cooler man than his former friend. It was more taunting than kind to write : ' How easy were it for me to hit many other palpable blots in that which you call an answer to my sermon ! And how above measure contemptible would you then appear to all impartial men, either of sense or learning ! But I spare you ; mine hand shall not be upon you; the Lord be judge between me and thee ! The general tenor, both of my public and private exhortations, when I touch thereon at all, as even my enemies know, if they would testify, is, " Spare the young man, even Absalom, for my sake ! " '

It may be safely affirmed that the two friends would not have quarrelled had they been left to themselves. They were the unwilling heads of rival parties among their own converts. ' Many, I know,' said Charles Wesley in his letter to Whitefield, ' desire nothing so much as to see George Whitefield and John Wesley at the head of different parties, as is plain from their truly devilish plans to effect it ; but, be assured, my dearest brother, our heart is as your heart.' Whitefield, as we have seen from his American letters, received embittering news from home ; and on his arrival his ear was assailed by reports from brethren who were already openly opposed to Wesley and those who held his views. True, there was also the anger of Wesley on account of Whitefield's indefensible breach of confidence ; and that and the meddling of partisans did more damage than the doctrines in dispute. The matter may be summed up thus: Wesley was wrong in the beginning— 1. In attacking Whitefield's views at the taunt of an anonymous enemy ; he struck the first blow, and struck it without sufficient cause. 2. In printing and publishing his sermon because of a lot. 3. In using irritating language to his opponent. Whitefield was wrong—1. In yielding his mind to the influence of inflaming representations sent to him from England, and made to him when he returned home. 2. In exposing private opinions and deeds. 3. In preaching his peculiar views in the chapel of the Wesleys.

It is but a sad task to record these things, and the high character of the chief actors makes it all the more painful. Happily, the course of events soon took a different direction ; and the shadow resting upon the close of this chapter and the opening of the next will soon be seen breaking and vanishing away.

CHAPTER VIII

March, 1741—August, 1744

LOSS OF POPULARITY—FIRST VISIT TO SCOTLAND—CONDUCT OF THE DISSENTERS

ON March 25, 1741, Whitefield wrote to Habersham at the Orphanage a dark yet hopeful account of his trials. The divisions among the Methodists affected his congregations so greatly that from twenty thousand they dwindled down to two or three hundred, and he was a thousand pounds in debt for the orphans, and not worth twenty pounds of his own; he was even threatened with arrest for three hundred and fifty pounds drawn for in favour of the orphan-house by his late 'dear deceased friend and fellow-traveller, Mr. Seward.' His bookseller, who had made hundreds by him, refused to print for him. Yet his faith never failed, neither did his charity. He says: 'I am enabled to strengthen myself in the Lord my God;' and early one morning, a morning that succeeded earnest prayer on the night before, a friend came to inquire if he knew where a lady of his acquaintance might lend three or four hundred pounds. Whitefield replied: 'Let her lend it to me, and in a few months, God willing, she shall have it again.' All the circumstances were told her, and she cheerfully put the money into his hands.

He was an outcast for awhile. Every church was closed against him ; the Wesleys could not have him in their pulpits, seeing he preached against them by name ; there was no way of gathering a congregation but by taking his stand in the open air daily ; and he determined to begin on the old battle-ground—Moorfields—on Good Friday. Twice a day he walked from Leadenhall to Moorfields, and preached under one of the trees. His own converts forsook him ; some of them would not deign him a look as they passed by ; others put their fingers into their ears, either to preserve them from the contamination of one Calvinistic word, or to ward off the witchery of that charming voice which never charmed in vain. Thus he held on his way amid contempt and hatred, not doubting that he must again win the hearts of the people for his Lord and Master. He called Cennick to his aid from Kingswood, and 'a few free-grace Dissenters' stood firmly by him. It was decided by them to build a large wooden shed for the congregations, which would serve until he should return to America ; and accordingly, they borrowed a piece of ground in Moorfields, and set a carpenter to work upon the erection, which, by the name of the Tabernacle, was opened and filled within two months of Whitefield's landing in England. Crowds were gathered together in it to hear early morning lectures. But it had one drawback in standing so near the Foundry, and Whitefield abhorred the appearance of opposition to his old friends the Wesleys. However, a fresh awakening began immediately ; the congregations grew rapidly ; and at the people's request, he called in the help of a number of laymen, necessity reconciling him to the idea. Here again, as in open-air preaching, he was the forerunner of Wesley.

His experience at Bristol, to which he paid a visit before his Tabernacle in London was erected, was similar to that at

London. The house at Kingswood which he had founded, for which he had preached and begged, and which was associated with his first holy works among the colliers, was denied him. Busybodies on both sides carried tales and stirred up strife. He listened too much to them, and a breach ensued. Still there was something stronger in the hearts of these mistaken, angry Methodists on both sides, than abhorrence of their respective tenets; for Whitefield gratefully records that, though different in judgment, they were one in affection; that both aimed at promoting the glory of their common Lord; and that they agreed in endeavouring 'to convert souls to the ever blessed Mediator.' As for Whitefield himself, no part of his career displays his completeness of devotion to the Lord Jesus more perfectly than this, in which he took the ingratitude of his spiritual children with sorrowful meekness, in which he welcomed rebukes as a 'very little child,' in which he carried his burden of debt for the orphans without once regretting his responsibility, in which he found time to intercede with one friend to write to his 'dear little orphans, both boys and girls,' and to thank another for his kindness to them, in which the peace and comfort of his heart through the gospel never failed him for an hour. All his healthfulness of soul got free play when once the storm had discharged itself. It was with profound relief that he wrote to his friend the Independent minister of Charleston, saying that he thought 'the heat of the battle was pretty well over,' and that the Word of God was running and being glorified. That kind hand which had supported him through so many difficulties, and on which he leaned like a little child, cleared his way surprisingly. One day, when he found himself forsaken and almost quite penniless, his suspense was broken by a stranger coming and putting a guinea into his hand; then something seemed to say, 'Cannot that God, who sent this person to give thee this guinea, make it up fifteen hundred?' And the inward voice was not untrue; soon he was making his apostolic circuit in Wiltshire, Essex, and other counties, and everywhere his orphans found friends. 'Field preaching,' he said, 'is my plan; in this I am carried as on eagles' wings. God makes way for me everywhere. The work of the Lord increases. I am comforted day and night.' In London he saw such triumphs of the gospel as he had never seen in England before. The whole kingdom also was opening its doors to him; and soon he was to have such a list of subscribers to his charity as perhaps no one else ever held in his hand; he could count on helpers in every county in England and Wales, in large districts of Scotland, and in America from Boston to Savannah.

The friendly relation between Whitefield and the Erskines, begun by a brotherly letter from Whitefield in the first instance, which letter Ralph Erskine, with true Scottish caution, answered only after making inquiries about his open-hearted correspondent, now caused pressing invitations to be sent from Scotland. The Erskines and their friends had just seceded from the Church of Scotland, on the ground of its corruptness, and had the difficult task of founding and establishing a new church. In this task they were naturally anxious to get all possible help, and looked with high expectation to the mighty preacher who had achieved such wonders in England and America, and whose theological views harmonised perfectly with their own, and with those of their fellow-countrymen generally. He was more intimate with them than with any one else in Scotland, and had often said how much pleasure it would afford him to visit them. Accordingly, Ralph wrote in very urgent terms: 'Come,' he said, 'if possible, dear Whitefield; come, and come to us also.' He strongly deprecated Whitefield's appearing in the pulpits of the kirk, lest it should be 'improven against the Associate Presbytery.' On the day of receiving this letter, Whitefield wrote to Ebenezer, and, referring to it, said that he could not fall in with its suggestion. 'I come only as an occasional preacher, to preach the simple gospel to all who are willing to hear me, of whatever denomination. It will be wrong in me to join a reformation in Church government any further than I have light given me from above.' The answer of Ebenezer was creditable to his candour; after expressing his pleasure on hearing the good news of Whitefield's success, he said :—

'How desirable would it be to all the sincere lovers of Jesus Christ in Scotland, to see Him "travelling in the greatness of His strength" among us also in your ministrations ! . . . All intended by us at present is, that when you come to Scotland, your way may be such as not to strengthen the hands of our corrupt clergy and judicatories, who are carrying on a course of defection, worming out a faithful ministry from the land, and the power of religion with it. Far be it from us to limit your great Master's commission to preach the gospel to every creature. We, ourselves, preach the gospel to all promiscuously who are willing to hear us. But we preach not upon the call and invitation of the ministers, but of the people, which, I suppose, is your own practice now in England.'

Whitefield thought that the Associate Presbytery was 'a little too hard' upon him, and said that if he was neuter as to the particular reformation of Church government till he had further light, it would be enough; he would come simply to preach the gospel, and not to enter into any particular connection whatever. Had none but the Erskines sought a visit from him, there can be no doubt that he would have gone to Scotland to preach only in connection with them, while abstaining from all interference with the points in dispute between them and the Kirk; but Kirk people were as anxious as their rivals to see him. An opportunity was thus made for him to go to any party who would have him, only the Erskines had the first claim, and must have the first visit.

Full of cares he took his passage from London to Leith. Chief of all cares, and yet chief of all earthly joys, was that distant family. He hopes, when he gets aboard, to redeem time to answer his 'dear lambs' letters.' They had rejoiced him exceedingly. He begs Mr. Barber to be particular in the accounts—and not without reason, since slander was soon busy with a tale about personal ends which Whitefield was serving. He sends word that he has ordered hats and shoes for the children, and intends to send brother H——'s order and other things with some cash very shortly. ' But the arrears hang on me yet. My Lord bears my burden; may He bear all yours for you. I am persuaded He will.' When he sailed he found time to gratify his desire about the orphans, and ten of his short letters are preserved. They cannot compare with such charming letters as Irving wrote to his little daughter, and now and again the harshest parts of his creed appear in a most unpleasing form; but love keeps breaking through every line to lend its own gentle light to the hearts of the little ones. It was in his best manner that he wrote to a child at Boston :—

'MY DEAR CHILD,—I thank you for your letter ; I neither forgot you nor my promise. O, that God may effectually work upon your heart betimes, for you cannot be good too soon, or too good. The little orphans at Georgia are crying out, " What shall we do to be saved? " How early was Jesus in the temple, first hearing and then asking questions ! How did He love the little children, how did He take them up in His sacred arms and bless them ! And when He was just ascending to the highest heaven, how tenderly did He speak to Peter, and bid him "feed His lambs." Let all this encourage you to come to Him.'

Sifting the rest of the correspondence, we come upon a sentence in a letter to the students at Cambridge and New Haven in America, who had partaken of the religious influence so sedulously diffused by Whitefield during his American tour, which is worth a place in every student's room, ' Henceforward, therefore, I hope you will enter into your studies, not to get a parish, nor to be polite preachers, but to be great saints.'

The *Mary and Ann*, after a pleasant passage, landed Whitefield at Leith on July 30, 1741, ten years before Wesley first visited Scotland.   He was come to a generation which Ebenezer Erskine described as 'being generally lifeless, lukewarm, and upsitten.'   Yet there was no little warmth about the stranger whom the Associate Presbytery and the Kirk both struggled for.   Persons of distinction welcomed him, and urged him to preach in Edinburgh on the day of his arrival.   But he stayed in the city only an hour, and went thence, as Ralph Erskine phrases it, 'over the belly of vast opposition,' and came to Ralph's house at Dunfermline at ten o'clock at night. Next morning guest and host conferred together alone on Church matters, when Whitefield admitted that he had changed his views of ordination ; at the time of his ordination he knew no better way, but now, 'he would not have it again in that way for a thousand worlds.'   As to preaching, he was firm in his resolution to go wherever he was asked, into the Kirk or into the meeting-house.   Were a Jesuit priest or a Mohammedan to give him an invitation he would gladly comply, and go and testify against them !   Whitefield wrote to Cennick, telling him that Erskine had received him 'very lovingly.'   He says :—

'I preached to his and the townspeople '—this was in the afternoon of the day after his arrival, and in the meeting-house—'a very thronged assembly.   After I had done prayer and named my text, the rustling made by opening the Bibles all at once surprised me ; a scene I never was witness to before.   Our conversation after sermon, in the house, was such as became the gospel of Christ. . . . They urged a longer stay, in order to converse more closely, and to set me right about Church government and the Solemn League and Covenant.   I informed them that I had given notice of preaching at Edinburgh this evening, but, as they desired it,

I would in a few days return and meet the Associate Presbytery in Mr. Ralph's house. This was agreed on. Dear Mr. Erskine accompanied me, and this evening I preached to many thousands in a place called Orphan-house Park. The Lord was there.'

The proposed conference took place at Ralph Erskine's house on the sixth day after Whitefield's arrival in the country. There were present Ralph and Ebenezer Erskine, Alexander Moncrieff, Adam Gib, Thomas and James Mair, and Mr. Clarkson; also two elders, James Wardlow and John Mowbray. Ralph called the 'tryst,' and Ebenezer began the proceedings with prayer. Some of the venerable men had come with the persuasion that they would succeed in making Whitefield an Associate Presbyterian; the wiser portion hoped for nothing more than to stagger his faith in any and every form of Church government which was different from theirs, to keep him in suspense, and in the meanwhile to secure his services in their meeting-houses for the establishment of their cause. These also meant his conversion, but knew that it must be an affair beyond the power of a morning's sitting of any Presbytery; it would be enough to enter into an alliance with him. Whitefield had evidently come to the meeting determined to keep himself from all alliances. The seceders were separating from the Established Church on the ground that no persons holding 'unscriptural tenets should be admitted members of the Church;' and the interpretation unscriptural tenets was so rigid as to mean that any man who differed from them in his views of Church government should not hold communion with them. Hence their reason for wishing to convert Whitefield was plain. Nor need any surprise be felt at such stickling for Church government; they were in an unenviable position of separation, and thus naturally anxious to prove their zeal for order as well as for orthodoxy. It was thus that the conversation turned upon Church govern-

ment, though Whitefield went away with the impression that
they also wanted to bring him round to the Solemn League
and Covenant! That was most likely a spectre in the mist.
To Whitefield's question, 'Whether, supposing Presbyterian
government to be agreeable to the pattern shown in the
mount, it excluded a toleration of Independents, Anabaptists,
and Episcopalians, among whom there are good men,'
Ebenezer Erskine replied, with fine dexterity: 'Sir, God has
made you an instrument of gathering a great multitude of
souls to the faith and profession of the gospel of Christ
throughout England, and also in foreign parts; and now it
is fit that you should be considering how that body is to be
organised and preserved, which cannot be done without
following the example of Paul and Barnabas, who, when
they had gathered Churches by the preaching of the gospel,
visited them again, and ordained over them elders in every
city; which you cannot do alone, without some two or three
met together in a judicative capacity in the name of the
Lord.' Whitefield answered that he could not see his way
to anything but preaching. But, it was urged, supposing he
were to die, the flock would be scattered and might fall a prey
to grievous wolves. Then he fixed himself on a resolution,
which, with the views that he had expressed about his
ordination, it was, no doubt, made sure he could never reach.
'I am of the communion of the Church of England,' he said;
'none in that communion can join me in the work you
have pointed to; neither do I mean to separate from that
communion till I am either cast out or excommunicated.'
All tempers were not cool under the reasoning that went on;
indeed, how could nine Scots, each one holding to the skirts
of his sacred Church, keep cool when dealing with a prelatist?
The interview ended in a scene. While it was being contended that one form of Church government was divine,

Whitefield, laying his hand on his heart, said : ' I do not find it here.' Alexander Moncrieff replied, as he rapped the Bible that lay on the table : ' But I find it here.'

It is evident that Whitefield's ecclesiastical position for the future is to be judged of by these three things : 1. That he did not believe that any form of Church government was of divine origin. 2. That his ordination to be a priest of the Church of England did not any longer accord with his conceptions of ordination to the ministerial functions. 3. That he was not free to leave the Church of England ; he must be cast off, if the connection must cease.

The unfortunate close of the conference was a great sorrow to Ralph Erskine, who wrote to Whitefield, and plainly, but kindly, told him that he was ' sorrowful for being disappointed about Whitefield's lying open to light, as appeared from his declining conversation on that head ; and also for his coming harnessed with a resolution to stand out against everything that should be advanced against —' (presumably the Established Church). Ralph must not be allowed to rest under the shade of bigotry which the words attributed to him, 'We are the Lord's people,' would cast over him. He may have used the very words in that warm discussion, when the ringing of bells and the expectation of sermon and the firmness of Whitefield threw him into confusion ; but in calmer moments, when meeting his seceding followers at the table of the Lord, he could speak as became his better self, and say, 'We are far from thinking that all are Christ's friends that join with us, and that all are His enemies that do not. No, indeed.' Had the Presbytery consisted only of the two brothers and young David Erskine, the son of Ebenezer, no disruption would have come about ; neither would Ralph have been provoked to insinuate in a letter to Whitefield, that the orphan-house was making him temporise. 'Indeed, dear sir,' Whitefield replied, 'you mistake, if you think I temporise on account of the orphans. Be it far from me. I abhor the very thought of it.'

There was commotion in all classes of society, and no small division, about this new preacher who depicted scenes, who appealed to the heart and conscience, and who offered to every man the riches of Divine grace with solemn urgency. Some were against him on the ground that his character was not sufficiently established; and even his friends commonly called him 'that godly youth.' Yet he was on a flood-tide of popularity in the Scottish capital. He had the ear of the people from the poorest to the noblest. At seven in the morning he had a lecture in the fields, which was attended by 'the common people and by persons of rank.' The very children of the city caught the spirit of his devotion, and would hear him eagerly while he read to them the letters of his orphans. At Heriot's Hospital the boys, who had been noted as the most wicked in the city, established fellowship meetings among themselves; indeed, children's meetings sprung up all over the city. Great numbers of young men met for promoting their Christian knowledge; and aged Christians, who had long maintained an honest profession of Christianity, were stimulated to seek closer brotherly communion.

Great as was the danger of this time, Whitefield bore himself with humility in the midst of applause, with love towards his enemies, and with patience and meekness so exemplary under the reproaches, the injuries, and the slanders which were heaped upon him, that one minister thought that God had sent him to show him how to preach, and especially how to suffer. In the pulpit he was like a flame of fire; among men he was most calm and easy, careful never to give offence, and never courting the favour of any. His temper was cheerful and grateful. His disinterestedness shone conspicuously in his refusal to accept a private contribution which some zealous friends thought of giving him. 'I make no purse,' he said; 'what I have I give away. "Poor, yet making many rich," shall be my motto still.' All that he cared for was his family; he would rather bear any burden than have it burdened. His pleadings on its behalf had the usual effect, and some 'evil men' soon had their tongues busy. Thousands of prayers were offered for him, and thousands of lies were spread abroad against him. It was said that he was hindering the poor from paying their debts, and impoverishing their families. But the fact was that his largest donations came from the rich. He said to his friends respecting all this slander, for he never noticed it publicly, 'I would have no one afraid of doing too much good, or think that a little given in charity will impoverish the country.'[1]

Edinburgh did not monopolise his labours; Glasgow, Dundee, Paisley, Perth, Stirling, Crieff, Falkirk, Airth, King-lassie, Culross, Kinross, Cupar of Fife, Stonehive, Benholm, Montrose, Brechin, Forfar, Cupar of Angus, Inverkeithing, Newbottle, Galashiels, Maxton, Haddington, Killern, Fintry, Balfrone, and Aberdeen received a visit from him. His visit to Aberdeen was at the oft-repeated request of Mr. Ogilvie, one of the ministers of the kirk, and is thus described by himself:—

'At my first coming here, things looked a little gloomy; for the magistrates had been so prejudiced by one Mr. Bisset, that, when applied to, they refused me the use of the kirk-yard to preach in. This Mr. Bisset

---

[1] This alarm about impoverishing the country does not look so absurd when it is remembered that in 1706 the total revenue of Scotland was only £160,000.

is colleague with Mr. Ogilvie, at whose repeated invitation I came hither. Though colleagues of the same congregation, they are very different in their natural tempers. The one is what they call in Scotland of a sweet-blooded, the other of a choleric disposition. Mr. Bisset is neither a Seceder nor quite a Kirk man, having great fault to find with both. Soon after my arrival, dear Mr. Ogilvie took me to pay my respects to him ; he was prepared for it, and immediately pulled out a paper containing a great number of insignificant queries, which I had neither time nor inclination to answer. The next morning, it being Mr. Ogilvie's turn, I lectured and preached ; the magistrates were present. The congregation very large, and light and life fled all around. In the afternoon Mr. Bisset officiated ; I attended. He began his prayers as usual, but in the midst of them, naming me by name, he entreated the Lord to forgive the dishonour that had been put upon Him by my being suffered to preach in that pulpit ; and that all might know what reason he had to put up such a petition, about the middle of his sermon he not only urged that I was a curate of the Church of England, but also quoted a passage or two out of my first printed sermons, which he said were grossly Arminian. Most of the congregation seemed surprised and chagrined, especially his good-natured colleague, Mr. Ogilvie, who, immediately after sermon, without consulting me in the least, stood up and gave notice that Mr. Whitefield would preach in about half an hour. The interval being so short, the magistrates returned into the sessions-house, and the congregation patiently waited, big with expectation of hearing my resentment. At the time appointed I went up, and took no other notice of the good man's ill-timed zeal than to observe, in some part of my discourse, that if the good old gentleman had seen some of my later writings, wherein I had corrected several of my former mistakes, he would not have expressed himself in such strong terms. The people being thus diverted from controversy with man, were deeply impressed with what they heard from the Word of God. All was hushed, and more than solemn ; and on the morrow the magistrates sent for me, expressed themselves quite concerned at the treatment I had met with, and begged I would accept of the freedom of the city. But of this enough.'

The spirit of love had been remarkably developed and strengthened in Whitefield since his return from America ; his troubles, keen and undeserved as they were, had proved a kindly chastening to his spirit. The fine frankness of his nature and the sincerity of his religion were shown at Aberdeen in a letter which he wrote to Wesley asking his forgive-

ness for a wrong he felt he had done him, and in another to
Peter Böhler, whose name he had mentioned in a very
inoffensive way in his famous letter to Wesley from Bethesda.
In the case of Böhler he had not sinned openly, but he knew
that he had broken the law of charity in his own heart; and
such faults are much to the true Christian.

His Scotch excursion did much for the kingdom of God, if
little for the Associate Presbytery; it also brought him more
worldly honour than he had ever before known. He was welcomed to their houses by several of the nobility, and became
the friend, correspondent, and religious helper of the Marquis
of Lothian, the Earl of Leven, Lord Rae, Lady Mary Hamil-
ton, Colonel Gardiner, Lady Frances Gardiner (wife of the
Colonel), Lady Jean Nimmo, and Lady Dirleton. Lord
Leven gave him a horse to perform his journeys on; the
Scotch people gave him above five hundred pounds for his
orphans.

Riding his gift-horse, he took his way from Scotland to
Wales to be married. Not a word has been found about his
courtship. Whether he preached on his journey or not, does
not appear, but in ten days (Nov. 14, 1741) he was at Abergavenny, ready to be joined in matrimony to Mrs. James, a
widow of about thirty-six years of age (he was twenty-six),
neither rich nor beautiful, 'once gay, but for three years last
past a despised follower of the Lamb,' one of whom he
cherished the hope that she would not hinder him in his
work. Wesley, who speaks of her in his journal but a month
before the marriage, had a favourable opinion of her; he calls
her 'a woman of candour and humanity,' and, we may add,
courage, seeing she compelled some complainers, who had
been free with their tongues in Wesley's absence, to repeat
everything to his face. There is an Eden-like story told about
the marriage with the matronly housekeeper, which, though not

to be depended upon, may serve to brighten a prosaic event. Ebenezer Jones, minister of Ebenezer Chapel, near Pontypool, was most happy in his marriage. His wife was a woman of eminent piety and strong mind ; they were married in youth, and years only deepened their affection. Mrs. Jones died first, and the afflicted widower would say, when speaking of the joys of another world, ' I would not for half a heaven but find her there.' Whitefield, it is said, was so enchanted with their happiness, when visiting at their house, that he immediately determined to change his condition, and soon paid his addresses to Mrs. James. And she seems to have been as good a wife to him as perhaps any woman could have been. Home-life they could never know so long as he would preach all day, and write letters at night, and this practice he kept up until he died.

There was probably no cessation of preaching ; only a few days after the celebration of the marriage he wrote to tell an Edinburgh friend that God had been pleased to work by his hand since his coming to Wales. Three days later still he was in Bristol, building up religious societies, and preaching in a large hall which his friends had hired; and Mrs. Whitefield was at Abergavenny, staying till he could conveniently take her with him on his journeys.[1]

His appeal from the jurisdiction of the commissary of Charleston was now returned to him from the Lords, who saw through the commissary's enmity; and there was an end of that trouble.

---

[1] Bristol had another distinguished visitor at this time. Savage was detained in Newgate for a debt of eight pounds ; his best friend was Mr. Dagge, the tender gaoler, whose virtues Johnson has praised in high terms, probably not knowing that he was praising a convert of Whitefield's. It is almost certain that Whitefield sometimes sat down at the keeper's hospitable table with that strange guest.

His work now lay in Bristol, where he began 'a general monthly meeting to read corresponding letters,' and between that place and London—the same district in which he won his first successes in itinerant preaching; and everywhere the desire to hear the truth was more intense than ever. Finally, he went to London, taking his wife with him, and probably lodged with some Methodist friend, one carefully chosen, as he was careful about the houses he went to, nor was it every one who could have his presence. To one London brother who wanted to have him and his wife, he replied :—

' I know not what to say about coming to your house ; for brother S——tells me you and your family are dilatory, and that you do not rise sometimes till nine or ten in the morning. This, dear Mr. N——, will never do for me ; and I am persuaded such a conduct tends much to the dishonour of God, and to the prejudice of your own precious soul. Be not slothful in business. Go to bed seasonably, and rise early. Redeem your precious time ; pick up the fragments of it, that not one moment may be lost. Be much in secret prayer. Converse less with man, and more with God.'

To this wise circumspection, and the fact that he was always the guest of men of undoubted piety or of untarnished reputation, may in part be ascribed his triumph over all the base slanders of his enemies.

He spent the winter 1741–42 mostly in preaching in his wooden tabernacle, London. Everything was helping to prepare him for another of those daring religious forays of which he is the most brilliant captain ; this was the enterprise he attempted—to beat the devil in Moorfields on Whit-Monday. The soldier is the best historian here :—

' LONDON, *May* 11, 1742.
'With this I send you a few out of the many notes I have received from persons who were convicted, converted, or comforted in Moorfields during the late holidays. For many weeks I found my heart much pressed to deter-

mine to venture to preach there at this season, when, it ever, Satan's children keep up their annual rendezvous. I must inform you that Moorfields is a large spacious place, given, as I have been told, by one Madam Moore, on purpose for all sorts of people to divert themselves in. For many years past, from one end to the other, booths of all kinds have been erected for mountebanks, players, puppet-shows, and such like. With a heart bleeding with compassion for so many thousands led captive by the devil at his will, on Whit Monday, at six o'clock in the morning, attended by a large congregation of praying people, I ventured to lift up a standard among them in the name of Jesus of Nazareth. Perhaps there were about ten thousand in waiting—not for me, but for Satan's instruments to amuse them. Glad was I to find that I had for once, as it were, got the start of the devil. I mounted my field pulpit; almost all immediately flocked around it. I preached on these words: "As Moses lifted up the serpent," &c. They gazed, they listened, they wept; and I believe that many felt themselves stung with deep conviction for their past sins. All was hushed and solemn. Being thus encouraged, I ventured out again at noon; but what a scene! The fields, the whole fields, seemed, in a bad sense of the word, all white, ready, not for the Redeemer's, but Beelzebub's, harvest. All his agents were in full motion—drummers, trumpeters, Merry Andrews, masters of puppet-shows, exhibitors of wild beasts, players, &c., &c.—all busy in entertaining their respective audiences. I suppose there could not be less than twenty or thirty thousand people. My pulpit was fixed on the opposite side, and immediately, to their great mortification, they found the number of their attendants sadly lessened. Judging that, like St. Paul, I should now be called, as it were, to fight with beasts at Ephesus, I preached from these words: "Great is Diana of the Ephesians." You may easily guess that there was some noise among the craftsmen, and that I was honoured with having a few stones, rotten eggs, and pieces of dead cat thrown at me, whilst engaged in calling them from their favourite, but lying, vanities. My soul was indeed among lions! but far the greatest part of my congregation, which was very large, seemed for awhile to be turned into lambs. This encouraged me to give notice that I would preach again at six o'clock in the evening. I came, I saw, but what —thousands and thousands more than before if possible, still more deeply engaged in their unhappy diversions; but some thousands among them waiting as earnestly to hear the gospel. This Satan could not brook. One of his choicest servants was exhibiting, trumpeting on a large stage; but as soon as the people saw me in my black robes and my pulpit, I think all to a man left him and ran to me. For awhile I was enabled to lift up my voice like a trumpet, and many heard the joyful sound. God's people kept praying, and the enemy's agents made a kind of a roaring at some distance from our camp. At length they approached nearer, and the Merry

Andrew, attended by others who complained that they had taken many
pounds less that day on account of my preaching, got upon a man's shoulders, and advancing near the pulpit, attempted to slash me with a long,
heavy whip several times, but always with the violence of his motion
tumbled down.   Soon afterwards they got a recruiting sergeant with
his drum, &c., to pass through the congregation.   I gave the word
of command, and ordered that way might be made for the king's
officer.   The ranks opened while all marched quietly through, and
then closed again.   Finding their efforts to fail, a large body, quite on
the opposite side, assembled together, and having got a large pole
for their standard, advanced towards us with steady and formidable
steps till they came very near the skirts of our hearing, praying, and
almost undaunted congregation.   I saw, gave warning, and prayed to
the Captain of our salvation for present support and deliverance.   He
heard and answered, for just as they approached us with looks full of
resentment, I know not by what accident they quarrelled among themselves, threw down their staff, and went their way, leaving, however, many
of their company behind, who, before we had done, I trust were brought
over to join the besieged party.   I think I continued in praying, preaching and singing—for the noise was too great at times to preach—about
three hours.   We then retired to the Tabernacle, with my pockets full of
notes from persons brought under concern, and read them amid the
praises and spiritual acclamations of thousands who joined with the holy
angels in rejoicing that so many sinners were snatched, in such an unexpected, unlikely place and manner, out of the very jaws of the devil.   This
was the beginning of the Tabernacle society.   Three hundred and fifty
awakened souls were received in one day, and I believe the number of
notes exceeded a thousand ; but I must have done, believing you want to
retire to join in mutual praise and thanksgiving to God and the Lamb with

'Yours, &c.

'G. WHITEFIELD.'

Bare facts support the statement that some had been
'plucked from the very jaws of the devil.'   Whitefield married
several who had been living in open adultery ; one man was
converted who had exchanged his wife for another, and given
fourteen shillings to boot ; and several were numbered in the
society whose days would in all probability have been ended
at Tyburn.   But his exploits were not ended.   Here is a
second letter :—

'LONDON, *May* 15, 1742.

' MY DEAR FRIEND,—Fresh matter of praise ; bless ye the Lord, for He
hath triumphed gloriously ! The battle that was begun on Monday was not
quite over till Wednesday evening, though the scene of action was a little
shifted. Being strongly invited, and a pulpit being prepared for me by an
honest Quaker, a coal merchant, I ventured on Tuesday evening to preach
at Mary-le-bone Fields, a place almost as much frequented by boxers,
gamesters, and such like, as Moorfields. A vast concourse was assembled
together, and as soon as I got into the field-pulpit their countenance bespoke
the enmity of their heart against the preacher. I opened with these words :
" I am not ashamed of the gospel of Christ ; for it is the power of God
unto salvation to every one that believeth." I preached in great jeopardy ;
for the pulpit being high and the supports not well fixed in the ground, it
tottered every time I moved, and numbers of enemies strove to push my
friends against the supporters in order to throw me down. But the
Redeemer stayed my soul on Himself, therefore I was not much moved,
unless with compassion for those to whom I was delivering my Master's
message, which I had reason to think, by the strong impressions that were
made, was welcome to many. But Satan did not like thus to be attacked
in his strongholds, and I narrowly escaped with my life ; for as I was
passing from the pulpit to the coach, I felt my wig and hat to be almost off.
I turned about, and perceived a sword just touching my temple. A young
rake, as I afterwards found, was determined to stab me ; but a gentleman,
seeing the sword thrusting near me, struck it up with his cane, and so the
destined victim providentially escaped. Such an attempt excited abhorrence ; the enraged multitude soon seized him, and had it not been for one
of my friends who received him into his house, he must have undergone a
severe discipline. The next day I renewed my attack in Moorfields ; but,
would you think it ? after they found that peltings, noise, and threatenings
would not do, one of the Merry Andrews got up into a tree very near the
pulpit, and shamefully exposed his nakedness before all the people. Such
a beastly action quite abashed the serious part of my auditory, whilst
hundreds of another stamp, instead of rising up to pull down the unhappy
wretch, expressed their approbation by repeated laughs. I must own at
first it gave me a shock ; I thought Satan had almost outdone himself ; but
recovering my spirits I appealed to all, since now they had such a spectacle
before them, whether I had wronged human nature in saying, after pious
Bishop Hall, " that man, when left to himself, is half a devil and half a
beast ; " or, as the great Mr. Law expressed himself, " a motley mixture
of the beast and devil." Silence and attention being thus gained, I concluded with a warm exhortation, and closed our festival enterprises in
reading fresh notes that were put up, praising and blessing God amidst
thousands at the Tabernacle for what He had done for precious souls, and

on account of the deliverances He had wrought out for me and His people, I could enlarge; but being about to embark in the *Mary and Ann* for Scotland, I must hasten to subscribe myself,

'Yours, &c.,

'G. WHITEFIELD.

'P.S.—I cannot help adding that several little boys and girls, who were fond of sitting round me on the pulpit while I preached, and handing to me people's notes, though they were often pelted with eggs, dirt, &c., thrown at me, never once gave way; but, on the contrary, every time I was struck turned up their little weeping eyes, and seemed to wish they could receive the blows for me. God make them in their growing years great and living martyrs for Him who out of the mouths of babes and sucklings perfects praise!'

Whitefield, accompanied by his wife, now went from the excitement of London to that of Scotland; and, happily, the voyage afforded him a few days for quieter engagements, before rushing into the heat of an immense revival. *Most of his time on board ship was spent in secret prayer.* He landed at Leith on June 3, 1742, amid the blessings and tears of the people, many of whom followed the coach up to Edinburgh, again to welcome him when he stepped out.

But all hearts were not glad for his return. The Associate Presbytery—still smarting under the rebuff of the preceding year, driven to the greater vehemence for their testimony the more they saw it unheeded, and made the more contentious by the 'foreigner's' low estimate of their 'holy contendings'— were full of wrath. Even the Erskines were unfriendly. But the most conspicuous enemy was Adam Gib, of Edinburgh, one of the venerable nine with whom Whitefield had the amusing interview at Dunfermline. Gib was resolved to expose Whitefield, and thus to deliver his own soul, and, it might be, the souls of the poor deluded, devil-blinded people that crowded to hear the deceiver. Accordingly he 'published, in the New Church at Bristow, upon Sabbath, June 6, 1742, "A Warning against countenancing the Ministrations of Mr.

George Whitefield ; " ' and certainly the trumpet gave no uncertain sound. The ' Warning ' caused such a commotion that
Gib was urged to print, and taking this as a hint from Providence that he should finish his holy task, he expanded a short
sermon of eight pages into an ' Appendix ' of fifty-seven ; thus
getting ample scope to make his charges, and to prove them, if
that were possible. Gib shows, in his own way, ' that Mr. Whitefield was no minister of Jesus Christ ; that his call and coming
to Scotland were scandalous ; that his practice was disorderly
and fertile of disorder ; that his whole doctrine was, and his
success must be, *diabolical ;* so that people ought to avoid
him, from duty to God, to the Church, to themselves, to fellow-
men, to posterity, and to him.'

Whitefield was not soured by such detraction and abuse, but
wrote to Ebenezer Erskine, to say how much concerned he was
that their difference as to outward things should cut off their
sweet fellowship and communion with each other. He pro-
tested that his love for Erskine and Erskine's brethren was
greater than ever ; that he applauded their zeal for God, though
it was not, in some respects, according to knowledge, and was
frequently levelled against himself ; and that his heart had no
resentment in it. Meanwhile the people, not heeding Gib's
' Warning,' flocked to the Hospital Park and filled the shaded
wooden amphitheatre which had been erected for their accommodation. Twice a day Whitefield went to the Park, and twice
a day they came to hear him.

A congregation moved by deeper religious feeling than that
which agitated Edinburgh was anxious to hear his voice in a
little village called Cambuslang, on the south side of the Clyde,
about five miles from Glasgow, and now a suburb of that city.
Wonderful things were beginning to take place in that small
parish of nine hundred souls. The Rev. William McCulloch,
who had been ordained its minister on April 29, 1731, was a

man of considerable learning and of solid, unostentatious piety, slow and cautious as a speaker, and more anxious to feed his people with sound truth than to move their passions with declamation. The news of the revivals in England and America had awakened a lively interest in him; he began to detail to his people what he knew, and they, in their turn, felt as interested as he did. A dilapidated church and an over-flowing congregation next compelled the good pastor and his flock to resort to the fields for worship; and nature, as if anticipating their wants, had made a fair temple of her own in a deep ravine near the church. The grassy level by the burn-side, and the brae which rises from it in the form of an amphi-theatre, afforded an admirable place for the gathering of a large mass of people; and there the pastor would preach the same doctrines which were touching rugged Kingswood colliers, depraved London roughs, and formal ministers and professors of religion in both hemispheres; but he dwelt mostly on regeneration. The sermon over, he would recount on a Sabbath evening what was going on in the kingdom of God elsewhere, and then renew his application of truth to the con-science. The great evangelist had also been heard by some of the people; nor could they forget his words, or throw off their influence. On his previous visit to Scotland, when he went to Glasgow, they had stood on the gravestones of the high churchyard in that immense congregation which trembled and wept as he denounced the curses and offered the blessings of the word of God. Others, again, had read the sermons after they were printed, and had been as vitally affected as if they had heard the thrilling voice which had spoken them. The religious leaven was touching the whole body of the people; and at the end of January, 1742, five months before White-field's second visit to Scotland, Ingram More, a shoemaker, and Robert Bowman, a weaver, carried a petition round the parish, praying the minister to set up a weekly lecture, and ninety heads of families signed it. The day which was most convenient for the temporal interests of the parish was Thursday, and on Thursday a lecture was given. Then wounded souls began to call at the manse to ask for counsel and comfort, and at last, after one of the Thursday lectures, fifty of them went; and all that night the faithful pastor was engaged in his good work. Next came a daily sermon, followed by private teaching, exhortation, and prayer ; and before Whitefield got there to increase the intense feeling and honest conviction which were abroad, three hundred souls, according to the computation of Mr. McCulloch, 'had been awakened and convinced of their perishing condition without a Saviour, more than two hundred of whom were, he believed, hopefully converted and brought home to God.' The congregations on the hillside had also increased to nine or ten thousand. All the work of preaching and teaching did not devolve upon one man ; ministers from far and near came to see and wonder and help. Great care was taken by them all to hinder hypocrisy and delusion from spreading ; and indeed the work, as examined by faithful men, presented every appearance of a work of the Holy Ghost. It embraced all classes, all ages, and all moral conditions. Cursing, swearing, and drunkenness were given up by those who had been guilty of these sins, and who had come under its power. It kindled remorse for acts of injustice. It compelled restitution for fraud. It won forgiveness from the revengeful. It imparted patience and love to endure the injuries of enemies. It bound pastors and people together with a stronger bond of sympathy. It raised an altar in the household, or kindled afresh the extinguished fire of domestic religion. It made men students of the word of God, and brought them in thought and purpose and effort into communion with their Father in heaven. True, there was chaff among the wheat, but the watchfulness and wisdom of the minister detected it, and quickly drove it away. And for long years afterwards humble men and women, who dated their conversion from the work at Cambuslang, walked among their neighbours with an unspotted Christian name, and then died peacefully and joyfully in the arms of One whom they had learned in revival days to call Lord and Saviour.

The most remarkable thing in the whole movement is an absence of terrible experiences. The great sorrow which swelled penitential hearts was not selfish, and came from no fear of future punishment, but from a sense of the dishonour they had done to God and their Redeemer. The influence of the Cambuslang meetings was at work in many a parish, and Whitefield's first ride from Edinburgh into the west was through places where the greatest commotion was visible. When he came to Cambuslang he immediately preached to a vast congregation, which, notwithstanding Gib's warning against hearing sermons on other days than the Sabbath, had come together on a Tuesday at noon. At six in the evening he preached again, and a third time at nine. No doubt the audience on the braeside was much the same at each service, and we are prepared to hear that by eleven at night the enthusiasm had reached its highest pitch. For an hour and a half the loud weeping of the company filled the stillness of the summer night, while now and again the cry of some strong man, or more susceptible woman, rang above the preacher's voice and the general wailing, and there was a swaying to and fro where the wounded one fell. Often the word would take effect like shot piercing a regiment of soldiers, and the congregation was broken again and again. It was a very field of battle, as Whitefield himself has described it. Helpers carried the agonised into the house, and, as they passed, the crying of those whom they bore moved all hearts with fresh emotion, and prepared the way for the word to make fresh triumphs. When Whitefield ended his sermon, McCulloch took his place, and preached till past one in the morning; and even then the people were unwilling to leave the spot. Many walked the fields all night, praying and singing, the sound of their voices much rejoicing the heart of Whitefield as he lay awake in the neighbouring manse.

The following Sunday was sacrament day, and he hurried back to Edinburgh to do some work there, before joining in the great and solemn ceremony. He says that there was such a shock in Edinburgh on Thursday night and Friday morning as he had never felt before. On Friday night he came to Cambuslang, and on Saturday he preached to more than twenty thousand people. Sabbath, however, was the day of days. New converts had looked forward to it as the time of their first loving confession of their Redeemer, and aged Christians were assembled with the freshness of their early devotion upon them. Godly pastors had come from neighbouring and also from distant places to assist in serving the tables, and to take part in prayer and exhortation. All around the inner group of believers who were to partake of the sacrament for a remembrance of our Lord was a mighty host, scarcely less earnest or less outwardly devout. Two tents were erected in the glen; seventeen hundred 'tokens' were issued to those who wished to communicate. The tables stood under the brae, and when Whitefield began to serve one of them the people so crowded upon him that he was obliged to desist and go to one of the tents to preach. All through the day, preaching by one or another never ceased; and at night, when the last communicant had partaken, all the companies, still unwearied, and still ready to hear, met in one congregation, and Whitefield, at the request of the ministers, preached to them. His sermon was an hour and a half long, and the twenty thousand were not tired of hearing it.

Such a day might well have been followed by quietness and repose, but his was no heart to cry for leisure, whatever his body might do. The following Monday was sure to be just such a day as he could most thoroughly enjoy, for the day after communion Sunday has had among Presbyterians almost more sanctity than the Sunday itself. Preachers have preached their most effective sermons on that day, and it was a memorable time at Cambuslang. 'The motion,' Whitefield says, 'fled as swift as lightning from one end of the auditory to another. You might have seen thousands bathed in tears. Some at the same time wringing their hands, others almost swooning, and others crying out and mourning over a pierced Saviour. It was like the Passover in Josiah's time.'

The sermon preached by him on the Sunday night was upon Isa. liv. 5—'For thy Maker is thy husband'—and was a sermon more frequently referred to by his converts than any other; yet we look in vain for a single passage of interest or power in it. The thought is meagre and the language tame; there is a total absence of the dramatic element which abounds in all his treatment of narrative and parable. But, remembering how perfectly his heart realised the idea of union with God, and how intense was his personal devotion to the will of God, it becomes easier to understand the unfailing unction with which his common thoughts were clothed. He could hardly fail to have power, when entreating sinners to yield to God and be joined to the Lord Jesus, who could say, without affectation or boast, 'The hopes of bringing more souls to Jesus Christ is the only consideration that can reconcile me to life. For this cause I can willingly stay long from my wished-for home, my wished-for Jesus. But whither am I going? I forget myself when writing of Jesus. His love fills my soul.'

His qualities of meekness and self-restraint were as hardly tested by the meddlesomeness of would-be advisers as by the

blind rage of enemies. Willison, of Dundee, a minister of
the Kirk, was jealous over him on two points : first, as to the
question of episcopacy ; and secondly, as to his habits of
private devotion. As to the first, Whitefield told his correspondent that he thought his ' letter breathed much of a
sectarian spirit,' and with his wonted charity added :—

' To which I hoped dear Mr. Willison was quite averse. As for my
answer to Mr. M——, dear sir, it is very satisfying to my own soul. Morning
and evening retirement is certainly exceeding good ; but if through weakness
of body, or frequency of preaching, I cannot go to God in my usual set times,
I think my spirit is not in bondage. It is not for me to tell how often I use
secret prayer ; if I did not use it, nay, if in one sense I did not pray without
ceasing, it would be difficult for me to keep up that frame of soul which,
by the Divine blessing, I daily enjoy. If the work of God prospers, and
your hands become more full, you will then, dear sir, know better what
I mean.' [1]

As soon as news of the Cambuslang work came from the
west, the Seceders called a Presbytery, which, with a promptitude that showed their prejudices and condemned their act
as rash and ignorant, appointed a fast for the diabolical
delusion which had seized the people. The notions of Gib
were evidently highly popular ; for between the 11th of
July and the 15th—the date of the act of the Presbytery—
no examination of the work could have been made. Whitefield

[1] What would Willison have thought of Whitefield, if he had heard the
following vagabond anecdote, which ought to be true, if it is not? Some
time after the quarrel upon the five points between Wesley and Whitefield,
and their happy reconciliation, the two combatants slept together in the
same bed (Methodist preachers sometimes slept three in a bed !), at the
close of a toilsome day. Wesley knelt down and prayed before lying
down to rest, but Whitefield threw himself upon the bed at once. ' George,'
said Wesley in a reproachful tone, ' is that your Calvinism ? ' During the
night Whitefield awoke, and found his friend fast asleep on his knees by
the bedside ; rousing him up, he said : ' John, is that your Arminianism ? '

expressed himself with much composure in a letter to a friend :—

'The Messrs. Erskine,' he says, 'and their adherents, would you think it ? have appointed a public fast to humble themselves, among other things, for my being received in Scotland, and for the delusion, as they term it, at Cambuslang, and other places ; and all this because I would not consent to preach only for them, till I had light into, and could take, the Solemn League and Covenant. But to what lengths may prejudice carry even good men ! From giving way to the first risings of bigotry and a party spirit, good Lord, deliver us !'

And the charity of this large-hearted man was not words on paper ; he could believe in the goodness of another, in spite of personal wrong done to himself, and wait with full confidence the time when evil should be overcome with good. Soon after the fast, which was proclaimed from Dunfermline, he had a short interview with Ralph Erskine, and brotherly love so prevailed that they embraced each other, and Ralph said, 'We have seen strange things.' Whitefield's faith in the power of love to bring brethren to a right state of mind was justified even in the case of violent Adam Gib, who, when an old man, confessed to his nephew that he wished that no copies of his pamphlet against Whitefield were on the face of the earth, and that, if he knew how to recall them, every copy should be obtained and burnt : 'My blood at that time was too hot,' said he, 'and I was unable to write with becoming temper.

The strain made upon Whitefield by his exhausting labours brought back again the spasms of sickness with which he had been so frequently seized in America. Writing to one of his friends, he said : 'Last night some of my friends thought I was going off ; but how did Jesus fill my heart ! To-day I am, as they call it, much better. In less than a month we are to have another sacrament at Cambuslang—a thing not practised before in Scotland. I entreat all to pray in an especial manner for a blessing at that time.' A fortnight later, when he had got to Cambuslang and shared in the much-desired sacrament, he said: 'My bodily strength is daily renewed, and I mount on the wings of faith and love like an eagle.' This second celebration was more remarkable than even the first. It came about in this wise.

Soon after the first celebration, Webster, of Edinburgh, proposed that there should be a second on an early day, and Whitefield seconded him. McCulloch liked the proposal, but must confer with his people before giving an answer. The several meetings for prayer were informed of it, and they, after supplication and deliberation, thought it best to favour it. It was therefore resolved to dispense the Lord's Supper again on August 15th. Meanwhile prayer-meetings were arranged for through the whole of the intervening month. Communicants came from distant as well as neighbouring places, from Edinburgh and Kilmarnock, from Irvine and Stewarton, and some even from England and Ireland. Great numbers of Quakers came to be hearers—not partakers, of course—so, too, did many of the Secession, and some of the latter went to the table. Ministers arrived from Edinburgh, Glasgow, Kilsyth, Kinglassie, Irvine, Douglas, Blantyre, Ruther-glen, and Cathcart. Old Mr. Bonar, of Torphichen, who took three days to ride eighteen miles, was determined to be present, and when helped up to one of the tents which had been pitched, preached three times with much energy ; he returned home with the 'Nunc Dimittis' on his lips. Between thirty and forty thousand people were gathered in the glen on the Sunday, and of these three thousand communicated.[1] The

[1] It will help us to understand how widespread was the religious work at this time, if we remember that the population of Glasgow was about twenty thousand. Had every man, woman, and child gone from the city and joined

energy of the truth which was all day long preached by several ministers in different parts was so great that possibly a thousand more would have done so if they could have had access to procure tokens. The staff of ministers were assisted at the tables by several elders of rank and distinction. There was not wanting that power which perhaps most, if not all, had come hoping to find. Whitefield himself was in a visible ecstasy as he stood in the evening serving some tables; and at ten at night, his great audience in the churchyard could heed only his words, though the weather, which had been favourable all day, had broken, and it rained fast. On the following morning, at seven o'clock, Webster preached with immense effect, and Whitefield followed in the same manner later in the day.

The greater the work the hotter the opposition and the more furious the denunciations of opponents. The Seceders were running greater and greater lengths in misguided zeal, and were beginning to split among themselves. This was a chance for the Kirk presbyters, some of whom had no love for the prelatist, excepting as he fortified their falling Church, to launch out at him; and they began to call to account some of the ministers who had employed him. The Cameronians, who rallied round the blue flag of the Covenant, rivalled in a 'Declaration' the 'Act' of the Associate Presbytery. They called their document 'The Declaration, Protestation, and Testimony of the Suffering Remnant of the anti-Popish, anti-Lutheran, anti-Prelatic, anti-Whitefieldian, anti-Erastian, anti-Sectarian, true Presbyterian Church of Christ in Scotland.

the people of Cambuslang, the whole would not have made more than two-thirds of one of the congregations assembled to hear Whitefield in that village. In many of the neighbouring places, notably Kilsyth, under the fostering care of that wise and devout minister, James Robe, a similar work of grace was proceeding.

Published against Mr. George Whitefield and his encouragers, and against the work at Cambuslang and other places;' and the ignorance and injustice of the declaration amply sustained its pugnacious title.

A more crafty way of damaging his reputation and impeding his work was hit upon by one or more persons in America, who wrote to friends in Scotland what they pretended to be true accounts of the condition of religion in New England. One of the letters was written to a minister in Glasgow, and another to Mr. George Wishart, one of the ministers of Edinburgh. Both letters were published without the names of their writers, and were offered for public acceptance, the one upon the word of its publisher, the other upon the word of Wishart. The first was deemed worthy of an answer, which Whitefield wrote at Cambuslang, where he had fixed his headquarters for some time, and whence he made constant excursions to places that wanted his services. Its authority was effectually shattered when Whitefield pointed out that, if it had come from America at all, it had been tampered with since its arrival; for reference was made in it to a sermon published in London on May 1st; yet the letter itself was written on May 24th, and no mode of transit in those days was swift enough to carry news across the Atlantic and back in twenty-three days. The letters were, indeed, more of an assault upon Whitefield, through Tennent, than of an attempt to assail him through his own work. The letter bearing Wishart's imprimatur only repeated the old cry, that Whitefield had taken people from their business, and filled every one's mouth with talk about religion: its real attack was upon Tennent, and his work and friends, only the people in Scotland were asked to regard Whitefield in the same light. Whitefield summed the whole manner up in a manly, impartial paragraph. He says :—

' There has been a great and marvellous work in New England ; but, as it should seem, by the imprudences of some, and the over-boiling zeal of others, some irregularities have been committed in several places, which Mr. Tennent himself, in a letter to Mr. Parsons, printed in the *Boston Gazette*, has borne his testimony against as strongly as any of these eminent ministers. This is nothing but what is common. It was so in old England some few years ago. Many young persons there ran out before they were called ; others were guilty of great imprudences. I checked them in the strictest manner myself, and found, as they grew acquainted with the Lord Jesus and their own hearts, the intemperance of their zeal abated, and they became truly humble walkers with God. But must the whole work of God be condemned as enthusiasm and delusion because of some disorder ? ' [1]

The opposition to Whitefield was of various kinds. Some sincere souls were anxious for pure religion, which they confounded with their familiar, quiet services ; some put Church government in too high a position relative to spiritual religion ; some were angry, disappointed, and envious, they would gladly have had a monopoly of the preaching they bitterly assailed ; and, in the dark background, were some who hated the preacher and his message, and struck at him with a deadly malignity. How strong in the grace of God must the man have been who never quailed before the storm, never became bitter, and never allowed his labours for men's salvation to relax in the least degree !

The labour of defending is work, as well as doing it, was

[1] How much Tennent himself was sobered in judgment upon some questions, though not at all in his way of expressing himself, appears in a letter published in the *Boston Evening Post*, July 26, 1742. He says : ' The late method of setting up separate meetings upon the supposed unregeneracy of pastors in places is enthusiastical, proud, schismatical. All that fear God ought to oppose it as a most dangerous engine to bring the Churches into the most damnable errors and confusions. The practice of openly exposing ministers, who are supposed to be unconverted, in public discourses, by particular application of such times and places, serves only to provoke them, instead of doing them good, and to declare our own arrogance.'

not all left in Whitefield's hands. Webster, of Edinburgh, vindicated the work in the west of Scotland with great calmness and charity towards adversaries. His words, after those of the Cameronians and Associate Presbyterians, were like summer breezes after an east wind. Jonathan Edwards also wrote his 'Thoughts on the Present Revival in New England,' &c.

The short retirement which Whitefield managed to snatch from the revival work was devoted to domestic concerns, as well as to the defence of preaching and its fruits. His mother had sought a temporary home in his house at Bristol—probably his sister's house had come into his possession—and the event so delighted him that he must write to welcome her as if he had been present :—

'HONOURED MOTHER,—I rejoice to hear that you have been so long under my roof. Blessed be God that I have a house for my honoured mother to come to. You are heartily welcome to anything my house affords as long as you please. I am of the same mind now as formerly. If need was, indeed, these hands should administer to your necessities. I had rather want myself than you should. I shall be highly pleased when I come to Bristol and find you sitting in your youngest son's house. O that I may sit with you in the house not made with hands, eternal in the heavens ! Ere long your doom, honoured mother, will be fixed. You must shortly go hence and be no more seen. Your only daughter, I trust, is now in the paradise of God : methinks I hear her say, "Mother, come up hither." Jesus, I am sure, calls you in His word. May His Spirit enable you to say, "Lord, lo I come." . . .'

The orphans were still a great, though pleasant burden, troubles having overtaken the institution from two sources. The magistrates had been acting with a high hand both towards the masters and the children, but General Oglethorpe had proved a warm and useful friend. The Spaniards had also raided the coast, and the orphans had to be carried to a place of safety. News of these alarms and troubles came with successive posts, and he had to wait for reassuring letters. In the long suspense he kept a quiet mind.

His philanthropic effort laid him open to all kinds of assaults. In America and at home the money was in every enemy's mouth. Accordingly, one of his last works was to write 'A Continuation of the Account of the Orphan-house in Georgia,' and to give a statement of his disbursements and receipts. The latter was satisfactory ; and from the former we learn that the workmen were all discharged, having fulfilled their contract, and carried on the work so far as to make every part of the house habitable ; that the stock of cattle was something considerable, and in a flourishing condition ; that the last Parliament had resolved to support the colony of Georgia ; that they had altered its constitution in two material points, namely, these : they had allowed the importation of rum, and free titles to the lands ; and that if they should see good hereafter to grant a limited use of Negroes, it must certainly, in all outward appearance, be as flourishing a colony as South Carolina, but that in the meantime a tolerable shift might be made with white servants. Hunting and shooting for much of their food, killing some of their own stock, growing their own vegetables, helped by the kindness of nearly all around them, and receiving constant remittances from England, the inmates of the orphan-house were always provided for. Whitefield's faith that God would not see them want was never put to shame ; and he delighted to tell how the house had answered to its motto, the burning bush, which, though on fire, was never consumed.

Winter was coming on fast, and it was time for Whitefield to think of returning to London to the only chapel which he could call his own ; in all other places he was dependent upon other clergymen, and, failing their support, must betake himself to Nonconformist chapels or to the fields. At the end of

October he took horse, and rode post from Edinburgh to London in less than five days. The city he left was now very dear to him : the writing its name would make him say, ' O Edinburgh ! Edinburgh ! I think I shall never forget thee ! ' He passed from a great contention with heart as peaceful as ever rested in human bosom. He went chastened and humbled to Scotland ; he returned in the power of quietness and confidence, persuaded that his was not the task of doing anything but preach the Lord Jesus, as he knew and loved Him. He had tried the disputing way in the Arminian struggle, and the quiet way in the Scotch contendings, and found the latter far preferable to the former. No small influence among men was justly in store for one who, feeling that disputing embitters the spirit, ruffles the soul, and hinders it from hearing the still, small voice of the Holy Ghost, could say, as Whitefield did to Wesley, with whom he was now on the best of terms, but quoting Wesley's own words to himself, ' Let the King live for ever, and controversy die.' ' I care not,' he said to another friend, ' if the name of George Whitefield be banished out of the world, so that Jesus be exalted in it.'

On his arrival in London he found the Tabernacle enlarged and ' a new awakening begun.' In his winter quarters, as he called them, he found himself as busy as he had been on the common and in the market-place. He worked from morning till midnight ; and was carried through the duties of each day with cheerfulness and almost uninterrupted tranquillity. The society was large and in good order, and daily improvements were made.

It was at this time that the congregation began to be sprinkled with visitors of distinction. Hitherto, Whitefield's intercourse with the nobility had been confined to those of Scotland, but now English peers and peeresses, led by the Earl and Countess of Huntingdon, and by the Earl's sisters, the Ladies Hastings, began to mingle with the humbler orders, among whom his efforts had won such astonishing success. The low, wooden Tabernacle was sometimes, during this winter of 1742, entered by the Duke of Cumberland, the 'hero of Culloden,' and by Frederick, Prince of Wales. Lord Hervey, too, wretched in health, which he supported by drinking asses' milk, his ghastly countenance covered with rouge, would sometimes sit on its benches. The Duke of Bolton, Lord Lonsdale, and Lord Sidney Beauclerk, who hunted the fortunes of the old and childless, but is best known as the father of Dr. Johnson's friend, Topham Beauclerk, also came. Most remarkable of all was the haughty face of the Duchess of Marlborough, 'great Atossa—

> ' Who with herself, or others, from her birth
> Finds all her life one warfare upon earth.
> Shines, in exposing knaves, and painting fools,
> Yet is whate'er she hates and ridicules ! '

Her letters to the Countess of Huntingdon are very characteristic of her pride and revenge; they show also that she did want to be good, but not to give up being wicked. She says :—

' My dear Lady Huntingdon is always so very good to me, and I really do feel very sensibly all your kindness and attention, that I must accept your very obliging invitation to accompany you to hear Mr. Whitefield, though I am still suffering from the effects of a severe cold. Your concern for my improvement in religious knowledge is very obliging, and I do hope that I shall be the better for all your excellent advice. God knows we all need mending, and none more than myself. I have lived to see great changes in the world—have acted a conspicuous part myself—and now hope, in my old days, to obtain mercy from God, as I never expect any at the hands of my fellow-creatures. The Duchess of Ancaster, Lady Townshend, and Lady Cobham were exceedingly pleased with many observations in Mr. Whitefield's sermon at St. Sepulchre's Church, which has made me lament ever since that I did not hear it, as it might have been the means of doing me good—for good, alas ! I do want ; but where among

the corrupt sons and daughters of Adam am I to find it? Your ladyship
must direct me.   You are all goodness and kindness, and I often wish I
had a portion of it.   Women of wit, beauty, and quality cannot hear too
many humiliating truths—they shock our pride.   But we must die—we
must converse with earth and worms.

'Pray do me the favour to present my humble service to your excellent
spouse.   A more amiable man I do not know than Lord Huntingdon.   And
believe me, my dear madam,

'Your most faithful and most humble servant,

'S. MARLBOROUGH.'

In a second letter to the Countess she says :—

'When alone, my reflections and recollections almost kill me, and I am
forced to fly the society of those I detest and abhor.   Now, there is Lady
Frances Saunderson's great rout to-morrow night—all the world will be
there, and I must go.   I do hate that woman as much as I do hate a
physician ; but I must go, if for no other purpose than to mortify and spite
her.   This is very wicked, I know, but I confess all my little peccadillos to
you, for I know your goodness will lead you to be mild and forgiving, and
perhaps my wicked heart may gain some good from you in the end.

'Lady Fanny has my best wishes for the success of her attack on that
crooked, perverse, little wretch at Twickenham.'

Another occasional hearer at the Tabernacle was the
Duchess of Buckingham, the rival of Atossa in pride, but less
patient than she under reproof, and hating Methodist doctrines
with all her heart.   To Lady Huntingdon's invitation to attend
one of Whitefield's services, she replies :—

'I thank your ladyship for the information concerning Methodist
preachers ; their doctrines are most repulsive, and strongly tinctured with
impertinence and disrespect towards their superiors, in perpetually
endeavouring to level all ranks, and do away with all distinctions.   It is
monstrous to be told that you have a heart as sinful as the common
wretches that crawl on the earth.   This is highly offensive and insulting ;
and I cannot but wonder that your ladyship should relish any sentiments
so much at variance with high rank and good breeding.   Your ladyship
does me infinite honour by your obliging inquiries after my health.   I shall

be most happy to accept your kind offer of accompanying me to hear your favourite preacher, and shall await your arrival. The Duchess of Queensberry insists on my patronising her on this occasion ; consequently she will be an addition to our party.'

The list of Whitefield's noble hearers is increased by the names of the Earl of Oxford, Lady Lisburne, and Lady Hinchinbroke. With the exception of the last two ladies, none of them accepted his teaching and lived according to it. To gratify their taste for the highest oratory, or to please the pious Countess who invited their attendance, was the motive that brought them to so strange a place.

In the spring, Whitefield started for his old ground in Gloucestershire, and found preaching there to be like preaching in the Tabernacle. His friends in the county had been roughly handled of late, yet he stood unmolested on a spot in Dursley from which his friend Adams had been driven but the Sunday before. On Hampton Common, from the top of a knoll named, after the preacher who first honoured it as his pulpit, 'Whitefield's tump,' he preached amid much solemnity to a congregation of ten thousand ; and when he stood at noon on old Mr. Cole's tump at Quarhouse, it was an 'alarming time,' and his soul enjoyed exceeding great liberty. Perhaps the memory of departed worth helped to expand his susceptible heart. His native city delighted in the sound of his voice ; and not until one o'clock on the Monday morning, after he bade them farewell, before starting for Wales, could he lay his weary body down to rest. Sick and unrefreshed he rose again at five, and, mounting horse, rode to meet a congregation which had come at seven, 'hoping to feel the power of a risen Lord.' He read prayers and preached ; then rode on to Stroud, where he preached in a field with uncommon freedom and power to twelve thousand people. At six in the evening he preached to the same number on Hampton

Common ; and still his word was with power. A general love-feast of the religious societies in Hampton was next presided over by him, and that engagement closed the day. All that he has to say about such abundant labours is beautifully like the simple loving spirit in which he delighted to be about 'his Father's business,' 'My soul was kept close to Jesus ; my bodily strength renewed ; and I went to bed about midnight very cheerful and very happy.' The next morning a congregation of some thousands was trembling and rejoicing under his word at Dursley ; and at night he was in Bristol, speaking with wonderful power to a full congregation at Smith's Hall. The following morning he met as large a congregation in the same place, and then set out for Waterford, in South Wales.

Only three months previously, January 5, 1743, four clergymen and three laymen had met at the same place to confer together on the best way of organising Welsh Methodism. Whitefield was chosen moderator, and a plan of classifying the various kinds of workers was decided upon. This was the germ of Welsh Calvinistic Methodism, and in point of arrangement English Methodism, as organised by Wesley, at a conference in London, eighteen months later, closely resembled it. One of the resolutions passed at this first Welsh Conference reveals in a curious way the relation of Nonconformity to the Established Church and of Methodism to both. It was this : 'That those brethren who scruple to receive the sacrament in the Church, on account of the impiety of the administrators and the usual communicants there ; and among the Dissenters, on account of their lukewarmness, should continue to receive it in the Church, until the Lord open a clear way to separate from her communion.'

Whitefield had come to Waterford a second time to preside over the *second* General Association of Methodists in Wales

(April, 1743). Judging from the amount of business done, its members were gifted with some capacity for work. Whitefield opened the Association at noon, on the day after his arrival, with a 'close and solemn discourse upon walking with God ;' then they betook themselves to business, and despatched several important things, among which was his appointment to the moderatorship whenever he was in England. There was an interval from seven till ten o'clock, from which hour they worked till two in the morning. The next day they sat till four in the afternoon ; a little refreshment followed and 'some warm talk about the things of God,' and then Whitefield preached to them a sermon upon the believer's rest. These —the refreshment for the body and the refreshment for the soul—prepared them for another sitting, which lasted until midnight, when the whole business of the Association was finished, and feeling that God had been with them in all that they had done, they did not forget to bless Him for His help before parting.

Wales did honour to her visitor. At Carmarthen, which Whitefield describes as 'one of the greatest and most polite places in Wales,' the justices, who were assembled at the great sessions, desired him to stay till they rose, and they would come to hear him at the cross. They came, and many thousands with them, including several persons of quality. On another day, when he was crossing Carmarthen Bay in the ferry, several ships hoisted their flags, and one fired a salute. Yet such attentions never turned him from his great purpose of seeking all the lost, and between the days when justices and sailors honoured him, he mentions with satisfaction that at Jefferson he preached to a Kingswood congregation, and at Llassivran to a Moorfields one. As soon as London was reached he wrote to his friend Ingham in Yorkshire, announcing his intention to stay there for a month, and in the holidays once more to attack the prince of darkness in Moorfields; for, said he, 'many precious souls have been captivated with Christ's love in that wicked place: Jerusalem sinners bring most glory to the Redeemer.' Besides, there was a bond of sympathy between that wicked place and Bethesda. Many a load of copper, sprinkled here and there with golden guineas, and whitened with a few crowns and shillings, had been gathered from among the crowd for the orphans; and the old kindness towards the preacher and his adopted ones was not extinct. Moorfields lifted the last straw of obligation in England from Whitefield's back on the second occasion of his getting free.

The incessant toil was making itself felt on that slim body which contained a spirit of seraphic devotion. In about three weeks, he says, he travelled about four hundred miles, spent three days in attending two associations, preached about forty times, visited about thirteen towns, and passed through seven counties! No wonder weariness and feebleness hung about it for a time, but preaching was continued at the same rate, the only relief being in the shorter distances travelled. The loving heart made light of the body's weakness, and enjoyed for itself all the more deeply the secret consolations which come from above. It became so full of heaven that Whitefield sometimes longed when in public to lie down anywhere, that on his face he might give God thanks; and when in private he wept for hours the tears of his consuming love for his Lord.

'In perils by mine own countrymen' was another experience through which he and his friends were now called to pass. Wiltshire had for some time been in commotion through the animosity of several clergymen, and Whitefield felt himself obliged to put the facts before the Bishop of Sarum, who, however, does not seem to have interfered to stop the disgraceful proceedings. Churchwardens and overseers were strictly forbidden to let the Methodists have anything out of the parish; they obeyed the clergy, and told the poor that they would punish them, if in no other way they could stop them from joining the new sect. Most of the poor, some of them with large families, braved the threat, and suffered for their constancy the loss of goods and friends. A few denied that they had ever been to meetings; and some promised that they would go no more.

Trouble arose in Wales also, and Whitefield appealed to the Bishop of Bangor against having certain good people indicted for holding a conventicle when they met to tell their religious experiences to each other. With some effect he urged that a continuance of such treatment must inevitably drive hundreds, if not thousands, from the Church, and compel them to declare themselves Dissenters.

But the greatest difficulty was with the Minchin-Hampton rioters, who were of the poorer class, aided and abetted by those of higher rank. Their special hatred was directed against one Adams, a convert of Whitefield's, and a preacher to his neighbours, who proved to be to Whitefield 'my very dear, steady old friend.' On a July Sunday afternoon, a hundred of them came with their rough music, forced their way into his house, carried him to a skin-pit full of stagnant water and the creeping things which breed in it, and threw him in. A friend of his who expostulated was thrown in twice, then beaten and dragged along the kennel. Adams quietly returned to his house to pray, and exhort his brethren to cheerfulness under suffering; but in half an hour the mob, anxious for more sport, entered his house a second time, dragged him downstairs, and led him to Bourn brook, and threw him in twice, cutting his leg severely against a stone. Meanwhile the constable and justices never heeded the appeals made for their interference, but countenanced the lawless suppression of Methodism.   The clergy was satisfied with the outrages.   Preaching was for a time suspended.   Whitefield now consulted with London friends as to the line of action it would be best to take, and all wisely determined to claim the protection of the law.   He and they moved for a rule of Court in the King's Bench to lodge an information against five of the ringleaders.   Counsel for the rioters prayed that the rule might be enlarged until the next term, and it was granted.   The interval was employed by the two sides in a characteristic way; the rioters increased their offences, and the Methodists stirred up the liberality of friends to bear the expenses of the trial, and the hearts of the faithful in England, Wales, and Scotland, to keep a day of fasting and prayer for its right issue.

It must have added to the excitement of a Methodist's coming to a town, in those days when 'such great liberty '—on one side —'was enjoyed under the mild and gentle government of King George,' to see how the Church and the roughs would receive him.   There must have been great glee in the belfry at Ottery when, just as Whitefield announced his text, the ringers pulled the ropes and made the bells utter a clanging peal, in which the finest voice became useless as a whisper. And there must have been profound satisfaction in the parsonage when the clergyman told an admiring circle how he had demanded of the arch-Methodist, as he and his friends made for the fields, where they might worship in peace, his authority for preaching, and called his meeting illegal and a riot.   The rabble of Wedgbury, too, must have been delighted when a sod fell on the reverently-bowed head of Whitefield, and another struck his clasped hands, as he stood among them and prayed.

But happily the clergy and the blackguards, if united for evil in some places, had not a national union.   If Ottery was inhospitable, St. Gennis prayed for Whitefield's coming ; and his visit renewed the days of Cambuslang. Exeter also answered to his call, many of its clergy, and nearly a third of its inhabitants, turning out to hear him. He thought that on the whole a healthy change was passing over society; that prejudices were falling off; and that people were beginning not only rationally to discern, but powerfully to feel, the doctrines of the gospel.

The expectation of a son's being born to him now filled his heart with all a father's pride; and, as well as his notions of public duty would permit, he was thoughtful for his wife's comfort and safety. But his was not the best of keeping for a delicate woman to be committed to; one day he nearly killed both her and himself. In expectation of the birth he restricted his work to London and the neighbourhood, and even indulged his domestic affections so far as to take Mrs. Whitefield for a drive, according to advice. But he was a poor driver, if a fine rider, and soon drove into a ditch fourteen feet deep. Mrs. Whitefield put her hand across the chaise, and thus saved herself and him from being thrown out. The horse went down as though held by a pulley, probably because the ditch narrowed very much towards the bottom. Bystanders shouted out that they were killed, and ran to the rescue; one of them seized the horse's head, two or three pulled Mrs. Whitefield up the side of the ditch, and others, with a long whip, drew the preacher from the back of the horse, on to which he had scrambled. Doubtless the accident broke off a close religious conversation; for Whitefield says that, 'being both in a comfortable frame, I must own to my shame that I felt rather regret than thankfulness in escaping what I thought would be a kind of translation to our wished-for haven. But, oh amazing love! we were so strengthened, that the chaise and horse being taken up, and our bruises being washed with vinegar in a neighbouring house, we went on our intended way, and came home rejoicing in God our Saviour.' It would appear that he never risked that mode of translation again.

A month afterwards, in October, 1743, his son was born; and as soon as the news reached him in the country to which he had made a short preaching excursion, he hastened to London. When the infant was about a week old, his father baptized him in the Tabernacle in the presence of a great congregation.

The little one was not born in a sumptuous house ; indeed, his home was not furnished when he came, and his father had to be content with borrowed furniture to complete his little stock in hand. The simple, grateful, humble heart of the mighty orator was just like itself when he wrote to an old friend in Gloucester : 'This afternoon I received your kind letter, and thank you a thousand times for your great generosity in lending me some furniture, having little of my own. I know who will repay you. Next week, God willing, my dear wife and little one will come to Gloucester, for I find it beyond my circumstances to maintain them here. I leave, God willing, this day seven-night. My brother will receive a letter about my wife's coming. She and the little one are brave and well.' The child's life was short as a dream. Within three weeks Whitefield was sitting at the 'Bell' in Gloucester, then his brother's house, writing an account of his death! He confessed and deplored his own need of the chastisement. His letter is touching for its disappointed love and humbled confidence. It runs thus :—

'Last night, February 8, 1744, I was called to sacrifice my Isaac—I mean to bury my own child and son, about four months old. Many things occurred to make me believe he was not only to be continued to me, but to be a preacher of the everlasting gospel. Pleased with the thought, and ambitious of having a son of my own so divinely employed, Satan was permitted to give me some wrong impressions, whereby, as I now find, I misapplied several texts of Scripture. . . . Upon my coming here, without knowing what had happened, I inquired concerning the welfare of parent and child, and by the answer found that the flower was cut down. I immediately called all to join in a prayer, in which I blessed the Father of mercies for giving me a son, continuing it to me so long, and taking it from me so soon. All joined in desiring that I would decline preaching till the child was buried; but I remembered a saying of good Mr. Henry, "that weeping must not hinder sowing," and therefore preached twice the next day, and also the day following, on the evening of which, just as I was closing my sermon, the bell struck out for the funeral. At first, I must acknowledge, it gave nature a little shake, but looking up, I recovered strength, and then concluded with saying that this text on which I had been preaching, namely, "All things work together for good to them that love God," made me as willing to go to my son's funeral as to hear of his birth.

'Our parting from him was solemn. We kneeled down, prayed, and shed many tears, but I hope tears of resignation; and then, as he died in the house wherein I was born, he was taken and laid in the church where I was baptized, first communicated, and first preached. . . .'

There was one sermon, at least, with which he often melted his vast congregation into tears, which would lose no force of tenderness and love now that his always affectionate heart, which might nourish the orphans of other fathers and mothers, was denied the delight of fondling a child of his own—the sermon on Abraham's offering up Isaac. All the grief and struggling of faithful Abraham during the three days' journey to the land of Moriah, with Isaac, the burnt-offering, by his side, was henceforth painfully real to Whitefield while, with trembling voice and glistening eye, he pictured them to his hearers. All could see the vision of—

'The good old man walking with his dear child in his hand, and now and then looking upon him, loving him, and then turning aside to weep. And, perhaps, sometimes he stays a little behind to pour out his heart before God, for he had no mortal to tell his case to. Then methinks I see him join his son and servants again, and talking to them of the things pertaining to the kingdom of God, as they walked by the way. . . . Little did Isaac think that he was to be offered on that very wood which he was carrying upon his shoulders; and therefore Isaac innocently, and with a holy freedom

—for good men should not keep their children at too great a distance—
spake unto Abraham, his father, and said, " My father ; " and he, with
equal affection and holy condescension, said, " Here am I, my son. . . ."
Come, all ye tender-hearted parents, who know what it is to look over a
dying child, fancy that you saw the altar erected before you, and the wood
laid in order, and the beloved Isaac bound upon it ; fancy that you saw the
aged parent standing by, weeping. For why may we not suppose that
Abraham wept, since Jesus Himself wept at the grave of Lazarus ? Oh,
what pious, endearing expressions passed now alternately between the
father and son ! Methinks I see the tears trickle down the patriarch's
cheeks ; and out of the abundance of the heart he cries, " Adieu ! adieu !
my son ! The Lord gave thee to me, and the Lord calls thee away ; blessed
be the name of the Lord ! Adieu, my Isaac ! my only son, whom I love
as my own soul ! Adieu ! adieu ! " I see Isaac at the same time meekly
resigning himself into his heavenly Father's hands, and praying to the Most
High to strengthen his earthly parent to strike the stroke.'

Then, when men had well entered into the greatness of the
human sacrifice, and were under the dominion of their finest
and purest emotions, the preacher said—

' I see your hearts affected, I see your eyes weep. And indeed, who can
refrain weeping at the relation of such a story ? But, behold ! I show you a
mystery hid under the sacrifice of Abraham's only son which, unless your
hearts are hardened, must cause you to weep tears of love, and that plentifully too. I would willingly hope you even prevent me here, and are ready
to say, " It is the love of God in giving Jesus Christ to die for our sins."
Yes, that is it.'

The evangelist had an ever-changing experience ; and before
his grief for his son was assuaged he was putting forth all his
energy to secure justice for his poor persecuted converts at
Hampton, going from place to place preaching, pleading, and
collecting money. The trial, which came off at Gloucester
Assizes, on March 3, 1744, was anticipated by the defendants
with much confidence, because they reckoned that the gentlemen and the jury would be prejudiced against the Methodists.
Whitefield entered court when the second witness was
being examined, and was the object of every one's attention,

while, amid much laughter, the defendants' counsel went on to describe the Methodists after the fashion which best suited his bad case. In spite, however, of hard swearing, of oratorical pleading, and of the genteel influence which the rioters undoubtedly had at their back, the jury found the defendants guilty of the whole information lodged against them.

Our narrative must now run back for a few months, that we may note the attitude of the Dissenters towards Whitefield. Many of them had shown him much kindness, but, with the exception of Doddridge and Watts, their leaders looked upon him with contempt, or dislike, or fear. And for the fear there was some reason. Dissenters were only permitted to hold their opinions under great disadvantages, and were studiously kept down in the State. In consequence, there was a great desire on the part of most of them to keep on friendly terms with the Established Church, and not to risk in any wise the good opinion of its bishops and clergy. Theirs was the worldly-wise, cautious spirit of men who felt that any false step might multiply their disabilities, not the fearless spirit of those who could safely dare to assume any position. Whitefield, the dread of orderly bishops and the reproach of idle clergymen, they therefore carefully shunned. To consort with him would have exposed them to double odium—the odium of Dissent and the odium of Methodism.

Great weight must also be attached to their laudable desire to grapple on safe ground with all forms of religious error ; and it was not deemed safe, in dealing with Deism, to lie open to the charge of enthusiasm. Only the calm, argumentative preacher, such as Butler, or Waterland, could be heard against the wit and arguments of Woolston, Shaftesbury, Collins, and Tindal. A feverish fear, only paralleled by that which any sensible man might now have of being esteemed a fanatic, agitated nearly all Christian apologists, of being suspected of any sympathy with ardent devotion and burning zeal. A reasonable faith, a faith well buttressed with arguments on the evidences of religion, and quiet, sedate religious habits, were supposed to constitute the proper, if not the perfect, Christian. Any such passion as glowed in the hearts of the early Methodists, common sense and reason must condemn and avoid. To have anything to do with the most religious, if not the most learned or the most intellectual, class of that time, was virtually to yield up the right of speaking on religion. Who dare write against Collins, if he had shaken hands with Whitefield or Wesley—the enthusiasts, the reproach of Christianity, men whose very profession of Christianity made it require a fresh apology from its accomplished defenders to its equally able assailants?

Doddridge, who had many friends in the Establishment, and who also took a lively interest in all public movements affecting the honour of religion and the welfare of mankind, stands out as a noble exception to the somewhat timid body with which he was allied. His sound and varied learning, together with his solid judgment, covered him from the sneer that he was a poor enthusiast, while his humble piety compelled him to countenance the new party in the Church. Persuaded of the usefulness of Whitefield's ministrations, he did not fear to entertain the Evangelist and to bid him God speed. His magnanimity surpassed that of Watts, who was very cautious with the 'erratic curate.' He even went to the extent of supplying Whitefield's place as preacher at the Tabernacle ; and Watts wrote saying—

'I am sorry that since your departure I have had many questions asked me about your preaching in the Tabernacle, and sinking the character of a minister, and especially of a tutor, among the Dissenters, so low thereby. I find many of our friends entertain this idea ; but I can give no answer, as not knowing how much you have been engaged there. I pray God to guard us from every temptation.'

Doddridge, always thoughtful, conscientious, and liberal, knew what the Methodists were, and what they were doing among the rude, ignorant, and irreligious part of the population; and was not to be moved out of his position either by ominous shakes of the head, or by open opposition on the part of his co-religionists. When the hackneyed charge of enthusiasm was levelled against them, his noble reply was—

'In some extraordinary conversions there may be and often is a tincture of enthusiasm, but, having weighed the matter diligently, I think a man had better be a sober, honest, chaste, industrious enthusiast, than live without any regard to God and religion at all. I think it infinitely better that a man should be a religious Methodist than an adulterer, a thief, a swearer, a drunkard, or a rebel to his parents, as I know some actually were who have been wrought upon and reformed by these preachers.'

On Whitefield's first visit to Northampton, Doddridge was only polite in personal intercourse, but on the second, he opened his pulpit to him, which daring charity soon brought a rebuke from London. Nathanael Neal, an attorney, and son of Neal, the historian of the Puritans, said, in a timeserving letter, dated October 11, 1743 :—

'It was with the utmost concern that I received the information of Mr. Whitefield's having preached last week in your pulpit, and that I attended the meeting of Coward's Trustees this day, when that matter was canvassed, and that I now find myself obliged to apprise you of the very great uneasiness which your conduct herein has occasioned them. . . . The Trustees are particularly in pain for it with regard to your academy, as they know it is an objection made to it by some persons in all appearance seriously, and by others craftily ; and yet they are afraid of giving their thoughts even in the most private manner concerning it, lest it should be made an occasion of drawing them into a public opposition to the Methodists, as they are likely to be in some measure by your letter to Mr. Mason (excusing your prefixing a recommendation of a book of theirs, without the advice of the Trustees), which letter they have desired me to inform you has given them great offence.'

A quick answer returned from Northampton, and on
October 15th Neal wrote again.   He says :—

'I am not insensible, sir, that the respect many of your people bore to
Mr. Whitefield, and your own acquaintance with him, must have made it
a matter of difficulty for you to have avoided showing him some polite
regards on his coming to Northampton ; and I greatly rejoice in being
furnished with so particular an account of the circumstances attending his
visit that may enable me to say you were so far at that time from seeking
his preaching in your pulpit, that you took several steps, and indeed all
that you thought you could prudently venture on, and such as might,
if they had succeeded, have been sufficient to have prevented it ; which
I doubt not will, and I am sure ought, to have some weight with those
who censure this step on the ground of imprudence.   I could only wish that
I were able to make these circumstances known as far as that censure
is likely to extend.'

Doddridge continued ' imprudent,' and dared ' the censure ' ; so that Neal returned again to the task of remon-
strating.   His third letter is more direct, and plainly tells
the feelings which he had only hinted at before.

The answer of Doddridge is plain and honest ; in one part
of it he says :—

'I shall always be ready to weigh whatever can be said against Mr.
Whitefield, as well as against any of the rest ; and though I must have
actual demonstration before I can admit him to be a dishonest man, and
though I shall never be able to think all he has written and all I have
heard from him nonsense, yet I am not so zealously attached to him as to
be disposed to celebrate him as one of the greatest men of the age, or to
think that he is the pillar that bears up the whole interest of religion
among us.   And if this moderation of sentiment towards him will not
appease my angry brethren, as I am sensible it will not abate the enmity
which some have for many years entertained towards me, I must acquiesce,
and be patient till the day of the Lord, when the secrets of all hearts shall
be made manifest ; in which I do from my heart believe that with respect
to the part I have acted in this affair I shall not be ashamed.'

Two sentences, in which the devout, tender, and humble
spirit of Doddridge expresses itself, are, when taken in con-

nection with many similar expressions of Whitefield, a sufficient explanation of the firm union between these distinguished Christians : ' I am one of the least of God's children,' said Doddridge, 'and yet a child ; and that is my daily joy. Indeed, I feel my love to Him increase ; I struggle forwards towards Him ; and look at Him, as it were, sometimes with tears of love, when, in the midst of the hurries of life, I cannot speak to Him otherwise than by an ejaculation.'

Other persons of a different communion, and more exalted in station than Neal, were trying as well as he what could be done in a secret way to damage the Methodists in general, and Whitefield in particular. The mean attempt to sever Doddridge from his friend was probably never known to its intended victim ; but this other meaner work of an enemy, or rather enemies, did come to his knowledge. On January 26, 1744, the following advertisement appeared in London :—

' Whereas some anonymous papers against the people called Methodists in general, and myself and friends in particular, have been for some weeks printed in a large edition, and handed about and read in the religious societies of the cities of London and Westminster, and given into the hands of many private persons, with strict injunctions to lend them to no one, nor let them go out of their hands to any, and whereas, after having had the hasty perusal of them, I find many queries of great importance concerning me and my conduct contained therein ; and as it appears that one paper has little or no connection with another, and a copy, when applied for, was refused me, and I know not how soon I may embark for Georgia, I am therefore obliged hereby to desire a speedy open publication of the aforesaid papers, in order that a candid, impartial answer may be made thereto by me.

'GEORGE WHITEFIELD.'

Rumour was not silent about the authorship of the secret papers ; no less a personage than the Bishop of London was singled out as their writer. Whitefield, accordingly, with the frankness and courage which always distinguished him, wrote to the Bishop himself to ask for information :—

'LONDON, *February* 1, 1744.

'MY LORD,—Simplicity becomes the followers of Jesus Christ, and therefore I think it my duty to trouble your lordship with these few lines. I suppose your lordship has seen the advertisement published by me, about four days ago, concerning some anonymous papers which have been handed about in the societies for some considerable time.   As I think it my duty to answer them, I should be glad to be informed whether the report be true that your lordship composed them, that I may the better know to whom I may direct my answer.   A sight also of one of the copies, if in your lordship's keeping, would much oblige, my lord,

'Your lordship's most obliged, dutiful son and servant,

'GEORGE WHITEFIELD.

' PS.—The bearer will bring your lordship's answer ; or if your lordship please to favour me with a line, be pleased to direct for me, to be left with Mr. J. Syms.'

To this letter the Bishop sent no answer at all; but two days after it was sent to him his printer left the following suggestive note for Whitefield :—

'*February* 3, 1744.

'SIR,—My name is Owen.   I am a printer in Amen Corner ; and I waited upon you to let you know that I have had orders from several of the bishops to print for their use such numbers of the "Observations upon the Conduct and Behaviour of the Methodists"—with some additions—as they have respectively bespoken.   And I will not fail to wait upon you with one copy as soon as the impression is finished.

'I am, sir, your most obedient, &c.'

The contents of the anonymous pamphlet are not difficult to discover from Whitefield's 'Answer,' which he addressed in a 'Letter to the Right Reverend the Bishop of London, and the other Right Reverend the Bishops concerned in the publication thereof,' namely, of the pamphlet.   Whitefield charged the pamphlet with having an intention to represent the proceedings of the Methodists as dangerous to Church and

State, in order to procure an Act of Parliament against them, or to oblige them to secure themselves by turning Dissenters, that is, putting themselves under the Toleration Act. His answer to such an attempt was the same as he gave to the Scotch Presbyterians : ' As yet we see no sufficient reason to leave the Church of England and turn Dissenters ; neither will we do it till we are thrust out.' The pamphlet charged the Methodists with breaking the statute law by their field-preaching ; and to be quite sure of the law on this point, Whitefield perused all the Acts of Charles II. in which the word ' field ' is mentioned. His conclusion was, that Acts against field-preaching related only to seditious conventicles ; and of this offence Methodism was not guilty. Then White-field enters upon a defence of his favourite mode of reaching the multitude, by quoting the example of our Lord and the apostles, and pungently inquires : ' I would humbly ask your lordships whether it would not be more becoming your lord-ships' characters to put your clergy on preaching against revelling, cock-fighting, and such like, than to move the Government against those who, out of love to God and precious souls, put their lives in their hand, and preach unto such revellers repentance towards God and faith in our Lord Jesus ? What if the Methodists by " public advertisement do invite the rabble ? " . . . These rabble, my lords, have precious and immortal souls, for which the dear Redeemer shed His precious blood, as well as the great and rich. These, my lords, are the publicans and harlots that enter into the king-dom of heaven, while self-righteous formal professors reject it. To show such poor sinners the way to God, to preach to them the power of Christ's resurrection, and to pluck them as fire-brands out of the burning, the Methodist preachers go out into the highways and hedges. If this is to be vile, by the help of my God I shall be more vile. . . . Is it not ridiculous, my lords, even in the eyes of worldly men, and does it not render the author of this pamphlet justly liable to contempt, to charge the Methodists with breaking canons and rubrics, which is really not their fault; when at the same time he knows that the generality of the clergy so notoriously break both canons and rubrics, and that too in the most important articles, such as not catechising, pluralities, non-residence, &c., every day themselves? With what face can he do it?'

The Rev. Thomas Church, vicar of Battersea, came, among others, to the rescue of the bishops with a 'Serious and Expostulatory Letter to the Rev. G. Whitefield.' He raised a few questions which throw some light upon Whitefield's ecclesiastical position. There were irregularities in curtailing the liturgy, or not using the Common Prayer in the fields— what had Whitefield to say about them? That when, and only when, his ecclesiastical superiors should arraign him at the bar of the proper courts would he give any answer at all to the question. There was his non-residence at Savannah—what could he say in defence of that? He replied :—

'I wish every non-resident minister in England could give as good an account of their non-residence as I can of my absence from Savannah. When I came over to England to receive priest's orders, and collect money for building an orphan-house, the honourable Trustees, at the request of many, presented me to the living of Savannah. I accepted it, but refused the stipend of fifty pounds per annum which they generously offered me. Neither did I put them to any expense during my stay in England, where I thought it my duty to abide till I had collected a sufficient sum wherewith I might begin the orphan-house, though I should have left England sooner had I not been prevented by the embargo. However, I was more easy, because the honourable Trustees I knew had sent out another minister, who arrived soon after I left the colony. Upon my second arrival in Georgia, finding the care of the orphan-house, and the care of the parish, too great a task for me, I immediately wrote over to the honourable Trustees to provide another minister. In the meanwhile, as most of my parishioners were in debt, or ready to leave the colony for want of being employed, and as I believed that erecting an orphan-house would be the best thing I could do for them and their posterity, I thought it my duty from time to time to answer the invitations that were sent me to preach Christ Jesus in several parts of America, and to make more collections towards carrying on the orphan-house. The Lord stirred up many to be ready to distribute and willing to communicate on this occasion. I always came home furnished with provisions and money, most of which was expended upon the people, and by this means the northern part of the colony almost entirely subsisted for a considerable time. 'And now, sir, judge you whether my non-residence was anything like the non-residence of most of the English clergy. When I was absent from my parishioners, I was not loitering or living at ease, but preaching and begging for them and theirs ; and when I returned, it was not to fleece my flocks, and then go and spend it upon my lusts, or lay it up for a fortune for myself and relations.'

The family at Bethesda, long wishful to see him, and the thousands living between Savannah and Boston, who wished again to hear him and sent him urgent requests to come among them, constrained him to take his fifth voyage to America ; and in June, 1744, he took passage in a ship which was to sail from Portsmouth. Second thoughts, but not better ones, led the captain to refuse him a berth in his ship for fear he might spoil the sailors. He then betook himself to Plymouth, and secured a passage in a mast-ship that was to sail under convoy to Piscataway in New England. The journey from London to the sea-port was a pleasant one, through the midst of warm friends and loving converts ; and as he went from place to place he encouraged believers and called sinners to repentance. Plymouth was not at first altogether gratified with the distinction that rested upon it for several weeks. It was presumed that Whitefield would be sure to appear on the Hoe on the night of his arrival, and to oppose him and draw away his congregation some one brought a bear and a drum. But the first announcement of his arrival was false news, and both crowd and bear were disappointed. The following night brought him ; and his first taste of Plymouth civility was the bursting open of his room door by several men under pretence of a hue-and-cry. He then withdrew from the inn to private lodgings ; but this was no protection against the purpose of a little knot of fast young men, who had resolved, probably in a bragging spirit, to put indignity upon him, if not to injure him. One of them, a lieutenant of a man-of-war, laid a wager of ten guineas that he would do the business for the Methodist preacher, and went and assailed him with a gold-headed stick as he lay in bed. Thinking he was some Nicodemite, Whitefield had permitted the coward to come up to his room. The cry of murder raised by Whitefield and his landlady and her daughter at last made him afraid, and as he retreated to the chamber door, the landlady helped him down-stairs with a push. Then a second bully—no doubt the whole band were outside listening to the scuffle—shouted out, 'Take courage, I am ready to help you,' and, rushing up-stairs while his friend was escaping, took one of the women by the heels and threw her so violently upon the stairs as almost to break her back. By this time the neighbourhood was alarmed, and thus the sport of the young 'gentlemen' came to an end. The house door was shut, and Whitefield went to sleep meditating on the propriety with which we are taught in the Litany to pray—'From sudden death, good Lord, deliver us !'

Preaching called Whitefield out next morning, and he went to it, saying to his friends who counselled the prosecution of the offenders, that he had better work to do, a restraint for which he is to be commended. The assault increased his popularity, curiosity drawing two thousand more to hear a man who 'had like to have been murdered in his bed.' There was undoubtedly some danger to be apprehended. Once his voice arrested the attention of a band of workmen who were passing near the field in which he preached, and thinking him mad, they filled their pockets with stones to pelt him, and arranged to throw him from his block. Their resolution, however, failed when they came to stand for a little while under the charm of his eloquence ; and one of them—Henry Tanner, a ship-builder—at least went home with a serious heart and a resolution in it that he would come again the next night and hear more. The next night the sermon was on the text 'Beginning at Jerusalem,' and contained, as it was sure to do in the hands of a pictorial preacher, and one who sought the recovery of 'Jerusalem sinners' with the greatest devotion, a description of the cruel murder of the Lord of life. It was an admirable topic for admitting a close application of truth to the conscience ; and when the last sad scenes in our Lord's life had been portrayed, Whitefield said to his congregation : 'You are reflecting on the cruelty of these inhuman butchers, who imbrued their hands in innocent blood.' As he spoke his eyes fell on the young ship-builder ; and then, while speaker and hearer seemed to be only with each other in the consciousness of each other's glance, he added : 'Thou art the man.' The effect was great and manifest ; and Whitefield, with his own swift aptitude for fastening on any passing event, and for preaching to one person in the midst of a multitude without any one but that person knowing of it, went on to speak words of tenderness and encouragement. A third time did the young man come to hear, and this time to enter into joy and peace in believing. By and by he in turn ventured to preach the gospel, and his ministry of sixty-five years, mostly exercised at Exeter, was one which could boast that hardly one of its sermons had fallen uselessly to the ground. His last end was according to an earnest and oft-repeated prayer, and such as became a good servant of the Lord Jesus Christ ; strength failed him in the pulpit, and he was carried thence to die.

The evangelist laboured bravely amidst his troubles, whilst a contrary wind hindered him from sailing; and as had happened a hundred times before, prejudice and opposition yielded to his love and effort. Freely and of themselves some who had been opposed offered him a piece of ground surrounded with walls for a society room. Great companies of people, with him in the midst, would return from the dock at night singing and praising God. The ferrymen, too, at the ferry, had an interest in the religious work which had been set on foot, and would not take toll from the crowds which passed over to hear the sermons. 'God forbid that we should sell the word of God,' said the kind-hearted fellows.

Though Whitefield was leaving the country, Christ's work was not interrupted; in every county where he had laboured, lay-preachers, who knew the grace of God as a living power in their hearts, went about, sometimes at the hazard of their lives, joyfully proclaiming the good news of redeeming love. In eight years a new ministry, and one of the most efficient, had been called into existence, and penetrated into villages and towns. Even the press-gang aided in diffusing the truth, for Methodists were looked on as fair game, and the Methodist soldier was not ashamed of his Saviour anywhere.

CHAPTER IX

August, 1744—July, 1748

THE fifth voyage was diversified with nautical adventures
and theological discussions. The usual dangers of
ocean travelling were at this time, August, 1744, increased by
the men-of-war which were cruising for spoil. France and
England were at their old folly of treating each other as
natural enemies. The fleet of one hundred and fifty ships
which sailed out of Plymouth Sound was therefore attended
by several convoys, and a good deal of nervousness was
evidently abroad. Whitefield was in poor health, suffering
from a violent pain in his side, and the tedious voyage
increased his trouble. Fully six weeks were consumed
between Plymouth and the Western Isles, and off the islands
they lay floating in a calm for days ; then, as the wind sprung
up a little, there came a mishap which might have sent a vessel
to the bottom. Orders were given to tack about, to take
advantage of the breeze, and one of the ships, missing her
stays in turning, ran directly against the *Wilmington*, on the

deck of which sat Whitefield, his wife and friends around him, singing a hymn. The *Wilmington*, being the larger vessel, suffered no damage, while the other was so broken that the cries and groans of her apprehensive crew were awful. Presently they came up with the convoy, and when Whitefield's captain informed them of what had happened, they answered, 'This is your praying, and be d—— to you!' Shocked by the profanity, the praying men got together, and Whitefield expressing their feelings, cried out, 'God of the sea, and God of the dry land, this is a night of rebuke and blasphemy; show Thyself, O God, and take us under Thy own immediate protection; be Thou our convoy, and make a difference between those who fear Thee and those who fear Thee not.' The next day a violent gale parted the *Wilmington* from the convoy, which was seen no more during the rest of the voyage—a circumstance which, with one day's exception, proved rather agreeable than otherwise to Whitefield. Until the adventure of that day comes in its proper order, we may go into Whitefield's cabin and consider the thoughts which he is planning for the benefit of the Bishop of London, and the bishop's brethren, who wrote the anonymous pamphlet once before mentioned, or, at any rate, gave authoritative countenance to it.

The pamphlet complained of the irregular practices of the Methodists, and then proceeded to inquire whether the doctrines they taught or the lengths they ran beyond what was practised among the religious societies or in other Christian Churches would be a service or dis-service to religion. The startling effects of Whitefield's preaching, the crying and fainting and convulsions, such as appeared at Cambuslang, were laid upon him as a reproach; and it is well to know what he himself thought of them. Referring to a question in the pamphlet on the subject, he says :—

'Would not one imagine by this query that these itinerants laid down such things as screamings, tremblings, &c., as essential marks of the co-operation of the Holy Spirit? But can any such thing be proved? Are they not looked upon by these itinerants themselves as extraordinary things, proceeding generally from soul distress, and sometimes, it may be, from the agency of the evil spirit, who labours to drive poor souls into despair? Does not this appear from the relation given of them in one of the journals referred to? Are there not many relations of the co-operation of the Spirit in the same journal, where no such bodily effects are so much as hinted at? And does not this give ground to suspect that the "due and regular attendance on the public offices of religion, paid by (what our author calls) good men, in a serious and composed way," is little better than a dead formal attendance on outward ordinances, which a man may continue in all his lifetime, and be all the while far from the kingdom of God? Did ever any one before hear this urged as an evidence of the co-operation of the Spirit? Or would any one think that the author of the observations ever read the relations that are given of the conversion of several in the Holy Scriptures? For may we not suppose, my lords, that many were cast into sudden agonies and screamings (Acts ii. 37) when "they were pricked to the heart, and said unto Peter and the rest of the apostles, Men and brethren, what shall we do to be saved?" Or what would this author think of the conversion of the jailor (Acts x. 29, 30), "who sprang in, and came trembling and fell down before Paul and Silas, and brought them out, and said, Sirs, what must I do to be saved?" Or what would he think of Paul, who, trembling and astonished (Acts ix. 6), said, "Lord, what wilt Thou have me to do?" and was afterwards three days without sight, and did neither eat nor drink? Is it not to be feared that if this author had been seated upon the bench, and heard this apostle give an account of his own conversion, he would have joined with Festus in crying out with a loud voice, "Paul, much learning doth make thee mad?" And are not all these things, and whatever else is recorded in the Book of God, written for our learning? Is not God the same, yesterday, to-day, and for ever? And may He not now, as well as formerly, reveal His arm and display His power in bringing sinners home to Himself as suddenly and instantaneously as in the first planting of the Gospel Church?'

With this important deduction from the instances quoted by Whitefield of persons undergoing great agony of mind at the time that they were turned from their own way of living to the way appointed by the Lord—that there was miracle to alarm—his explanation may be accepted. The pamphlet further complained of Whitefield's notions of justification, and of the height to which he carried them. The gravamen of the charge is directly against the supposed immoral tendency of justification bestowed solely upon the ground of another's merit, and has been already dealt with ; but all the conceptions which in Whitefield's mind stood related to the conception of justification may now have our consideration. His system was severely logical. The atonement was so much suffering endured on the part of our Lord at the hands of His angry Father on behalf of so many sinners ; he says : ' When Christ's righteousness is spoken of, we are to understand Christ's obedience and death—all that Christ has done, and all that Christ has suffered for an elect world, for all that will believe on Him.' The position of our Lord was that of a substitute —the view which has always been effectual, through the Holy Spirit, to the conversion of souls. The sins of the elect were laid on Him in the most literal sense : He was there as a sinner in the Father's sight, and before the Father's law ; and upon the head of such a One it was meet that the indignation should be poured. The active obedience of our Saviour constituted the extra righteousness in the moral world, which, not being required for Himself, since He was always pure and sinless, might be imputed to any who would believe on Him. Whitefield's words are : ' In that nature '—*i.e.*, our human nature—' He obeyed, and thereby fulfilled the whole moral law in our stead ; and also died a painful death upon the Cross, and thereby became a curse for, or instead of, those whom the Father had given to Him. As God He satisfied at the same time that He obeyed and suffered as man ; and, being God and man in one person, He wrought out a full, perfect, and sufficient righteousness for all to whom it was to be imputed.' The language in which, in his favourite and thrilling sermon on ' The True Way of Beholding the Lamb of God,' he describes the sufferings of the Redeemer, is, in some parts, melting and attractive for its tender sympathy of love. It has one short clause which seems to indicate that Whitefield was not quite satisfied with what he said :—

'The paschal lamb was further typical of Christ, its great Antitype, in that it was to be killed in the evening, and afterwards roasted with fire.' So Christ, our Passover, was sacrificed for us in the evening of the world, only with this material difference, the paschal lamb was first slain and then roasted, whereas the holy Jesus, the spotless Lamb of God, was burnt and roasted in the fire of His Father's wrath before He actually expired upon the cross. To satisfy you of this, if you can bear to be spectators of such an awful tragedy, as I desired you just now to go with me to the entrance, so I must now entreat you to venture a little further into the same garden. But—stop—what is that we see? Behold the Lamb of God undergoing the most direful tortures of vindictive wrath! Of the people, even of His disciples, there is none with Him. Alas! was ever sorrow like unto that sorrow wherewith His innocent soul was afflicted in this day of His Father's fierce anger? Before He entered into this bitter passion, out of the fulness of His heart he said, "Now is My soul troubled." But how is it troubled now? His agony bespeaks it to be exceeding sorrowful, even unto death. It extorts sweat, yea, a bloody sweat. His face, His hands, His garments are all over stained with blood. It extorts strong crying and many tears. See how the incarnate Deity lies prostrate before His Father, who now laid on Him the iniquities of us all. See how He agonises in prayer! Hark! Again and again He addresses His Father with an "If it be possible, let this cup pass from Me!" Tell me, ye blessed angels, tell me, Gabriel, or whatsoever thou art called, who wast sent from heaven in this important hour to strengthen our agonising Lord, tell me, if ye can, what Christ endured in this dark and doleful night; and tell me what you yourselves felt when you heard this same God-man, whilst expiring on the accursed tree, breaking forth into that dolorous, unheard-of expostulation, "My God, my God, why hast Thou forsaken Me?" Were you not all struck dumb? And did not a universal awful silence fill heaven itself when God the Father said unto His sword, "Sword, smite My fellow"? Well might nature put on its sable weeds; well might the rocks rend to show their sympathy with a suffering Saviour; and well might the sun withdraw its light, as though it was shocked and confounded to see its Maker suffer. But our hearts are harder than rocks, otherwise they would now break; and our souls more stupid than any part of the inanimate creation, or they would even now, in some degree at least, sympathise with a crucified Redeemer, who for us

men, and for our salvation, was thus roasted, as it were, in the Father's
wrath, and therefore fitly styled the Lamb of God.'

Note the short clause, 'as it were.'

Congregations had no time to settle down upon Whitefield's
theological mistakes or inconsistencies, and find fault with
them. Before the questioner had well begun to consider
what hope of acceptance with God any one durst cherish if
the atonement was only for the elect, his soul was called to
repent and believe ; for Whitefield was too wise at winning
souls to leave his 'application' to the last : he would put an
application to every paragraph rather than fail in getting practical results. Love was stronger than logic. In his sermon
on 'The Lord Our Righteousness' he rushes straight in among
his hearers' doubts and struggles—doubts and troubles which
his own rebukes and pleadings have created, and exclaims :—

'Who knows but the Lord may have mercy on, nay, abundantly pardon
you? Beg of God to give you faith ; and if the Lord gives you that, you
will by it receive Christ with His righteousness and His all. You need
not fear the greatness or number of your sins. For are you sinners? so
am I. Are you the chief of sinners? so am I. Are you backsliding
sinners? so am I. And yet the Lord—for ever adored be His rich, free,
and sovereign grace—is my righteousness. Come, then, O young men,
who, as I acted once myself, are playing the prodigal, and wandering away
afar off from your heavenly Father's house, come home, come home, and
leave your swine-trough. Feed no longer on the husks of sensual delights ;
for Christ's sake arise and come home ! Your heavenly Father now calls
you. See yonder the best robe, even the righteousness of His dear Son,
awaits you. See it ; view it again and again. Consider at how dear a
rate it was purchased, even by the blood of God. Consider what great need
you have of it. You are lost, undone, damned for ever, without it. Come,
then, poor guilty prodigals, come home. Indeed I will not, like the elder
brother in the gospel, be angry ; no, I will rejoice with the angels in
heaven. And O that God would now bow the heavens and come down !
Descend, O Son of God, descend ; and as Thou hast shown in me such
mercy, O let Thy blessed Spirit apply Thy righteousness to some young
prodigals now before Thee, and clothe their naked souls with Thy best
robe !'

Here we have, though he might formally have denied it, the doctrine of the Fatherhood of God. But see the tender, passionate pleading!

The writing of theological letters was very rudely interrupted one day. The good ship *Wilmington* was toiling through the Atlantic without her convoy, when, to the alarm of all, Whitefield included, two ships were sighted which the captain took to be enemies, bearing down on them with all the sail they could crowd. Preparations were at once made for an engagement. Guns were mounted; chains were put about the masts; the great cabin was emptied of everything; hammocks were slung about the sides of the ship. Mrs. Whitefield dressed herself to be prepared for all events, and then set about making cartridges. All but one stood ready for fire and smoke. Whitefield retreated to the hold of the ship when told that that was the chaplain's place; but not liking his quarters, and being urged by one of his New England friends to say something to animate the men, he crept on deck, and beat to arms with a warm exhortation. His words warmed the hearts of braver men. On came the dreaded enemy, when lo! a nearer view showed that they were two friends!

The chaplain had another kind of enemy to fight with, and gladly betook himself to his desk and his quill to write 'Some Remarks upon a late Charge against Enthusiasm, delivered by the Right Reverend Father in God, Richard, Lord Bishop of Lichfield and Coventry, in a Triennial Visitation of the same in 1741; and published at their request in the present year 1744. In a Letter to the Rev. the Clergy of that Diocess.' The position taken by the bishop is almost the same as that chosen by Dr. Gibson, and the reply was the one with which we are familiar: 'Though it is the quintessence of enthusiasm to pretend to be guided by the Spirit without the

written word, yet it is every Christian's duty to be guided by
the Spirit in conjunction with the written word.'

At the end of eleven weeks the *Wilmington* came within
sight of port.   The long confinement had made Whitefield impatient to land; and, with some friends, he eagerly and, in spite
of remonstrance, transferred himself from the ship to a little
fishing-smack that had come alongside, and which, it was said,
would distance the ship by several hours.   His haste delayed
him.   It soon grew dark, the pilots missed the bar of York
harbour, and the smack and its passengers were tossed about
all night.   Exposure increased the pain of a severe attack of
nervous colic, from which he had been suffering for some
time.   He was also so hungry that he could almost have
gnawed the boards of the boat, and perhaps wood might have
done him no more harm than the raw potatoes, the only food
on board, of which he partook freely.   It pleased him, as he
lay shivering, to hear a fisherman, in answer to a question
about what was going on ashore, say that the 'New-lights'
were expecting one Mr. Whitefield, and that the day before
many had been praying for his safe arrival.   Towards morning
the men found the inlet, and Whitefield was received into the
house of a physician, formerly a notorious Deist, but converted at Whitefield's last American visit.   Half an hour after
his arrival he was put to bed, racked with nervous colic, con-
vulsed from his waist to his toes, and a total convulsion
was expected every moment.   As his wife and friends stood
around him, weeping, he begged them not to be distressed.
Fearing that he might fall into a delirium, and say things that
were wrong, he told them—so anxious was he never to exert
a baneful influence—that such a thing must not surprise
them.   Happily the worst did not come, yet for four days
he could not bear the sound of a footstep or of a voice.

As soon as he was somewhat better, the minister of York,

old Mr. Moody, called to bid him welcome to America, and then urged him to give them a sermon. He consented. Meanwhile news had gone to Boston that he was dying; and when it reached that city two of his friends started for York, to nurse him if he were alive, or to attend his funeral if he were dead. On their arrival they found him in the pulpit! Soon a relapse came on, through his catching cold, and his friends again thought that his end was come; yet while he lay in agony of body, his greater pain was that he had been announced to preach and could not go. The hour of service drew near; the minister who had been appointed to preach was leaving the house for church, when of a sudden Whitefield said to his friend and doctor, 'Doctor, my pains are suspended; by the help of God I'll go and preach, and then come home and die.' And he did go, pale as death, and looking to the astonished congregation like one risen from the grave. It was taken for a last sermon by both people and preacher. The invisible things of another world lay open to his view, and expecting to be with his Master before morning, he spoke with peculiar energy for an hour. The effect of his word was, he says, worth dying for a thousand times over. But nature was hard pressed by the effort, and when, on his return home, he was laid on a bed before the fire, animation seemed to be suspended, and he could hear his friends say to each other, 'He is gone!' Gradually he recovered; and the first visitor who would see him, yea or nay, was a poor Negro woman. Sitting on the ground beside him, and looking earnestly into that kind face which always wore its gentlest aspect when such as she approached it, she said in her broken English, 'Master, you just go to heaven's gate, but Jesus Christ said, Get you down, get you down; you must not come here yet; but go first and call some more poor Negroes.' The sick man prayed that it might be as the simple-hearted

Negress wished it to be; and prayer and wish were fulfilled.

In about three weeks, though still very weak, he was able to
proceed to Boston. Here he was convinced that since his
departure for England a glorious work had been going on,
both in Boston and in almost all parts of New England. That
there had been irregularities and follies, an unhappy mixture
of human infirmity with Divine work, he could not but
sorrowfully admit; but good predominated over evil. What
reproach was incurred, either justly or unjustly, was thrown
upon him; and many clergy who had before met him at
Governor Belcher's table—Belcher was not now in the post
of governor—and 'paid him the nod,' were shy and distant,
and refused him their pulpits. There was certainly great
excitement in the city, and party feeling ran high. A great
number of strongly-worded pamphlets had appeared against
him. Some of the clergy began to publish 'halfpenny testi-
monials' against him, and the president, professors, and
students of Harvard College joined in the assaults. But they
assailed a man who was too good not to wish to be better,
and too candid to be afraid of confessing his faults. Their
exposure of real blame on his part only gave him the opportunity to acknowledge (which he did with beautiful humility)
wherein he had offended; and their shameful treatment of
him in other respects so roused many of his friends, that they
came to him to say that they would, with his consent, build in
a few weeks the outside of the largest place of worship in
America for his use. The democratic feeling was too strong
for ministers to control. He gratefully declined their offer as
unsuited to his taste and work. Here, as in so many other
instances, his humility saved him.

There were strange instances of the effect of his preaching.
One morning the crowd was too dense to be penetrated, and

he was obliged to go in at the window. Immediately after him came the high sheriff, who had been hostile to the 'new lights,' and the sight of whose face, as it appeared through the window, almost made the astonished people cry out, 'Is Saul also among the prophets?'

Another day his friend Mr. Prince told him he should shortly be visited by a very pensive and uncommon person, one of good parts, ready wit, and lively imagination, who, to procure matter for tavern amusement, had often gone to hear Whitefield preach, and then returned to his bottle and his friends, and recounted what he could remember, at the same time adorning it with further exposition. He went once too often for his fun. The crowd which bore him easily into Dr. S——'s meeting-house as Whitefield entered, was like a solid rock behind him, when he wished to return with what he thought was sufficient food for sport. Obliged to stay, he kept looking up at Whitefield and waiting for anything he could ridicule. But soon he began to feel miserable under what he heard, and when he withdrew, it was to go to Mr. Prince and confess his sins, and his desire to ask Whitefield's pardon, only he was afraid to see him. Mr. Prince encouraged him to venture. He went, and Whitefield, on opening the door for him, saw in his pale, pensive, and horrified countenance, the story of his life. In a low, plaintive voice he said, 'Sir, can you forgive me?' 'Yes, sir, very readily,' said Whitefield with a smile. The visitor thought that the tale of all his wrong-doings would make that impossible; but Whitefield asked him to sit down, and then spoke to him such comfort as the gospel has provided for broken hearts.

The stay among his New England friends was more prolonged than usual. Upon the renewal of his journeys his course is not easily traced. Such glimpses of him, however, as we do get lend fresh charm both to him and his work.

One day he is to be seen at a settlement of Delaware Indians, the converts of the devout Brainerd, preaching to them through an interpreter, and watching with that kindly interest which the orphans at Bethesda knew so well, a class of fifty Indian children learning the Assembly's Shorter Catechism. Soon afterwards we find him at Philadelphia, welcomed by twenty ministers of the city and neighbourhood, who own him as their spiritual father; surrounded with enthusiastic, solemn congregations; and offered by the gentlemen who had the management of the free temple there, eight hundred pounds a year and liberty to travel six months in the year if he would become a minister in the city, an offer which he treated as he had done that of the Boston people. We see him availing himself of his short stay in the city to write to his mother, and tell her that, though for two years she had not written to him—doubtless his incessant and distant wanderings had helped to hinder her—his attachment to her was as great as ever; and then some snatches of news about the 'golden bait' which 'Jesus had kept him from catching at;' about his door of usefulness which opens wider and wider; about his wife being very weak through a miscarriage, or she would have enclosed a few lines in his letter; and about the many mercies he receives from God. He rejoiced in roaming the woods, hunting for sinners, as he called his work; and next we find him among a little band of Christians in the backwoods of Virginia. These men were first gathered together in a remarkable way. Relations and friends in the dear old country, Scotland, had got a volume of those Glasgow sermons which had helped to kindle the revival in the valley of the Clyde, and sent them across the waters. When the precious book was received under the shadow of the great forest, its owner, Samuel Morris, called his friends and neighbours to rejoice with him, and share his feast. As his own house was soon crowded to excess, a meeting-house had to be built, and many quiet, solemn evenings were spent in it, tears flowing from many eyes as freely as if Whitefield's pathetic voice were speaking the words that were only read. The sermons soon took a wider range, and upon invitation Morris carried them to distant little groups of colonists, who could not enjoy such teaching in the churches, which by law they were expected to frequent. The little church of Lutherans, as it was called, lifted up its head, like a flower refreshed with rain, when Whitefield came ; others also 'engaged themselves to the Lord.'

Somewhere on the road his wife, with a Boston young lady, left him, to travel to Georgia, and tidings came to him that they 'traverse the wood bravely.' Whether he felt lonely without her with whom he had been 'more than happy' he nowhere says; but then he never said as much about his troubles as his comforts. We next come upon him at Bethesda, where he wintered in 1746-47. Most likely his letters to friends in London—the only letters he wrote at this time—would have contained news about his dear family, had not London friends needed counsel and comfort in the midst of troubles which had arisen at the Tabernacle. So he said not a word about his own heavy burden with the orphans, but added another load to all that his tender heart already carried. Bethesda had long wished to see him, and as soon as he crossed its threshold the cry came from London to return and succour his distressed flock there. What could he do but direct his people to One whose love was his own daily support ? 'Oh, that your eyes,' he exclaims, may be looking towards and waiting on the blessed Jesus : from Him alone can come your salvation ; He will be better to you than a thousand Whitefields.'

The same generosity which made him accessible to all in

trouble made him most grateful for any help afforded him in
carrying out his benevolent purposes.   In a letter he shows
both his kindness and his perverted notions about slaves :—

'God has put it into the hearts of my South Carolina friends to contribute liberally towards purchasing a plantation and slaves in this province,
which I purpose to devote to the support of Bethesda.   Blessed be God,
the purchase is made.   I last week bought at a very cheap rate a plantation of six hundred and forty acres of ground ready cleared, fenced, and
fit for rice, corn, and everything that will be necessary for provisions.
One Negro has been given me.   Some more I purpose to purchase this
week.'

While benefactors were thanked with exuberant gratitude,
detractors were quietly faced with an audited account of
receipts and disbursements in behalf of the orphan-house.   A
very serious affair was auditing in these days, before the introduction of limited liability companies.   First, Whitefield and
Habersham were put upon oath that the accounts laid before
the bailiffs contained, to the best of their knowledge, a just
and true account of 'all monies collected by, or given to
them, or any other, for the use and benefit of the said house ;
and that the disbursement had been faithfully applied to and
for the use of the same.'   Then comes the statement of the
auditors, given upon oath, in which they say: 'It doth not
appear that the Rev. Mr. Whitefield hath converted any part
thereof to his own private use and property, or charged the
said house with any of his travelling, or other private expenses ;
but on the contrary, hath contributed to the said house many
valuable benefactions.'

The return of spring saw him mounted for another excursion.   The news of his coming spread from settlement to
settlement ; and when the early light of the fresh spring mornings flushed the sky, farmers and planters bestirred themselves, and prepared for a ride to the distant preaching-place.

Many a lonely forest path and highway, striped with shadows of tall trees and bands of sunshine, was enlivened by groups of horsemen and solitary riders—some of them men of staunch piety, who longed after religious stimulus and instruction, and were going to the open glade as devoutly as ever David went up to Mount Zion; others of them men of heavy heart and sad countenance, who were getting their first insight into themselves and the mysteries of religion, and were uneasy as they saw the vision; and others again men of thoughtless spirit and easy life, who supposed that religion might very well be left to a more serious time than joyous days of health and vigour, when the blood is warm, but who had a fancy to hear the far-famed preacher. Nor were wives and daughters absent from the bands of travellers. As they tied their neighing horses to the trees and hedges, and formed themselves into a great congregation, few sights could be either more picturesque or more impressive. All hearts were more or less accessible to the glowing eloquence of the evangelist, who pleaded before them, with tears and earnest words, the claims of his gracious and exalted Master on the trust and love of every soul of man. Holy thoughts were carried back home by many of the worldly, as well as by many of the devout ; and the plantation and farm began to give signs that a God-fearing man lived in the principal house on it.

But the evangelist's health soon began to suffer when the cool spring changed to sultry summer. American summers always exhausted him, and that of 1747 formed no exception. By the middle of May the heat was trying his 'wasting tabernacle,' but, he says, 'through Christ strengthening me, I intend persisting till I drop.' The condition of the southern colonies was so destitute, and his sense of the love of our Lord so vivid, that he carried out his purpose, and in five weeks made a circuit of five hundred miles ; but by that time fever was consuming him, convulsions shaking him, and nervous colic and gravel griping him. At length that which he dreaded came upon him; he could not preach. His chief solace was gone. It is with an infinite pathos that the burdened, harassed, persecuted man writes : ''Tis hard to be silent, but I must be tried every way.' Compelled to hold his peace, he made his way as far north as New York, and there again resumed his beloved work. To follow him from this point would simply be to recount, with an alteration of the names of places, the experience of alternate sickness and partial recovery, of preaching and its pleasures, which has just been before us.

His attention had to be given to things in London, though his heart had become so united to America that he sometimes thought he should never again leave it. Cennick, who had quarrelled with Howel Harris, the chief manager of the Tabernacle, during Whitefield's absence, had gone over to the Moravians. Whitefield's letter to him upon that step is highly creditable both to his charity and good sense. He says :—

' I am sorry to hear there are yet disputings amongst us about brick walls. I was in hopes, after our contests of that kind about seven years ago, such a scene would never occur again; but I find fresh offences must come, to search out and discover to us fresh corruptions, to try our faith, teach us to cease from man, and to lean more upon Him who by His infinite wisdom and power will cause that "out of the eater shall come forth meat, and from the strong sweetness." I am glad you find yourself happy in the holy Jesus. . . . It has been my meat and drink to preach among poor sinners the unsearchable riches of Christ. Mayst thou continue and abide in this place.'

It is pleasant to know that old divisions were being healed, if, unhappily, new ones were breaking out. The letter just

quoted from, and others presently to be referred to, amply
sustain the generous eulogy of his friend Charles Wesley :—

> ' When Satan strove the brethren to divide,
>   And turn their zeal to " Who is on my side ? "
>   One moment warmed with controversial fire,
>   He felt the spark as suddenly expire ;
>   He felt revived the pure ethereal flame,
>   The love for all that bowed to Jesus' name,
>   Nor ever more would for opinions fight
>   With men whose life, like his, was in the right.'

On September 11, 1747, he wrote to John Wesley, and
said :—

' Not long ago I received your kind letter, dated in February last. Your
others, I believe, came to hand, and I hope ere now you have received my
answer. My heart is really for an outward as well as for an inward
union. Nothing shall be wanting on my part to bring it about, but I
cannot see how it can possibly be effected till we all think and speak the
same things. I rejoice to hear that you and your brothers are more moderate with respect to sinless perfection. Time and experience, I believe,
will convince you that attaining such a state in this life is not a doctrine of
the everlasting gospel. As for universal redemption, if we omit from each
side the talking for or against reprobation, which we may do fairly, and
agree as we already do in giving a universal offer to all poor sinners that
will come and taste the water of life, I think we may manage very well.'

Thus reprobation sank into oblivion—really died without a
struggle. The same day he wrote a shorter but perhaps still
warmer letter to Charles.

At the end of his summer's labours he turned his face again
to Bethesda. A little riding tired him, but still he felt that,
near as he had been to the kingdom of heaven, some of his
friends had prayed him back again into the world. His heart
was all gratitude for the success of his word : 'the barren
wilderness was made to smile all the way.' What he did
during the winter of 1747–48, whether he went about Georgia

preaching to little companies, as in the days when he first
entered the colony, at the same time watching the affairs of the
orphan-house, or rested to recruit himself, cannot be told.   It
is certain that in the spring following he was much weighed
down with travelling, with care, and with his orphan-house
debts—was, in fact, in such poor health that his friends advised
him to try the air of Bermudas—

> ' So sweet the air, so moderate the clime,
>   None sickly lives, or dies before the time.'

Were we to judge of the clime of the Summer Islands by
Whitefield's labours in them, Waller's praise might be taken for
literal truth; but Whitefield was an energetic invalid.   The
diary of his two months' stay on the island is an agreeable
renewal of that journal which he unfortunately ceased too soon
to write.   Its only remarkable difference from his general run
of narrative is the half-amused way in which he records the
wonder of the great men at his preaching without notes.   A
clergyman invalid who could preach twice a day and travel
considerable distances was a great marvel, but a clergyman
who used no 'minutes' in the pulpit was a greater.   There was
only one greater degree of marvel possible, and that would
have been a clergyman preaching from notes to Kingswood
colliers on Hannam Mount, to London rabble at Moorfields
Fair, to thirty thousand Scotchmen who were full of anxiety
about their salvation, and holding them in rapt attention.

One entry from the journal may be given :—

' Sunday, May 15th.—Praise the Lord, O my soul, and all that is within
thee praise His holy name !   This morning I preached my farewell sermon
at Mr. Paul's meeting-house ; it was quite full, and as the president said,
above one hundred and fifty whites, besides blacks, were round the house.
Attention sat on every face; and when I came to take my leave, oh ! what
a sweet unaffected weeping was to be seen everywhere.   I believe there

were few dry eyes. The Negroes without doors, I heard, wept plentifully. My own heart was affected, and though I have parted from friends so often, yet I find every fresh parting almost unmans me, and very much affects my heart. Surely a great work is begun in some souls in Bermudas. Carry it on, O Lord; and if it be Thy will, send me to this dear people again! Even so, Lord Jesus. Amen.'

The voyage home was not to be without alarms, though it proved, on the whole, both rapid and pleasant. Those dreadful men-of-war were hanging about like hungry sharks, and on the first day of the voyage one of them gave chase; and when the *Betsy* approached the English Channel, where they swarmed, 'a large French vessel shot twice at, and bore down upon us. We gave up all for gone.' But some pang of compassion or a panic seized the Frenchman; he turned about and left his trembling prey unhurt.

Whitefield might not preach during this voyage, because his health was so impaired. He says: 'This may spare my lungs, but it grieves my heart. I long to be ashore, if it was for no other reason. Besides, I can do but little in respect to my writing. You may guess how it is when we have four gentlewomen in the cabin!' However, he did write, and finished his abridgement of Law's 'Serious Call,' which he endeavoured to 'gospelise.' His journals, too, were revised; and in reference to that work, he makes some remarks which will illustrate his ingenuousness of temper. The revision had brought under his notice many things that his maturer judgment and calmer, though not less earnest, spirit could not but disapprove of.

'Alas, alas!' he says, 'in how many things have I judged and acted wrong. I have been too rash and hasty in giving characters, both of places and persons. Being fond of Scripture language, I have often used a style too apostolical, and at the same time I have been too bitter in my zeal. Wild-fire has been mixed with it; and I find that I frequently wrote and spoke in my own spirit, when I thought I was writing and speaking by the assistance of the Spirit of God. I have likewise too much made inward impressions my rule of acting, and too soon and too explicitly published what had been better kept in longer, or told after my death. By these things I have given some wrong touches to God's ark, and hurt the blessed cause I would defend, and also stirred up endless opposition. This has humbled me much since I have been on board, and made me think of a saying of Mr. Henry's, "Joseph had more honesty than he had policy, or he never would have told his dreams." At the same time, I cannot but bless and praise and magnify that gracious God, who filled me with so much of His holy fire, and carried me, a poor weak youth, through such a torrent both of popularity and contempt, and set so many seals to my unworthy ministrations. I bless Him for ripening my judgment a little more, for giving me to see and confess, and I hope in some degree correct and amend, some of my mistakes. I thank God for giving me grace to embark in such a blessed cause, and pray Him to give me strength to hold on and increase in zeal and love to the end.'

He had been made to prove the truth of one of his wise remarks, ' God always makes use of strong passions for a great work.' Strong passions have great dangers ; but he was now beginning to understand how to rule them with a firm hand. Less robust in health than when he last returned from America, and less disposed to contend with those that differed from him, but not a whit less zealous or self-sacrificing, only showing the first tints of mellow ripeness in all goodness, he stepped again upon English soil on July 6, 1748.

CHAPTER X

July, 1748–1752

APPOINTED CHAPLAIN TO THE COUNTESS OF HUNTINGDON—A
SLAVE-OWNER—STONED BEFORE A BISHOP

THE English newspapers, Whitefield learned on his arrival
in England, had interred him as early as April in that
year. From the people he found a welcome the very reverse
of that which had pained him seven years before. Thousands received him with a joy that almost overcame both him
and them. Their love and devotion to him humbled him to
the dust. The damaged fortunes of the Tabernacle instantly
revived when he resumed the pulpit and the management of
affairs. One church also, St. Bartholomew's, was open to him;
and there he preached to immense congregations, and assisted
in administering the sacrament to a thousand communicants.
Moorfields was as white as ever to the harvest.

Many tender memories were awakened by the return home;
and his affectionate heart yearned towards his family and
friends. Though his mother had remained silent during all
his long absence, and he had vainly entreated a letter from her,
one of his first acts was to remember her, and announce by a
letter his arrival. A kindly greeting was sent to Wesley.
Hervey, one of Whitefield's converts, the author of 'Medi-

tations among the Tombs,' was complimented on his appearance as an author, and encouraged to persevere, because his writings were so adapted to the taste of the polite world. Times have greatly changed since then, and taste too. Thus he tried to keep his place in hearts that had once received him.

An unexpected call was made upon him on the occasion of this return. Howel Harris had instructions to take him, as soon as he landed, to the house of the Countess of Huntingdon, at Chelsea. That remarkable woman was already acquainted with the power of his oratory over popular assemblies, for she had often seen and felt it; now she wanted to see what it could avail in her drawing-room upon the hearts of high-born ladies and gentlemen. It does not appear what kind of an audience he had when he preached in her house the first two times, but after the second service the Countess wrote to inform him that several of the nobility wished to hear him, if he would come again. In a few days a brilliant circle was gathered round him, and he spoke to them with all his usual unaffected earnestness and natural gracefulness, while they listened with attention and some degree of emotion. The Earl of Chesterfield thanked him, and paid him one of his studied, high-mannered compliments at the close. 'Sir,' he said, 'I will not tell you what I shall tell others, how I approve of you.' The wife of Lord Chesterfield and two of his sisters, Lady Gertrude Hotham and the Countess Delitz, became consistent lifelong disciples of the new teaching. The Earl himself went so far as to allow Whitefield the use of Bretby Hall in Derbyshire for meetings. Bolingbroke was afterwards prevailed upon to come; 'he sat like an archbishop,' and at the conclusion condescended to assure Whitefield that he had done great justice to the Divine attributes in his discourse. In a letter to Lady Huntingdon he said: 'Mr. Whitefield is the most extraordinary man in our times. He has the most commanding eloquence I ever heard in any person.' Hume, also, became an admirer of this eloquence, which had a charm for colliers and peers; in his opinion Whitefield was the most ingenious preacher he had ever heard; it was worth going twenty miles to hear him. He gives a remarkable instance of the effect with which Whitefield once employed apostrophe, not, of course, in the drawing-room of Chelsea.

'Once after a solemn pause, he thus addressed his audience: "The attendant angel is just about to leave the threshold of this sanctuary, and ascend to heaven. And shall he ascend and not bear with him the news of one sinner amongst all this multitude reclaimed from the error of his way?" To give the greater effect to this exclamation, Whitefield stamped with his foot, lifted up his hands and eyes to heaven, and cried aloud, "Stop, Gabriel, stop, ere you enter the sacred portals, and yet carry with you the news of one sinner converted to God." This address was accompanied with such animated, yet natural, action, that it surpassed anything I ever saw or heard in any other preacher.'

Within a fortnight the Countess added Whitefield's name to the number of her chaplains, of whom Romaine was the first.

This work among the nobility will shortly demand attention again; and in the meantime we notice in a few words that, besides a flying visit to Wales this autumn, he paid a third visit to Scotland, where he had to mourn the death of many of his foremost friends, and endure the usual ecclesiastical torment about Church government. The Synods of Glasgow, of Perth and Stirling, of Lothian and Tweedale, and a Presbytery—Edinburgh—wrangled, or, as they thought, had a holy contending, about him, whether ministers should be prohibited or discouraged from employing him. 'The more I was blackened,' he says, 'the more the Redeemer comforted me.' The hearts of the multitude responded to him as before; and his visit gave him great cause for joy and thankfulness.

One symptom began to show itself on his return, which was premonitory of sad mischief. When he went into Scotland, and began to preach, he suffered from a very severe hoarseness, and when he reached Topcliff, on his way back, he wrote to a friend : 'Though I do not preach, yet I hope I am preparing for it. Reading, prayer, and meditation are the three necessary ingredients for it. Riding and getting proper rest have recruited me ; but I am apt to believe I have strained myself inwardly. I feel sensible pain in my breath. But no matter ; it is for a good Master, who bore inexpressible pain for me.' That pain was to become a grievous burden through many years of incredible labour. It was too late now to take the prudential measures which he felt were necessary even before he started for Scotland.

As soon as he reached London, November 10th, Lady Huntingdon came to town, and made arrangements for him to preach in her house to 'the great and noble.' As her name and his become inseparably associated from this time forward to the end of his life, it is time to indicate her religious position. Lady Selina Shirley was born on August 24, 1707—seven years before Whitefield—and was married to Theophilus, ninth Earl of Huntingdon, on June 3, 1728. She entered heartily into the pleasures and duties of her high station, was often at Court, took a lively interest in politics, and cared for the poor on her husband's estate. She determined to win the favour of the Almighty and everlasting life simply by her attention to moral maxims, without any reference to our Lord Jesus Christ, in whom alone is life. It happened, however, that Lady Margaret Hastings, one of her husband's sisters, came under the influence of those new doctrines which were winning such remarkable triumphs; and not only so, she became an earnest and affectionate teacher of them to her family and friends. Among other things she one day made a remark to the Countess which produced a deep impression; it was this: 'That since she had known and believed in the Lord Jesus Christ for life and salvation, she had been as happy as an angel.' The Countess knew that she herself could pretend to no such joy. The thought haunted her, and made her resolve to live a more religious life, which, according to her notions, was to multiply her good works and increase her austerities. This brought her no relief. A dangerous illness then fell upon her; she was brought nigh to death; the prospect was terrible; her conscience was restless; and no remembrance of her almsgivings and fastings could calm it. Then Lady Margaret's words came back into her mind with fresh meaning and force, and she learned that Jesus Christ is our life and our salvation. Her illness left her, and she arose to enter upon a career as remarkable as that of any peeress in England.

The change was soon manifest; nor were Court beauties, such as the Duchess of Buckingham, well pleased to see it. They thought that the Earl might very properly exert his authority to unconvert her; for it was not to be borne that the Methodists should gain a Countess. The Earl did not care to undertake the task, but thought that a conversation with his former tutor, Bishop Benson, might do her good, and accordingly recommended her to see his lordship. The bishop came, but to a much harder task than he had anticipated. Turning to the Scriptures, to the articles and the homilies, the neophyte preached to him his duties in a style not familiar to bishops' ears: she would not relax her devotion; he must increase his. The kind man was ruffled, and was departing in haste and in anger at having ever laid hands on Whitefield, whom he blamed for the conversion of the Countess, when the lady said in her own firm way, 'My lord! mark my words: when you are on your dying bed, that will be one of the few ordinations you will reflect upon with complacence.'

The Earl of Huntingdon, who rather yielded to his wife's religious zeal than toned it down to harmonise with his colder feelings, died on October 13, 1746, leaving the Countess in command of immense wealth, and free to carry out her wishes without interference from any one. Everything favoured her assumption of that position she was soon to gain, and towards which she took her first decisive step, when, in 1748, she appointed Whitefield her chaplain. Liberal to profusion in her gifts, arbitrary in temper, Calvinistic in creed, consummate in administrative ability, devout in spirit, and thoroughly consecrated to the glory of Christ, she was unmistakably the proper leader of the Calvinistic side of the Methodist body, whether in or out of the Established Church. Whitefield might be its great preacher, but he could not, and cared not to form a party. The Countess must form any organisation that might be required, or guide any movement.

In a letter to Wesley, Whitefield thus refers to the question of union :—

'What have you thought about a union ? I am afraid an external one is impracticable. I find by your sermons that we differ in principles more than I thought ; and I believe we are upon two different plans. My attachment to America will not permit me to abide very long in England ; consequently I should but weave a Penelope's web if I formed societies ; and if I should form them I have not proper assistants to take care of them. I intend, therefore, to go about preaching the gospel to every creature. You, I suppose, are for settling societies everywhere : but more of this when we meet.'

About this time Whitefield ceased to be moderator of the Calvinistic Methodists, and henceforth his efforts and those of Lady Huntingdon were directed, with much success, to the object of giving an evangelical ministry to the Church of England.

The following are some of the great and noble who came to the preaching in the drawing-room of the Countess of

Huntingdon : The Duchess of Argyll, Lady Betty Campbell, Bubb Doddington, George Selwyn, the Duchess of Montagu, Lady Cardigan, Lord Townshend, Charles Townshend, Mr. Lyttleton, Mr. Pitt, Lord North, Lord Sandwich. The doctrines which Whitefield taught found other believers besides the Countess. The first Earl of Bath, formerly Mr. Pulteney, was one of these. Lord St. John, half-brother of Bolingbroke, seems to have been a convert. His last words, spoken to the clergyman who attended him, were, ' To God I commit myself ; I feel how unworthy I am ; but He died to save sinners, and the prayer of my heart now to Him is, God be merciful to me a sinner.' Bolingbroke was only moved so far by his brother's death as to offer himself as a champion of the Calvinistic doctrines ; not that he cared for them, but they had a philosophical side, and he would not object to stand as the philosopher of Calvinistic Methodism. ' You may command my pen when you will,' he said to the Countess ; 'it shall be drawn in your service. For, admitting the Bible to be true, I shall have little apprehension of maintaining the doctrines of predestination and·grace against all your revilers.' What would have been the issue of a contest between Wesley and his lordship on the five points?

The eccentric Lady Townshend was one of the first to admire Whitefield's oratory ; and probably she did so quite as much because such admiration was unusual among her friends as because the oratory was noble and commanding. When her freakish fancy pointed to an opposite course, she was equally ready to dislike and disparage her favourite. With equal facility could she turn Papist as Methodist ; a cathedral or a tabernacle for her place of worship, it mattered not which, if she pleased her whim. Once Whitefield cherished some hope of her conversion, through a serious illness which she had ; and as late as 1775, Lady Huntingdon wrote to her, when she was again in a similar condition, and evidently indulged in hopes such as had previously buoyed Whitefield up. She seemed to prefer Methodism for times of trial.

The Countess of Suffolk was neither so calmly impartial as Bolingbroke, nor so obligingly changeful as Lady Townshend. Her circumstances—the loss of her husband and only son—at the time that Lady Guildford took her to the Countess's to hear the Methodist chaplain, might have been thought favourable to her acceptance of the truths of religion ; but she was stung and enraged by every word which Whitefield, ignorant both of her presence and her condition, said.   Her self-control gave way as soon as he withdrew, at the close of the service. She then abused Lady Huntingdon to her face, in the presence of the illustrious congregation, and ' denounced the sermon as a deliberate attack upon herself.'   Her relatives who were present—Lady Betty Germain, Lady Eleanor Bertie, and the Dowager Duchess of Ancaster—attempted in vain alternately to pacify her, by explaining to her that she was mistaken, and to silence her by command.   Thinking herself insulted, she would not for some time hear.reason ; but at length she was prevailed upon to apologise, though only with a bad grace, to Lady Huntingdon for her rudeness.   She was never seen again among Whitefield's hearers, nor did she ever really forgive the Countess ; on her death-bed she denied the Countess permission to come and speak with her.

Lady Fanny Shirley, an aunt of Lady Huntingdon, the friend and neighbour of Pope, and the rival of Lady Mary Wortley Montague, became, through the efforts of the Countess Delitz, a conspicuous member of the aristocratic Methodist circle, and had her change of mind duly chronicled in the gossiping letters of Walpole.

' If you ever think of returning to England,' he writes to Sir Horace Mann, ' as I hope it will be long first, you must prepare yourself with Methodism.

I really believe by that time it will be necessary; this sect increases as fast almost as any religious nonsense did. Lady Fanny Shirley has chosen this way of bestowing the dregs of her beauty; and Mr. Lyttleton is very near making the same sacrifice of the dregs of all those various characters that he has worn. The Methodists love your big sinners, as proper subjects to work upon—and indeed they have a plentiful harvest.'

To the Countess Delitz, Whitefield writes in a manner which shows that he only cared for his introduction to 'society' as a means of winning souls. 'Ceiled houses, gaudy attire, and rich furniture, do not make the world appear less a wilderness to a mind enlightened to see the beauties of Jesus of Nazareth.'

There can be no doubt that Walpole spoke the truth, both about the rapid increase of Methodism and its love for big sinners; and some one who shared his alarm at its advance, through the popularity and success of Whitefield, even ventured to suggest to the king that the preacher should be restrained. 'I believe the best way,' said the king, 'will be to make a bishop of him.'

The Countess of Huntingdon told Mr. Barry, R.A., a story which confirms the sneer about big sinners. He reports it thus :—

'Some ladies called one Saturday morning to pay a visit to Lady Huntingdon, and during the visit she inquired of them if they had ever heard Mr. Whitefield preach. Upon being answered in the negative, she said, I wish you would hear him; he is to preach to-morrow evening at such a church or chapel, the name of which the writer forgets—nor is it material. They promised her ladyship they would certainly attend. They were as good as their word; and upon calling on the Monday morning on her ladyship, she anxiously inquired if they had heard Mr. Whitefield, and how they liked him. The reply was, "Oh, my lady, of all the preachers we ever heard, he is the most strange and unaccountable. Among other preposterous things—would your ladyship believe it?—he declared that Jesus Christ was so willing to receive sinners that He did not object to receive even the devil's castaways. Now, my lady, did you ever hear of such a thing since you were born?" To which her ladyship made the following reply : "There is something, I acknowledge, a little singular in the invitation, and I do not recollect to have ever met with it before ; but as Mr. Whitefield is below in the parlour, we'll have him up, and let him answer for himself." Upon his coming up into the drawing-room, Lady Huntingdon said : "Mr. Whitefield, these ladies have been preferring a very heavy charge against you, and I thought it best you should come up and defend yourself. They say that in your sermon last evening, in speaking of the willingness of Jesus Christ to receive sinners, you expressed yourself in the following terms : That so ready was Christ to receive sinners who came to Him, that he was willing to receive even the devil's castaways." Mr. Whitefield immediately replied, "I certainly, my lady, must plead guilty to the charge ; whether I did what was right or otherwise, your ladyship shall judge from the following circumstance : Did your ladyship notice, about half an hour ago, a very modest single rap at the door ? It was given by a poor, miserable-looking aged female, who requested to speak with me. I desired her to be shown into the parlour, when she accosted me in the following manner : 'I believe, sir, you preached last evening at such a chapel ?' 'Yes, I did.' 'Ah, sir, I was accidentally passing the door of that chapel, and hearing the voice of some one preaching, I did what I have never been in the habit of doing—I went in ; and one of the first things I heard you say was, that Jesus Christ was so willing to receive sinners, that he did not object to receive the devil's castaways. Now, sir, I have been on the town for many years, and am so worn out in his service, that I think I may with truth be called one of his castaways. Do you think, sir, that Jesus Christ would receive me ?'" Mr. Whitefield assured her that there was no doubt of it, if she was but willing to go to Him. From the sequel, it appeared that it was the case, and that it ended in the sound conversion of this poor creature, and Lady Huntingdon, was assured, on most respectable authority, that the woman left a very charming testimony behind her that, though her sins had been of a crimson hue, the atoning blood of Christ had washed them white as snow.'

Whitefield's labours among the rich were relieved by the more congenial work of visiting some of the provincial towns. From Gloucester he wrote a letter to the Trustees of Georgia, which is painful to read, for its defence of slavery ; nay, worse than that, its entreaty that slavery might be introduced where it did not already exist. The profit of the slave trade was now becoming so great that all who had any interest in its extension were clamouring to have restrictions removed. The mercenary spirit was blind and deaf to the griefs and wrongs of the poor African ; and it is deplorable that Whitefield, one of the most generous and self-denying of men, should have been affected with the popular tone of thought and feeling. It was often said, when slavery was the ' domestic institution ' of America, that contact with it too frequently dulled conscience, and turned anti-slavery men into pro-slavery men ; and from that letter which, under the first burst of indignation at the sight of shameful cruelties, Whitefield wrote to the inhabitants of South Carolina, it would seem that he was no exception to the rule.

Whitefield is seen, at the end of 1748, in kindly and close communion with the two foremost Nonconformists of his day. On November 25th, he called at Lady Abney's to see Dr. Watts, who described himself as ' a waiting servant of Christ.' He helped to raise the venerable man to take some medicine ; and within half an hour of his departure from the house, the ' servant ' had ceased his waiting, and entered into the joy of his Lord.

Whitefield's letter to Doddridge, on December 21st, is full of brotherly sympathy with the doctor in his trouble through the Moravians, who had disturbed his congregation. Whitefield had felt all the annoyance of having his work damaged and broken by meddling men, and could thoroughly enter into Doddridge's feelings. He speaks as a chastened, humbled, submissive, charitably-minded man, not blaming his troublers more than he condemns himself, and gratefully acknowledging the personal benefit that their conduct, under the Divine blessing, had been to him. It is with touching humility that he refers to those dark days when he came from America and found his converts turned against him. He says—

' The Moravians first divided my family, then my parish at Georgia, and after that the societies which, under God, I was an instrument of gathering.

İ suppose not less than four hundred, through their practices, have left the Tabernacle. But I have been forsaken other ways. I have not had above a hundred to hear me where I had twenty thousand, and hundreds now assemble within a quarter of a mile of me who never come to see or speak to me, though they must own at the great day I was their spiritual father. All this I find but little enough to teach me to cease from man, and to wean me from that too great fondness which spiritual fathers are apt to have for their spiritual children.'

It is not less pleasant to find Whitefield and his old tutor together again at Bristol. Dr. R—— was now a prebendary, and when Whitefield called upon him he received him gladly. They talked about the Church and Methodism ; and Whitefield told him that his judgment was riper than it had been at the outset of his career, and that as fast as he found out his faults he should be glad to acknowledge them. The prebendary replied that as Whitefield grew moderate, the offence of the bishops and other dignitaries would wear away—a change which Whitefield would have hailed with satisfaction, though he was content to be under displeasure ; his great anxiety was to act an honest part and keep from trimming. This is the last glimpse we shall get of the kindly man, who did Whitefield no slight service by his fatherly oversight, when misguided earnestness and anxiety in religion might have ruined White-field's energies for life.

The winter's work among the nobility damaged Whitefield's health not a little. He was glad to get away into the west, to revisit some of his former places of labour—Bristol, Plymouth, Exeter, Gloucester. Between January 28 and March 10, 1749, this feeble, suffering man performed a journey of six hundred miles, preaching as frequently as he ever had done in the days of health, and, notwithstanding the unseasonable time of the year for open-air services, often in the open air. His life was a faithful embodiment of some of his happy sayings—such as, 'I do not preach for life, but from life ; '

'Like a pure crystal, I would transmit all the glory that God is pleased to pour upon me, and never claim as my own what is His sole property.' It was with much reluctance that he thought of turning from his beloved 'ranging' to renew his work in the Countess's house. The same diffidence which made him shrink from encountering the shocks of life, when he approached the American coast on his second visit to America, made him write to his friend Hervey—

'Lady Huntingdon writes me word that "the prospect of doing gcod at my return to London is very encouraging." Thither I am now bound. I go with fear and trembling, knowing how difficult it is to speak to the great, so as to win them to Jesus Christ. . . . My dear brother, fail not to pray for me, that I may hold on and hold out to the end, and in prosperity and adversity, press forward with an even, meek, and lowly mind towards the mark for the prize of our high calling in Christ Jesus.'

In quite the same spirit he says to the same friend, a few weeks later—

'You judge right when you say, it is your opinion that I do not want to make a sect, or set myself at the head of a party. No; let the name of Whitefield die, so that the cause of Jesus Christ may live. I have seen enough of popularity to be sick of it, and did not the interest of my blessed Master require my appearing in public, the world should hear but little of me henceforward.'

To one brother minister he says: 'I am glad your children grow so fast; they become fathers soon; I wish some may not prove dwarfs at last. A word to the wise is sufficient. I have always found awakening times like spring times: many blossoms, but not always so much fruit.'

But other work than preaching demanded his attention; for it was no idle word which he spoke to his old tutor, when he told him that he would acknowledge his faults as fast as he found them out. The Bishop of Exeter, Dr. Lavington, furnished him with a fine opportunity of retracting many blameworthy words and deeds; and no part of his life is more remarkable than this for its exhibition of frankness and humility. The bishop wrote, in 1747, when Whitefield was absent in America, a treatise on 'The Enthusiasm of the Methodists and Papists,' in which he attempted to draw a parallel between the old Church and the new sect, or rather the new men of his own Church. The subject was tempting to an enemy; and the argument adopted valid, if everything belonging to Popery be evil. The syllogism was: Everything belonging to Popery is bad; the enthusiasm of the Methodist and Papists is the same; therefore the enthusiasm of the Methodists is bad. The identity of Methodist and Popish enthusiasm is traced with much patience and astounding malevolence through nine characteristics. Dominicans, Franciscans, and Jesuits are shown to be the true forerunners of Whitefield and Wesley!

There is only one thing more painful than the reading of such unscrupulous attacks, and it is the assurance of Archdeacon More that the assertion that 'Bishop Lavington in his latter days repented of his writings against the Methodists, I know to be without foundation, as far as his conversation could afford assurance to the contrary. To the very last he always spoke of them as a fraternity compounded of hypocrites and enthusiasts.'

A crushing answer might have been penned by any honest man; but Whitefield's 'Remarks upon the Pamphlet,' as he calls his reply, are better than any formal answer. Their spirit is something wonderful; and it is impossible to turn from perusing the bishop's slanders and abuse, to read Whitefield's reply, without feeling how good and blessed a thing is an honest, forgiving heart. Lavington had said that the Methodist preachers, like St. Anthony, were attended by 'a sturdy set of followers, as their guards, armed with clubs under their clothes, menacing and terrifying such as should speak lightly of their apostle.'

'You add,' says Whitefield, ' " I have heard it often affirmed ; " and so might the heathens have said that they heard it often affirmed, that when the primitive Christians received the blessed sacrament, they killed a young child, and then sucked its blood. But was that any reason why they should believe it? It is true, indeed, some of the Methodist preachers have more than once been attended with a sturdy set of followers, armed with clubs and other weapons, not as their guards, but opposers and persecutors ; and who have not only menaced and terrified, but actually abused and beat many of those who came to hear him whom you, I suppose, would call their apostle. Both Methodist preachers and Methodist hearers, too, for want of better arguments, have often felt the weight of such irresistible power, which, literally speaking, hath struck many of them dumb, and I verily believe, had it not been for some superior, invisible guard, must have struck them dead. These are all the sturdy set of armed followers that the Methodists know of. And whatever you may unkindly insinuate about my being aware of a turbulent spirit, a fighting enthusiasm amongst them, because I said, " I dread nothing more than the false zeal of my friends in a suffering hour," I think many years' experience may convince the world that the weapons of their warfare, like those of their blessed Redeemer and His apostles, have not been carnal ; but, thanks be to God, however you may ridicule His irresistible power, they have, through Him, been mighty to the pulling down of Satan's strongholds in many a sturdy sinner's heart.'

Whitefield confessed that 'there is generally much—too much—severity in our first zeal ; at least there was in mine ; ' also that his and Seward's treatment of Archbishop Tillotson 'was by far too severe. We condemned his state, when we ought only, in a candid manner, which I would do again if called to it, to have mentioned what we judged wrong in his doctrines. I do not justify it. I condemn myself most heartily, and ask pardon for it, as I believe he (Seward) would do, were he now alive. But then, do not you still go on, sir, to imitate us in our faults ; let the surviving Methodists

answer for themselves; let Seward and Tillotson lie undis-
turbed.' Whitefield adds, on the subject of desiring persecution :
'Whatever can be produced out of any of my writings to prove
that I have desired or prayed for ill-usage, persecution,
martyrdom, death, &c., I retract it with all my heart, as
proceeding from the overflowings of an irregular, though well-
meant zeal.' He also thanks Lavington for pointing out the
'very wrong expression' about the 'hosannas of the multitude.'
'Your remark,' he says, 'runs thus : "Very profane, unless it
be a false print for huzzas." I could wish it had been so, but
the word was my own ; and though not intended to convey a
profane idea, was very wrong and unguarded, and I desire
may be buried in oblivion, unless you, or some other kind
person, are pleased to remind me of it, in order to lay me low
before God and man.' The last admission of all, that he was
wrong in making public the lot Wesley cast in private, is worth
all the rest, and does honour to Whitefield's candour; it is a
perfect atonement for his fault.

The whole of the summer, and the early part of the autumn,
of 1749, were spent in a tour through the west and through
Wales, thousands answering his call, and coming as of old,
even when the rain rendered an open-air service both uncom-
fortable and dangerous. For two days he sought retirement in
his wife's house at Abergavenny (she was now on her way
from Bethesda to join him), and found it 'so very sweet,' that
he would have been glad never to have been heard of again.
From thence he wrote to his brother at Bristol a letter which
exhibits so many sides of his life and character that it demands
a place in his biography :—

'MY VERY DEAR BROTHER,—Enclosed you have a letter from our
good Lady Huntingdon, whom, I suppose, you will have the honour of
receiving in a few days under your roof. Both before and ever since I left
Bristol, I have been frequently thinking of the unspeakable mercies that

the infinitely great and glorious God is pleased to pour down upon us. Surely the language of both our hearts ought to be, "What shall we render unto the Lord?" For my part, I am lost in wonder, and want a thousand lives to spend in the Redeemer's service. Oh, let not my dear brother be angry if I entreat him at length to leave off killing, and begin to redeem, time. A concern for your eternal welfare so affects me, that it often brings bodily sickness upon me, and drives me to a throne of grace, to wrestle in your behalf. Even now, whilst I am writing, my soul is agonising in prayer for you, hoping I shall see that day when you will have poured out on you a spirit of grace and of supplication, and look to Him whom we have pierced, and be made to mourn as one mourneth for a first-born. Till this be done, all resolutions, all schemes for amendment, will be only like spiders' webs. Nature is a mere Proteus, and till renewed by the Spirit of God, though it may shift its scene, will be only nature still. Apply then, my dearest brother, to the fountain of light and life, from whence every good and perfect gift cometh.

'A worthy woman, in all probability, is going to throw herself under God into your hands. A considerable addition will then be made to your present talents, and consequently a greater share of care and circumspection necessary to improve all for the glory of Him who hath been always preventing and following you with His blessings. Should you prove any otherwise than a pious husband, it will be one of the greatest afflictions I ever met with in my life. At present you can only hurt yourself, which is hurt enough; but then, forgive me, my dear brother, I am jealous over you with a godly jealousy. My tears shall be turned into prayers, and I will follow this letter with strong crying unto God in your behalf. My retirement here these two days hath been very sweet; but to-morrow I begin a three weeks' circuit. Next Sabbath I am to be at Carmarthen; the Friday following at Haverford West. For the present, adieu. That you may take Christ to be your all in all, and that the remainder of your life may be one continued sacrifice of love to Him who hath shed His precious blood for you, is the hearty prayer of, my dear brother,

'Yours most affectionately
'George Whitefield.'

These prayers appear to have been answered.

His work among the rich was done with a scrupulous disregard of all self-interest. To a friend, who thought that Whitefield had carried religion very near the Court, if not quite into it, and that he might have influence enough to secure the appointment of a religious governor to some colony where a governor was wanted, he replied that he should be very shy to ask favours, even if he had interest at Court, lest he should be thought to preach for himself and not for Christ Jesus, his Lord, and because he would fain convince all that he sought not theirs, but them. Yet he would use his influence with equal freedom in other quarters, and especially if it was for any one in more than usually humble circumstances. Such a worthy object came under his notice during this tour, an obscure Dissenting minister, who had sold part of his library to finish the meeting-house in which he preached, whose dress was very mean—as well it might be, seeing he had but three pounds per annum from a fund, and the same sum from his people—who lived very low, but enjoyed much of God, and who was something of a poet; for Whitefield found that he had as good an understanding of the figurative parts of Scripture as any one that 'he knew of in the world.' How could he forbear using his interest with a rich and benevolent friend for such a 'poor, despised, faithful minister of Christ?' So he hints that four or five guineas might be bestowed on this Zachary, who had also a faithful Elizabeth.

A hard task was it for him to inspire other hearts with as much moral courage as always bore up his own. By word, as well as by example, by reproach, and by loving persuasion, he would try to free the fearful from the fear of man, which hindered their full and self-denying consecration to the will of Jesus Christ. One of the most difficult cases he ever had to manage was that of Dr. Stonehouse, of Northampton, an eminent physician, a friend of Doddridge, and a man of great refinement. Many were the expostulations of the bold evangelist before the shrinking man could be brought to a firm stand, but at last it was done.

On the day of his arrival at Bristol after a month's circuit he gives this account of his work :—

'Yesterday God brought me here, after having carried me a circuit of about eight hundred miles, and enabled me to preach, I suppose, to upwards of a hundred thousand souls. I have been in eight Welsh counties, and I think we have not had one dry meeting. The work in Wales is much upon the advance, and likely to increase daily. Had my dear Mr. Hervey been there to have seen the simplicity of so many dear souls, I am persuaded he would have said, "*Sit anima mea cum Methodistis!*" But every one to his post. During this excursion I have been kept happy inwardly, and well in body till the latter end of last week, when the Lord was pleased to lay His hand upon me, so that I was almost brought to the grave. But He that wounds heals also.'

Soon afterwards Whitefield resumed his work in London for a little while, and then returned into the west, where Methodist doctrines were agitating all minds, and where he was an especial object of interest, on account of his reply to the first part of Bishop Lavington's pamphlet. The journey has as many incidents as would form the remarkable parts of many a life, but in this career they are in danger of being passed over as commonplace. It would be a rare thing in the life of any clergyman were he, on being recognised as he passed through a town, to be asked and entreated by a humble, unknown woman to stay and give the people a sermon ; and upon consenting to do so, soon to find himself surrounded 'with a great company.' And the next day the congregation at the same place was still greater. This happened at Wellington when Whitefield rode through it.

All along his way he found the good seed of past sowing times springing up and promising an abundant harvest. At Plymouth the wonderful power which attended his first visit was making things look quite new. His pamphlet in reply to the bishop had been useful to some ; its candour and simplicity deserved nothing less. The bishop, when asked by some one if he had seen it, replied, 'Yes : Whitefield writes like an honest man, and has recanted several things ; but he goes on in the same way yet.' His lordship also promised a second part of his pamphlet, which in due time appeared ; but as it was mainly directed against Wesley, in Wesley's hands Whitefield was content to leave it.

The bishop was troubled with Methodists in his own diocese, and among his own clergy, the Rev. Mr. Thompson, vicar of St. Gennis, being one of these undesirable 'sons.' When Lavington threatened him to his face that he would pull off his gown, Thompson immediately pulled it off himself, and throwing it at the feet of the astounded bishop, exclaimed, ' I can preach the gospel without a gown.' The bishop thought it was best to send for him, and try to soothe him. Next he had the mortification of seeing Whitefield welcomed to Thompson's house, from whence he had thought to banish him, and the two friends fraternising with such cordiality as only men whose endangered friendship has stood firm can feel.

The bishop was not, however, to go without his gratification. In his presence, and in that of many of his clergy, Whitefield was for the fourth time violently assaulted while preaching the gospel. The blow of a cudgel at Basingstoke, the thump of a sod from a Staffordshire heathen, and the pelting with the refuse of a Moorfield's fair, were followed by a stunning blow from a great stone, which struck deep into Whitefield's head, and almost rolled him off the table, from which, amidst an awful stillness, he was addressing ten thousand hearers at Exeter. A second stone, also meant for him, struck a poor man quite to the ground. A third, aimed at the same object, fell and did no damage. This was done in the presence of the man who had unblushingly repeated the lie, that Methodist preachers were often attended with a set of sturdy fellows carrying clubs under their clothes to make the congregations reverence their preaching apostle ; nor did he mount the table to express his shame and regret at being the witness of such an outrage, neither did he act the part of the kind Samaritan to the injured man. The only alleviating thought to this story is that the bishop and his clergy do not seem to have been accessory to the assault. Whitefield, never wishful to magnify his deeds and sufferings, nor to exaggerate another's fault, simply says that it was 'a drunken man' who threw three great stones at him; but the assailant must have been tolerably sober when once he aimed so well as to hit his man on the head, and the next time threw with such force as to lay a man on the ground; neither do drunken men often manage to carry three large stones into a dense crowd.[1]

Weak and suffering, yet a moral conqueror, Whitefield returned to London, not forgetting on his way to call at Dorchester Gaol to comfort John Haime, a soldier who had headed a

---

[1] It would have been more becoming a Christian bishop had Dr. Lavington tried to reform the heathen of Exeter, instead of wasting his time in slandering others who did his neglected work. For the sake of truth it should be stated that the city had a band of ruffians called 'Church Rabble,' or 'The God-damn-me Crew,' who carried persecution to every length short of death. In 1745, the crew, led by a bailiff, a sexton, a parish-clerk, and several tradesmen, and encouraged by many 'gentlemen,' who ¡ laced themselves in windows to see the obscene sport, abused the Methodists as they would, neither the mayor nor the magistrates interfering to stop them. They kicked the men and subjected them to every abuse and indignity. They rubbed the faces of the women with lamp-black and oil ; they beat their breasts with their clenched fists ; they stripped them almost naked, then turned the rest of their clothes over their heads, and in that condition kicked or dragged them along the street, or rolled them in the gutters or in mud-heaps prepared for them. To save herself from one of the mob who attempted even worse outrage, one woman leaped from the gallery of the meeting-house to the floor. The riot lasted for hours, and in the presence of thousands.—See 'An Account of a late Riot at Exeter,' by John Cennick, 1745 ; and 'A brief Account of the late Persecution and Barbarous Usage of the Methodists at Exeter,' by an Impartial Hand, 1746. The riot occurred in 1745 ; Lavington's Treatise was written in 1747 ; Whitefield was assaulted in 1749.

revival movement among his comrades in Flanders, and since his return home had preached in Methodist fashion, and been rewarded for his zeal by a place among knaves and felons !

Whitefield's 'grand catholicon' under both public and domestic trials—preaching—was now used by him with unremitting diligence ; and in the autumn of 1749 we find him in a new district, and among a people as different from those of the west of England as Yorkshire moors are different from Devonshire lanes and orchards.   It was the splendid autumn season when he first clambered up that steep road 'winding between wave-like hills that rise and fall on every side of the horizon, with a long, illimitable look, as if they were a part of the line of the great serpent, which, the Norse legend says, girdles the world ;' and was received at bleak little Haworth, sacred both to piety and genius, by William Grimshaw, the incumbent.   The old parsonage (not the one in which the Brontës afterwards lived), standing half a mile from the church, and commanding from its windows a wide view of the valley of the Worth, and from its door the interlacing hills towards Keighley, the sheltered valley at their feet, and the swelling moors, traced with winding roads, that lie bordering on the moors of Ilkley, was solid and weather-beaten, like the sturdy man who then inhabited it.   We do not know whether his eye often lingered on the beauty and grandeur that lay around his home ; perhaps at the most it would be a hurried glance that he would give, when he halted for a moment on the doorstone, as he went forth to preach, or returned from the same duty ; for he was an untiring apostle of the truth, and it would be little time that he could find for communion with nature.   His work was to soften and change the rugged, hardened sinners of the village, and of all the district round, as far as his iron strength could carry him ; and for that he must only exchange the saddle where he made his sermons for the pulpit where he preached them. An all-absorbing thing was the enjoying and teaching those truths which had turned his own soul from sin to holiness, and which had changed a clergyman, a mere professional, who had entered holy orders with the unholy wish to get the best living he could, into a loving shepherd, who sought the lambs and the sheep by night and day, in summer and winter, in weariness and painfulness, nor ever thought of his sacrifice, if so be he might save that which was lost. Thirty times a week would he preach in cottage or church, or on hillside; it was an idle week when he preached but twelve times. Neither was he satisfied simply to preach, to get through his subject; he would dwell with unwearied patience on each part of his message, loving the tenderness and mercy of which it spoke, and anxious that the feeblest mind should also love and understand it. 'Affectionately desirous' of his people, he would have imparted to them, not the gospel of God only, but also his own soul, because they were dear to him. Truer and kinder shepherd never tended flock than this overseer of the flock among the hills. Much has been said about his eccentricities, but these were little noticed by his people, who lived daily in the light of his shining purity, and received in their every sorrow and in their every joy the sympathy of his faithful heart.

His church always presented a remarkable appearance on the Sunday. The shepherding of the week made a full fold that day. Weavers and farmers, shepherds and labourers, came from the remotest parts of his wild district to hear his words of grace and truth, and listened as if they felt the power of another world upon their spirits. When Whitefield first visited them, which was in September, 1749, six thousand people stood in the churchyard to hear him, and above a thousand communicants approached the table with feelings of awe and joy. So great a number could have been collected together in this thinly-populated district only by a strong desire to hear an unequalled preacher, whose fame was familiar through the lips of their pastor, and by a deep and real interest in the great subjects on which he discoursed, as the congregations at Cambuslang and in the American woods were called together. 'It was,' says Whitefield, 'a great day of the Son of man.'

Whitefield paid his first visit to Leeds at the request of one of Wesley's preachers and of all Wesley's people; he was welcomed by all, and had a congregation of ten thousand to hear him. About the same time he visited Armley, Pudsey, and Birstall.[1]

Proceeding northwards, he met Charles Wesley returning from Newcastle, where Methodism had already won a remarkable triumph, and where he had been confirming the believers. Charles immediately turned his horse's head round towards Newcastle, and went (a pleasant sight to see) to introduce his brother in Christ to the Methodist pulpit in that town. He wrote a letter giving an account of what took place which reflects the highest credit upon the spirit in which the three friends were now doing their work :—

'I snatch a few moments before the people come to tell you what you will rejoice to know—that the Lord is reviving His work as at the beginning; that multitudes are daily added to His Church; so that G. W. and my brother and I are one—a threefold cord which shall no more be broken. The week before last I waited on our friend George to our house in Newcastle, and gave him full possession of our pulpit and people's hearts; as full as was in my power to give. The Lord united all

---

[1] Tradition long retained a story about the preaching at Birstall. Nancy Bowling, a pious old maid of Heckmondwike, who died sixty years ago at the advanced age of eighty, used to tell how the wind blew from Birstall towards Heckmondwike when Whitefield preached, and that his voice could be heard on Staincliffe Hill, a mile and a half from where he stood, crying, 'O earth, earth, hear the Word of the Lord !' The story must have been told her; but most likely she heard him preach, as she was ten years old when he died.

our hearts. I attended his successful ministry for some days. He was never more blessed or better satisfied. . . . At Leeds we met my brother, who gave honest George the right hand of fellowship, and attended him everywhere to our societies. Some at London will be alarmed at the news; but it is the Lord's doing, as they, I doubt not, will by and by acknowledge.'

'Brother Charles' and 'honest George' did something more at Newcastle than preach; they got Mrs. Grace Murray, a widow, to whom Wesley was engaged, married to John Bennet, to the great anguish of Wesley's heart. Whitefield played only a secondary part in this blamable transaction, and under the strain it caused he kept the two brothers together. Wesley showed astonishing magnanimity towards all concerned, but especially towards Charles and Mrs. Bennet.

This second visit to Leeds, to which Charles refers, was after a ride with Whitefield through part of Lancashire and part of Cheshire. It made the Established and Dissenting clergy very angry, and their churches and chapels echoed with the thunder of their displeasure.

It was November now, and, says Whitefield, 'indeed it begins to be cold abroad.' Winter was warning him home to his Tabernacle; so he only called at Sheffield, Nottingham, and Ashby on his way southwards. At Sheffield, then a town of ten thousand inhabitants, he unwittingly gave the Wesleys a most appropriate return for their kindness at Leeds and Newcastle. In 1743 Charles had been stoned there, and the society house pulled down by a mob, while the constable looked on approvingly. Three years later Charles found the hardened sinners at Sheffield still the same; and felt himself constrained to warn them from the awful words: 'Except the Lord of hosts had left unto us a very small remnant, we should have been as Sodom, and we should have been like unto Gomorrah!' God filled his mouth with judgments against them, which he trembled to utter, and they to hear; yet he had no deeper satisfaction than that of having delivered his own soul. Other labourers toiled, then came Whitefield, the success of whose preaching is thus noticed by Charles Wesley, eighteen months after Whitefield's visit :—

'At two I rejoiced to meet some of my dear children in Sheffield. I encouraged them by that most glorious promise—"Behold He cometh with clouds, and every eye shall see Him." The door has continued open ever since Mr. Whitefield preached here, and quite removed the prejudices of our first opposers. Some of them were convinced by him, some converted and added to the Church. "He that escapes the sword of Jehu shall Elisha slay."'

He was no mighty man, glorying in his strength, who won these conquests over fierceness, rage, and hate, but one who passed his days in humble watchfulness and dependence upon heavenly aid. When others were wondering at his unflagging devotion, he was 'more afraid of declining in the latter stages of his road than of anything else.' There was not a grain of self-satisfaction in him. He was hungering and thirsting after simplicity and godly sincerity. He was subjecting all personal interests to the glory and kingdom of his Lord. 'If souls were profited he desired no more.' Every expense was contracted with miserly vigilance, that he might have the more to give to the poor, and for the furtherance of the gospel. And in every sacrifice made, in every reproach endured, there was before his soul the image of his humbled, homeless, suffering Redeemer, cheering and reviving and defending him. He had struggled upwards to a glorious height of consecration and love, yet was he ever mindful of the past, when self-will and fear of contempt marred the beauty and excellence of his piety, and anxious for the day of his final emancipation from sin. 'Oh, my dear sir,' he exclaims to a friend, 'this pretty character of mine I did not at first care to part with; 'twas death to be despised, and worse than death to think of being laughed at by all. But when I began to consider Him who endured such contradiction of sinners against Himself, I then longed to drink of the same cup; and blessed be God, contempt and I are pretty intimate, and have been so for above twice seven years.' Humility was now one of the most conspicuous among all that radiant cluster of virtues and graces which crowned his head like stars. 'Oh, that I may learn from all I see to desire to be nothing!' he cries out, 'and to think it my highest privilege to be an assistant to all, but the head of none. I find a love of power sometimes intoxicates even God's own dear children, and makes them to mistake passion for zeal, and an overbearing spirit for an authority given them from above. For my own part, I find it much easier to obey than govern, and that it is much safer to be trodden under foot than to have it in one's power to serve others so. This makes me fly from that which at our first setting out we are too apt to court. Thanks be to the Lord of all lords for taking any pains with ill and hell-deserving me! I cannot well buy humility at too dear a rate.'

He went to 'golden seasons' in London, in the winter 1749–50. Large congregations were gathered together in the Tabernacle, at six in the morning. The nobility were preached to, and poor people and orphans not forgotten. He tells Lady Huntingdon that he 'hopes to write to the poor baker soon;' and to Habersham at the orphan-house he sends word that he has agreed to take 'little Joseph and his sister,' also that he hears there is a little infant beside the other two, and that he would willingly have it too, if it could be kept till it was about three years old; 'for,' says he, 'I hope to grow rich in heaven by taking care of orphans on earth.' Habersham is further instructed to let Mrs. V—— (probably some widow) and the other poor of Savannah reap the benefit of the crop, if it answers expectation. 'Pray let one barrel of rice be reserved for them.'

Something now induced him to offer to preach in Wesley's chapel. His friendly advance was kindly met; and he preached four or five times to large congregations, and administered the sacrament twice. Wesley also came to the Tabernacle, and preached for Whitefield, and administered the sacrament to twelve hundred communicants.

His work among the nobility, which was in a fair measure satisfying even to him, with his spiritual conceptions of the work of God, was now the subject of conversation at Court, as well as in private circles. The following anecdote, which he communicated to the Countess, will show how his friends were observed. He says :—

'His Majesty seems to have been acquainted with some things about us, by what passed in his discourse with Lady Chesterfield. The particulars are these : her ladyship had a suit of clothes on, with a brown ground and silver flowers, which was brought from abroad. His Majesty coming round to her, first smiled, and then laughed right out. Her ladyship could not imagine what was the matter. At length his Majesty said : "I know who chose that gown for you—Mr. Whitefield ; and I hear that you have attended on him this year and a half." Her ladyship answered : "Yes, I have, and I like him very well ; " but after she came to her chair was grieved she had not said more ; so that I find her ladyship is not ashamed.'

Early in 1750 London was several times shaken with earthquakes; and the state of excitement into which it and other causes threw the people, gave Whitefield a grand opportunity for displaying the fulness of his love and the strength of his faith in God. The first shocks were felt on the 8th of February, and on the 8th of March there came another, at a quarter past five in the morning. There was no more harm done than the rocking of the houses and the tumbling down of some chimneys; but men's hearts failed them for fear. There was talking about judgment and the last day. A soldier, bolder and more fanatical than the rest of the people, announced the coming overthrow of a great part of the city on a certain night between twelve and one o'clock. Multitudes fled the city altogether, while others crowded the fields and open places for safety from falling houses. The Methodist chapels had enormous congregations. Whitefield sought his congregation in Hyde Park on the dreaded night of the soldier's prediction. He warned and entreated them all to prepare for the coming of the Son of man, an event much more stupendous and important than that which they now expected every moment to see. Neither moon nor star shed any light upon audience or preacher, and only one voice was heard in the still darkness, like a voice crying in the wilderness. It spoke of mercy and judgment, and could hardly have spoken in vain.

The winter in London had been very trying to Whitefield's health, if refreshing to his heart; throughout the whole of it his body was a daily trial to him, and sometimes he could 'scarce drag the crazy load along.' It was with delight that he saw spring return, and that he went off into the west for a time of ranging. He went with his hands so full of work, and moved so rapidly from place to place, that he could hardly find time to eat. He found it exceedingly pleasant, and hoped now, in his Master's strength, 'to begin beginning to spend and be spent for Him!' Twelve times in six days did he preach at Plymouth, and the longer he preached, the greater became the congregations and the mightier his word. Still he was not satisfied. He wanted 'more tongues, more bodies, more souls for the Lord Jesus;' had he been gifted with ten thousand, Christ should have had them all.

It was inevitable that his flaming zeal, kindled as it was by the love of the Lord Jesus, and burnin only for His glory,

should fire all the district through which he passed. Gloucester, Bristol, Plymouth, and Cornwall right to the Land's End,
were all ablaze with religious fervour. He seemed to travel in
the strength of the Holy Ghost, and to be independent of that
crazy body which had oppressed him in London. Friends
were jubilant at his coming; and when he was speaking at
Bideford, where there was one of the best little flocks in
all England, the bold vicar of St. Gennis almost fell under
the mighty power of God which came down upon the
people.

Such exertions as he put forth could not fail to do him
physical mischief. That pain which he felt as he came last
from Scotland was not inactive; it now and again pierced
him, and stayed his headlong pace. It had plagued him in
London when he was preaching four times a day; and when
he was over the first burst of effort in the west, and thought
himself so much better for the change, it returned upon him
with increased power. He had continued vomitings which
'almost killed him,' he says; and yet the pulpit was his only
cure, so that his friends began to pity him less, and to leave
off 'that ungrateful caution, "Spare thyself!"'

He does not appear to have permitted one day's rest to his
body when he returned to London from the west. Early in
May, 1750, he started for Ashby, where Lady Huntingdon
was lying ill, whom he hoped God's people would keep out of
heaven as long as possible by their prayers. He had some
pleasant interviews with Doddridge, with Stonehouse (now a
clergyman, and not afraid to attend Whitefield's preaching in
the fields, nor to take the evangelist's arm down the street),
with Hervey and Hartley. At Ashby there began the first of
a series of little incidents in this town which well illustrate
what kind of a life his was. 'The kind people of Ashby,' he
says, 'stirred up some of the baser sort to riot before her

ladyship's door while the gospel was preaching; and on Wednesday evening some people, on their return home, narrowly escaped being murdered. Her ladyship has just received a message from the justice, in order to bring the offenders before him.' After passing through Nottingham, Mansfield, and Sutton, at which places his message was reverently listened to by vast numbers, another rough reception was given to him at Rotherham. The crier was employed to give notice of a bear-baiting. At seven o'clock on a Saturday morning the 'bear' had his congregation round him; then the drum sounded, and several watermen came with great staves to the baiting. The constable was struck; two of the mobbers were apprehended, but afterwards rescued. One of the most active opponents of Whitefield at Rotherham, but afterwards one of his best friends, was one Thorpe, who also thought to make merry with his public-house friends at the evangelist's expense. He and three others engaged to compete, in a public-house, for a wager, at mimicking Whitefield. His competitors took their turn first; then he jumped on the table, saying, 'I shall beat you all.' According to the terms of the contest, he opened the Bible at haphazard, and took the first text that his eye fell upon, which was this, 'Except ye repent, ye shall all likewise perish.' The words pierced his conscience at once, and instead of mimicking, he began to preach in right earnest, neither thoughts nor language failing him. His audience hung their heads in silence and gloom; none attempted to interrupt him as he went on to make remarks which filled his own mind with amazement and terror. His sermon—which he always affirmed was preached by the help of the Spirit of God—ended, he descended from the table, and left the room in silence, without noticing any one. Afterwards he joined Ingham's society, then Wesley's, and finally becoming an Independent, settled as the pastor of

the Independent Church at Masbro.[1]   The people of Bolton
rivalled those of Rotherham in rudeness and violence; a
drunkard stood up behind Whitefield to preach; and a woman
twice attempted to stab the person who erected the preaching-
stand in her husband's field.   At Newby Cote, from whence
he wrote the letter detailing the treatment he had received at
Bolton, he had to append to his letter, at seven on the morning
after writing it, a postscript which ran thus: 'This last night
Satan hath showed his teeth.   Some persons got into the
barn and stable, and have cut my chaise and one of the
horse's tails.   What would men do, if they could?'   It was
reserved for 'a clergyman at Ulverstone, who looked more
like a butcher than a minister,' to render the last of those
insults which Whitefield bore during this journey.   He came
with two others, and charged a constable to take Whitefield
into custody; 'but,' adds Whitefield, 'I never saw a poor
creature sent off in such disgrace.'   Thus the poor pilgrim
went on from town to town, from county to county.

The journey had also its bright side.   Sheffield hardened
sinners were visibly altered in their looks since the last visit,
and received the word with such gladness that many went
away because they could not come near enough to hear.   The
moors around Haworth were thronged on Whit Sunday with
thousands of people, and the church was thrice almost filled
with communicants.   Increasing in power as he went, he
reached Edinburgh at the end of two months, during which

[1] Whitefield's house was often the village inn, and there he was exposed
to annoyance both from drunkards and gamblers.   One night the room in
which he and a friend slept was next to that in which a set of gamblers
were carousing; and their foul language so troubled him that he felt he
must go and reprove them.   In vain did his friend try to dissuade him.
He went and spoke, but apparently without any effect.   When he returned
and lay down again, his friend said, 'What did you gain by it?'   'A soft
pillow,' he answered, and soon fell asleep.

time he had preached more than ninety times, and to perhaps as many as one hundred and forty thousand people..

His coming was hailed with joy in Scotland ; larger congregations than ever waited on his word ; and results, not so striking, but quite as useful, followed his efforts as formerly. His general plan was to preach twice every day, the first time early in the morning, and the second in the evening at six ; but one day he preached thrice, and another day four times. This exertion proved too much. Ralph Erskine and he met, and shook hands. The pamphleteers were quiet ; and many of his enemies were glad to be at peace with him. 'The parting was rather more affectionate than ever,' he says, 'and I shall have reason to bless God for ever for this last visit to Scotland.'

His active life did not altogether remove him from the quiet sphere of an ordinary pastor ; and sometimes we find him comforting the dying, and preparing them for their change. Such work awaited him on his return to England. The Honourable Miss Hotham, daughter of Lady Hotham, received her last religious teaching from him, and passed into the joy of her Lord. It is striking to see Whitefield kneeling at her bedside, and praying 'as low as he could,' and then giving her the communion.

The end of 1750 and the beginning of 1751 do not appear to have been so stirring as other times in Whitefield's life ; but the fact is that his public labours, numerous and exhausting as ever, when he was well enough to work at all, were considerably overshadowed by personal affliction and the affliction of his wife and friends. At first, and for some short time after his return from Scotland, all was most pleasant and most quiet. He looks at home in his house adjoining the Tabernacle. There he entertains his dearly beloved friend Hervey ; Wesley, too, comes up one morning to breakfast with him, and then to

pray with him. 'His heart,' as Wesley says, 'was susceptible
of the most generous and the most tender friendship. I have
frequently thought that this of all others was the distinguishing part of his character. How few have we known of so kind
a temper, of such large and flowing affections!' Charles
Wesley, too, had the same judgment on this point, and said
of him—

> 'For friendship formed by nature and by grace,
> His heart made up of truth and tenderness,
> He lived, himself on others to bestow.'

It is in the spirit of this beautiful expression of his, 'It is my
comfort that those who are friends to Jesus shall live eternally
together hereafter,' that he comes in from the Tabernacle to
enjoy the conversation of his friend; and by and by goes
down to Ashby to see the Countess and four clergymen who
are enjoying her hospitality. He says that she looks like 'a
good archbishop with his chaplains around him.' 'They have
'the sacrament every morning, heavenly conversation all day,
and preaching at night.' He calls this living at Court indeed.
Nor is the heavenly conversation without wit and pleasantry,
for Whitefield was one of the cheerfullest of men. 'Strong
good sense, a generous expansion of heart, the most artless
but captivating affability, the brightest cheerfulness, and the
promptest wit,' Toplady says, 'made him one of the best
companions in the world.'

But it is only for a few days that we see him spending a life
so free from the strain of preaching to thousands. He is
hardly withdrawn from the fields, yet is longing to die preaching in them. His favourite caution to ministers—'Beware of
nestling'—is never out of mind; and although he has won
converts in this short stay at Ashby, he is soon off to
London, and plunged into all the excitement of his countless
labours.

Two months' work brought on a violent and dangerous fever, which confined him to his room for two weeks. He soon was well enough to engage again in his work; but he had thought to cast anchor in the haven of eternal rest. Half regretfully he received the summons 'to put out to sea again;' but his thought for himself was quickly forgotten in the old passion of his soul—love of others—and he wished that he might live to direct them to the haven he had almost sighted.

His wife, too, was in very delicate health, near her third confinement, and after that event she still continued for some time in a precarious state. Not a word fell from his pen about his third child, which, like the second, was probably still-born.

Trouble next fell upon Lady Huntingdon, and what affected her affected him. She was, indeed, unwell at the same time as Whitefield, but in January, 1751, she became much worse, and he was sent for to see her at once. When he arrived at Ashby, he found her somewhat better, but her sister-in-law, Lady Frances Hastings, lying dead in the house. He remarks concerning her: 'She was a retired Christian, lived silently, and died suddenly without a groan. May my exit be like hers! Whether right or not, I cannot help wishing that I may go off in the same manner. To me it is worse than death to live to be nursed, and see friends weeping about one. Sudden death is sudden glory.'

Whitefield's preaching this winter was as remarkable as on any previous winter for its efficacy in comforting mourners, in cheering the faithful, and in converting the impenitent. When he finished and started for Bristol, in March, he wrote a characteristic letter to his friend Hervey, urging him to come to Lady Huntingdon at Bristol; 'for,' he says, 'she will have nobody to give her the sacrament unless you come!' Whitefield proceeds: 'I ventured the other day to put out a guinea to interest for you.   It was to relieve an excellent Christian, who, by living very hard and working near twenty hours out of four-and-twenty, had brought himself very low.   He has a wife and four children, and was above two guineas in debt.   I gave one for myself and one for you.   We shall have good interest for our money in another world.'

This year his mind was much relieved about Georgia, because the introduction of slaves was at length permitted by the Government.   The pertinacity of those who wanted to make money out of their fellow-men out-wearied the better feelings and holier principles of those who saw in the trade a violation of human rights, a political and social curse; and free scope was given for the capture of Negroes in Africa and for their introduction into America.   Whitefield's remarks upon his new acquisition are too strange, as coming from one who had just helped the poor indebted Christian, to be omitted. They cause a sigh of regret that he never appears to have met his contemporary, that beautiful character, John Woolman, the American Quaker, who certainly would have talked and prayed him into a different state of mind.

'Thanks be to God,' he says, 'that the time for favouring that colony seems to be come.   I think now is the season for us to exert our utmost for the good of the poor Ethiopians.   We are told that even they are soon to stretch out their hands to God.   And who knows but their being settled in Georgia may be overruled for this great end ?   As for the lawfulness of keeping slaves I have no doubt, since I hear of some that were bought with Abraham's money, and some that were born in his house.   And I cannot help thinking that some of those servants mentioned by the apostles in their epistles were or had been slaves.   It is plain that the Gibeonites were doomed to perpetual slavery, and though liberty is a sweet thing to such as are born free, yet to those who never knew the sweets of it, slavery perhaps may not be so irksome.   However this be, it is plain to a demonstration that hot countries cannot be cultivated without Negroes.   What a flourishing country might Georgia have been, had the use of them been permitted years ago !   How many white people have been destroyed for want of them, and how many thousands of pounds spent to no purpose at all! Had Mr. Henry'—Matthew Henry?—'been in America, I believe he would have seen the lawfulness and necessity of having Negroes there. And though it is true that they are brought in a wrong way from their own country, and it is a trade not to be approved of, yet as it will be carried on whether we will or not, I should think myself highly favoured if I could purchase a good number of them, in order to make their lives comfortable, and lay a foundation for breeding up their posterity in the nurture and admonition of the Lord. You know, dear sir, that I had no hand in bringing them into Georgia; though my judgment was for it, and so much money was yearly spent to no purpose, and I was strongly importuned thereto, yet I would not have a Negro upon my plantation till the use of them was publicly allowed in the colony.' (It will be remembered that he had a hand in urging on the alteration of the law.) 'Now this is done, dear sir, let us reason no more about it, but diligently improve the present opportunity for their instruction. The Trustees favour it, and we may never have a like prospect. It rejoiced my soul to hear that one of my poor Negroes in Carolina was made a brother in Christ. How know we but we may have many such instances in Georgia ere it be long? In the fall, God willing, I intend to see what can be done towards laying a foundation.'

In a copy of the earliest orphan-house accounts may be found, on the same page which records the number of pounds paid for so many horses, cows, calves, and pigs, an entry 'For two servants *bought* of George Cuthbert, £12.' And this was done sincerely in the name of philanthropy and religion, nor does one protest from any quarter appear to have been raised against it. To Whitefield himself it never seemed to occur that the brotherly love he showed to Negroes personally was a spirit utterly opposed to the spirit of slavery, and that soon or later one must destroy the other. Love and slavery never can co-exist in peace. And little did he dream what a ghastly failure this attempt to unite Christianity and slavery would prove to be. From this dark deed flowed, for more than a century, a river of wrong, misery, and shame. In the original Declaration of Independence of the United States there was a clause reprobating the enslavement of African

Negroes, but at the instigation of South Carolina and Georgia, which had never attempted to restrain the importation of slaves, and still wished to continue it, the clause was struck out. Georgia became one of the worst of the slave States. It offered, in 1831, a reward of five thousand dollars for William Lloyd Garrison, the leader of American Negro Emancipation, which was a bribe to any ruffian to seize him and convey him South, whence it is certain he never would have come out alive. The reward was on his head for thirty-four years, when Lincoln's Proclamation of Emancipation annulled it. But Providence had a strange revenge for Whitefield's fault, for in the house next to that in which he died at Newbury Port, Garrison was born, and over the ramparts of Fort Sumter, Charleston, S.C., from which the first shot was fired by the South on the Federal flag, Garrison and a band of Abolitionists, invited by the Government to be present, had the joy of seeing that flag raised again as the symbol of liberty for all, black and white alike. In New England, which had shared so largely in the revival, was generated the force that destroyed slavery. The good overcame the evil. Nevertheless, evangelists and ministers should be warned by this painful part of Whitefield's life not to give their support, either directly or indirectly, to anything, under any pretext whatsoever, that is a violation of justice, lest thereby they do more harm than by all their labours they do good. Whitefield might not have been able to prevent the introduction of slavery into Georgia, but he would have been honoured for failing in an attempt to stop it, and he need not have availed himself of the right to hold slaves.

On March 30, 1751, Whitefield writes from Plymouth : 'I suppose the death of our Prince has affected you. It has given me a shock.' The Prince of Wales counted many of Lady Huntingdon's friends among his political supporters, and she herself, before her conversion, often attended his

Court. Her absence from Court after her conversion was not unnoticed by the Prince; and inquiring one day of Lady Charlotte Edwin where she was, he received the laconic, mocking answer, 'I suppose praying with her beggars.' The Prince shook his head, and turning to her said, 'Lady Charlotte, when I am dying, I think I shall be happy to seize the skirt of Lady Huntingdon's mantle, to lift me up with her to heaven.'

From January, 1751, to December, 1752, there occurred nothing that deserves detailed record in a life like this, where effort was generally at the full stretch, and where sufferings, both mental and bodily, as well as joys, abounded. We are prepared to hear of journeys and voyages made with the promptness of a general at the head of an attacking army; and of weariness and sickness paid as the price for the risks run. A few pages of Whitefield's letters carry us into Wales, where, since nothing is said about it, we must imagine what work he did; and into Ireland, where he was received into the house of Mr. Lunell, a Dublin banker, and where the people welcomed him, everything, apparently, having prepared his way. Dublin was soon aroused by his earnest words, and 'Moorfield's auditories' rewarded him for his toil, as they stood with solemn countenances, like men who were hearing as for eternity. Athlone and Limerick, where, as a hunger-bitten, weary traveller, he had preached fourteen years before, next heard his voice. Then Waterford and Cork, where he stood unhurt in the midst of a populace which had shamefully treated the Methodists whom the Wesleys and their helpers had gathered into a society. Hundreds in that city prayed him to continue among them; and many Papists promised to leave their priests if he would consent to the request; but their pleading and promising were alike ineffectual. He was soon in Dublin again, and as quickly away to Belfast and

other places in the north.   What the efforts of the people
of Cork, and the tears of the people of Dublin could not
procure—a few days longer stay—the importunity of the
people of Belfast won from him.   The numbers that attended
were so large, and the opportunities for good were so promising,
that he grieved he had not come among them sooner.   And
all the while he had been performing these journeys and
labours in the heat of summer, and under physical weakness
which caused violent vomiting, attended with great loss of
blood after preaching!   Yet in five days he was at Glasgow,
in the house of his old friend, Mr. Niven, a merchant, who
lived above the cross.   The enthusiasm of Cambuslang days
still burned in the hearts of the peasantry and the weavers in
the country, and by three o'clock in the morning many of
them were on their way to the city, to hear him on the day of
his farewell preaching.   In Edinburgh, whither he went next,
the selecter society living in the capital evinced, along with
the poor and the degraded, a strong desire to receive his
message.   More work brought on more hæmorrhage and more
prostration, till his body was almost worn out.   Riding recruited
him ; and he was no sooner in London, than he took ship for
his fourth voyage to America, his seventh across the Atlantic.
Dr. Doddridge thought his constitution was quite worn out
with labour.   After spending the winter in America, he
embarked for his eighth voyage in the spring, and was in
England preaching and journeying as usual the whole of
the summer.   His special object in returning so soon
was 'to put the orphanage upon a proper footing.'   He
retired to London for the winter of 1752 ; but at the end of
what exertion and triumph did that laborious repose come!
For about twenty-eight days he preached in Scotland to not
less than ten thousand a day.   His progress through the north
of England towards London was a sublime march.   From

Sheffield he wrote that since his leaving Newcastle he had sometimes scarce known whether he was in heaven or on earth. As he swept along from town to town, thousands and thousands flocked twice and thrice a day to hear the word of life. 'A gale of Divine influence everywhere attended it.' He continued his work till he reached Northampton, where he took coach for London. No wonder that, on his arrival in the city, it seemed as if the broken tabernacle of the body must release the ardent spirit that quickened it. Moreover, the inner life was as intense as the outward was active and busy. 'Oh, my dear friend,' he exclaims to a correspondent, 'what manner of love is this, that we should be called the sons of God! Excuse me. I must pause awhile, my eyes gush out with water; at present they are almost fountains of tears. But thanks be to God they are tears of love!'

Looking round upon the circle of Whitefield's friends at Christmas, 1752, we miss some kind, familiar faces. His mother's face is not there; she had died a year before, while he was paying his last visit to America. Doddridge's face is not there; he died at Lisbon, and the news of his decease followed Whitefield to America. Like the soldier on the battlefield who can but drop a word of pity for a fallen comrade, and lift up a prayer for himself, Whitefield could only say, 'Dr. Doddridge, I find, is gone; Lord Jesus, prepare me to follow after!' The face of good Bishop Benson is not there; he died on August 30, 1752. His last days verified the remark of the Countess of Huntingdon: 'My lord, mark my words; when you are on your dying bed, Whitefield's will be one of the few ordinations you will reflect upon with complacence' On his dying bed he sent Whitefield a present of ten guineas for his orphan-house as a token of his regard, and begged to be remembered in his prayers. The face of Whitefield's only sister is not there. Her house in Bristol had been his home, and also his early Sunday morning preaching-room, while in that city ; and when she died he believed that she had entered into 'the rest that remaineth for the people of God.' The face of Ralph Erskine is not there. His death occurred on November 6, 1752; and when the intelligence was brought to Ebenezer, he said with great emotion, 'And is Ralph gone? He has twice got the start of me ; he was first in Christ, and now he is first in glory.' But the start was not a long one ; for Ebenezer Erskine was now an old man, and worn with heavy labours. On June 2, 1754, he followed his brother quietly and gently; as one sleeping and resting himself after toil, he went to his reward.

CHAPTER XI

1753–1770

CHAPEL-BUILDING—ATTACKS BY ENEMIES—INFIRMITIES—HIS DEATH—THE RESULTS OF HIS WORK

NO small portion of the year 1753 was spent by Whitefield in what he called cross-ploughing the land; and what that work was is well enough known without our following him from field to field. But while he thought that he was the happiest man who, being fond neither of money, numbers, nor power, went on day by day without any other scheme than 'a general intention to promote the common salvation amongst people of all denominations,' his attention was forcibly called to the work of providing a permanent place of worship for his followers in London. The churches were as inaccessible to Methodists as ever; but had they been open probably few would have cared to enter them, for the freedom of the Tabernacle was in their estimation preferable to the unalterable forms of the Church. The Tabernacle was still the wooden building that was hastily erected at the time of the division between the Calvinists and Arminians. The idea of a permanent building seems to have been first suggested by the Countess of Huntingdon; but Whitefield was slow to move. In the winter of 1752, she and Lady Frances Shirley

again urged the work upon him, and this time he was brought
to their side, and began to collect money. His people responded with their usual liberality, and contributed a hundred
and seventy-six pounds on one Sunday. With eleven hundred
pounds in hand, he, on March 1, 1753, laid the first brick of
the new Tabernacle, which was to be eighty feet square, and
built round the old place. The ceremony was performed with
great solemnity, and Whitefield preached a sermon from the
text, ' In all places where I record My name, I will come unto
thee and bless thee.' Three months later the Tabernacle
was ready to receive its congregation ; and he opened it by
preaching in it morning and evening, to four thousand people
or more.

In the spring of this year Whitefield came into serious
collision with the Moravians. The reports of their proceedings
and of their financial position which he published in ' An Expostulatory Letter' to Count Zinzendorf, were brought to his
ears by one whom Peter Böhler stigmatises as an apostate ;
but there can be no doubt that Whitefield had his information
from more sources than one ; and as Böhler was assailed in
the letter, his phrase must be somewhat discounted. A man
might be an apostate from Moravianism, and yet a true witness.
Whitefield opened his letter with a protestation that a real
regard for his king and country, and a disinterested love for
his Saviour and his Saviour's Church, would not let him keep
silence longer with respect to the shocking things of which he
had heard, and the offences which had swelled to such an
enormous bulk. According to the statements which he had
received, there had been much foolishness and some wickedness practised by the Brethren, and they were seriously in debt.
But these are things that need not be further named here.
Whitefield evidently acted with candour and kindness, and his
remonstrances did the Brethren good.

His open-air preaching was concluded this year in a way too beautiful to be left without notice. He had opened in Bristol another chapel, called by the same name as that in London,[1] and then started for Somersetshire. He writes, on December 1st, that on the Tuesday before, he had preached at seven in the evening to a great multitude in the open air ; that all was hushed and exceeding solemn ; that the stars shone with great brightness ; that then, if ever, he had by faith seen Him who calls them all by their names ; and that his soul was filled with holy ambition, and he longed to be one of those who shall shine as the stars for ever and ever. His hands and body had been pierced with cold ; ' but what,' he asks, ' are outward things when the soul within is warmed with the love of God ? '

Much and sincerely as he desired his crown and joy, it seemed at this time as if another were to precede him. His friend Wesley was ill of what the physicians thought was galloping consumption. Whitefield pitied the Church and himself, but not Wesley. He almost grieved to think that he must stay behind in 'this cold climate,' while Wesley took 'his flight to a radiant throne prepared for him from the foundations of the world.' Then, again, he thought how 'poor Mr. Charles' was to be pitied, upon whom double work would come. The time was full of sorrow, and it gave Whitefield and the Countess an excellent opportunity

---

[1] Lord Chesterfield contributed twenty pounds towards the erection of Bristol Tabernacle ; but begged that his name might not appear in any way. Sainte Beuve says that he feared ridicule ; and very likely that feeling made him wish his name to be withheld. He seems also to have been afraid of Lady Huntingdon's importunities, and a little impatience with her is perceptible. ' Really,' he said, ' there is no resisting your ladyship's importunities. It would ill become me to censure your enthusiastic admiration of Mr. Whitefield. His eloquence is unrivalled, his zeal inexhaustible ; and not to admire both would argue a total absence of taste, and an insensibility not to be coveted by anybody.'

to serve their friends. The Countess and another lady, just arrived in Bath from London, went from Bath to Bristol, to inform Charles of his brother's dangerous state. He immediately started for London, and found John at Lewisham; he fell on his neck and wept. Prayer was now offered in all the Methodist societies for the recovery of their great leader; and Charles records that a change for the better came when the people were praying for him at the Foundry. Hope, however, had been relinquished by all; and Wesley had written his epitaph, which was a longer composition than Whitefield had penned for his own tombstone, but similar in spirit. Whitefield wrote from Bristol to both the brothers, but enclosed John's letter in Charles's. To John he wrote :—

'If seeing you so weak, when leaving London, distressed me, the news and prospect of your approaching dissolution hath quite weighed me down. I pity the Church, and myself, but not you. A radiant throne awaits you, and ere long you will enter into your Master's joy. Yonder He stands with a massy crown, ready to put it on your head amid an admiring throng of saints and angels. But I, poor I, that have been waiting for my dissolution these nineteen years, must be left behind to grovel here below! Well, this is my comfort, it cannot be long ere the chariots are sent even for worthless me. If prayers can detain them, even you, reverend and very dear sir, shall not leave us yet; but if the decree is gone forth that you must now fall asleep in Jesus, may He kiss your soul away, and give you to die in the embraces of triumphant love. If in the land of the living, I hope to pay my last respects to you next week; if not, reverend and dear sir, farewell! *I præ, sequar, etsi non passibus æquis.* My heart is too big, tears trickle down too fast, and I fear you are too weak for me to enlarge. May underneath you be Christ's everlasting arms! I commend you to His never-failing mercy.'

Wesley disappointed his friends' fears by slowly regaining his health. He who seemed so nigh to his rest returned to work for almost forty years longer, and, among other services, preached the funeral sermon of his brother Whitefield. It was the cause of sincere joy to Whitefield to see his fellow-labourers spared to stand by his side; he prayed that the Wesleys might both spring up afresh, and their latter end increase more and more. 'Talk not of having no more work in the vineyard,' he wrote to Charles; 'I hope all our work is but just beginning. I am sure it is high time to do something for Him who hath done and suffered so much for me. Near forty years old, and such a dwarf! The winter come already, and so little done in the summer! I am ashamed; I blush, and am confounded!'

This winter of affliction for the Wesleys was one of much physical prostration to Whitefield also; every sermon, he says, was fetched out of the furnace. He itinerated between Portsmouth and Scotland and back in this state. When spring came he sailed with twenty-two orphans for Georgia, *viâ* Lisbon. This was his ninth voyage; and his reason for making it by way of Lisbon was that as a preacher and a Protestant he might see something of the superstitions of the Church of Rome. For this purpose he could have chosen no better season and no better place; he was in time for all the pageantry and activity of Easter week. A gentleman of the factory, whose brother had received good through Whitefield's preaching, welcomed the evangelist to his house, and afforded him every opportunity of gratifying his wishes. Nor were these the wishes of idle curiosity. Whitefield delighted in travelling for the sake of preaching and also for the sake of seeing men and things. He thought that it expanded a man's mind to see strange places and fresh customs; and there can be no doubt that his own wide charity was due in no small degree to his intercourse with men of all classes, of all Churches, and of many nations. At first he did not care much for the distinctions between Churches; and when Quakers, Independents, Presbyterians, and Baptists showed him equal kindness wherever he travelled, and displayed the great qualities of purity and love, he cared yet less. A more impartial Christian it would be hard to find. He expected perfection in none, and hailed every tendency to it in all. Even Lisbon was to do more than present him with things to be hated and shunned. Amid so much that was against his judgment and conscience, there were things to delight his taste. The singing in St. Domingo Church by the Dominican friars while the queen performed her devotions there, was 'most surprisingly sweet.' The action of the preachers, a great number of whom he heard, struck him as most graceful. '*Vividi oculi, vividæ manus, omnia vivida.*' He thought, as he beheld their impressive gesticulation and heard their tender tones, that English preachers, who have truth on their side, would do well to be a little more fervent in their address, and not let falsehood and superstition run away with all that is pathetic and affecting. The city was a scene to make him all eye and ear. There were images of saints with lanterns burning in front of them, and churches hung with purple damask trimmed with gold. There were the richest and noblest of the land bowing before the gorgeous altars, or hurrying from church to church to offer their sacrifices. There was the spectacle of the king, attended with his nobles, washing the feet of twelve poor men, and of the queen and her royal daughters doing the same to twelve poor women. There were processions of penitents, headed by preaching friars bearing crucifixes in their hands, which they held up before the eyes of the devotees as they exhorted them to fresh acts of sacrifice. His soul was moved with pity as he saw by moonlight one night some two hundred penitents, dressed in white linen vestments, barefooted, and with heavy chains attached to their ankles, which made a dismal noise as they passed along the streets; some carried great stones on their backs, and others dead men's bones and skulls in their hands; most of them whipped and lashed themselves with cords or with flat bits of iron. Even in the moonlight the effects of their heavy penances could be seen on their red and swollen backs. It struck him as a horrible sight, in the same church where he so greatly admired the singing, that over the great window were the heads of many Jews, painted on canvas, who had been condemned by the inquisition, and carried out from that church to be burnt. 'Strange way this of compelling people to come in!' he exclaimed. 'Such was not Thy method, O meek and compassionate Lamb of God! But bigotry is as cruel as the grave.' The whole time was, as he said, instructive, though silent.

His wife was not with him this voyage, indeed she seems to have performed but one long journey with him after their marriage. Her health was unequal to the trials of an American summer; and it would have been useless for her to have travelled with him as a companion from place to place. He could but leave her to her own resources and the kindness of his friends—not a pleasant position for a wife, but the best in which he could place her, unless he relinquished his evangelistic work, and that would simply have overturned his whole plan of life, and violated his most solemn convictions. He implored one of his London friends to visit his wife frequently. 'Add to my obligations,' he said, 'by frequently visiting my poor wife. Kindnesses shown to her in my absence will be double kindnesses.'

With a family, but not with his wife, he arrived at Bethesda, which he found in a flourishing state, as was also the colony. He had a hundred and six persons, black and white, to provide for and to guide; and he seems to have known the ages and capabilities and condition of all at the orphan-house, and often to have sent specific and peremptory directions concerning particular cases. Honour, too, was beginning to come to early and faithful colonists. His friend Habersham, who came over with him at his first voyage, and to whom he committed the temporal affairs of the orphan-house, was now appointed secretary of the colony; afterwards he became president of the Council and Commons House of Assembly. Whitefield himself received from the new college of New Jersey, for which he had greatly exerted himself before leaving England, the degree of Master of Arts. Altogether a better reception was given him by the country than he had received fourteen years before, and that, as we have seen, was gratifying enough. His weaknesses still clung to him, that is, his weaknesses of the flesh, and from this time he may be considered a confirmed invalid who refused to be invalided; but his strength of heart was not at all diminished, and when he got as far north as Portsmouth, he said in the quietest way, 'I am now come to the end of my northward line, and in a day or two purpose to turn back, in order to preach all the way to Georgia. It is about a sixteen hundred miles' journey.' This was he who was ashamed of his sloth and lukewarmness, and longed to be on the stretch for God! Yet again, when his ride of two thousand miles was ended, scenes of wonder having opened all the way, and when he had preached for nearly five months, he longed to have time to spend in retirement and deep humiliation before that Saviour for whom he had done so little! He had learnt to be humble.

Whitefield's tenth voyage was performed in the spring of 1755. About two months after his arrival in England his friend Cennick died. 'John Cennick,' he said, 'is now added to the happy number of those who see God as He is. I do not envy, but want to follow after him.' If not a strong Christian, Cennick was a very devout one; and the Church cannot forget her indebtedness to him for a few good hymns which he added to her treasury. Some tender, beautiful lines, headed '*Nunc dimittis,*' were found in his pocketbook when he died. Here are some of them :—

> ' I never am forsaken or alone ;
> Thou kissest all my tears and griefs away ;
> Art with me all night long, and all the day ;
> I have no doubt that I belong to Thee,
> And shall be with Thee to eternity.
> I would not Thee offend—Thou know'st my heart—
> Nor one short day before Thy time depart :
> But I am weary and dejected too,
> O let me to eternal Sabbath go.'

Whitefield found the Methodists very lively in England, and had the pleasure of hearing that several clergymen were preaching those truths which he had done so much to propagate. But enemies were also alert. He found it difficult to keep clear of collision with Wesley's friends, his own admirers and they being, as usual, as careless about unneighbourly acts as their leaders were anxious to love and serve one another. He also had open and dangerous opposition from some ruffians in the metropolis. It was to be expected that one who eclipsed the best actors of the day in grace of action and naturalness of expression (Garrick said he would give a hundred guineas to be able to say 'Oh' as did Whitefield), and who, at the same time, assailed theatre-going with unsparing severity, would be attacked in turn. The trouble with admirers of the stage this time was of a complicated kind, and it is difficult to say how much they were to blame ; for playhouses, a bishop and his vestry, and Roman Catholics, who hated King George, are mingled in a strange medley in the story. It is possible to get consistency only by supposing that all these hated the Methodist for special reasons of their own, and were, by this common feeling, banded against him. Even

hatred of the same thing will make enemies wondrous kind for
a season. The Seven Years' War was also raging, and feeling
ran high. Some religious people, apparently the Dissenters,
had built a chapel, called Long Acre Chapel, near the playhouses. It was an unconsecrated building, duly licensed for
preaching; its minister was the Rev. John Barnard, an Independent, one of Whitefield's converts. Mr. Barnard asked
Whitefield to preach in his chapel twice a week, and Whitefield
consented to do so on the understanding that he might use
the liturgy if he thought proper; for he judged that he might
'innocently preach the love of a crucified Redeemer, without
giving any just offence to Jew or Gentile, much less to any
bishop or overseer of the Church of God.' Every one was not
of his mind. A band of roughs were hired to disturb him
while he preached, by making a noise with a copper furnace,
bells, drum, &c., at the chapel door. Part of their pay came
from some gentlemen of the vestry of the Bishop of Bangor
and Dean of Westminster, Dr. Zachary Pearce; and they did
their work to perfection. They used more dangerous means
of silencing the obnoxious preacher than drums; they threw
stones through the windows at him, and always missed him,
though some one else suffered; they rioted at the door, and
abused him and his congregation as they were leaving the
chapel. Things were serious, though Whitefield with his
strong sense of humour called their behaviour 'a serenading
from the sons of Jubal and Cain.' An appeal made by him
to a magistrate procured protection for a time. An appeal to
Dr. Pearce was less successful; that prelate forbade his
preaching in the chapel again; but his inhibition was useless. Whitefield continued his work. The bishop's vestry
now revived the persecution by the mob; and Whitefield
made repeated appeals to this exemplary overseer to stay
the violence, and he appealed in vain! Several persons

were seriously injured, and he himself was threatened with
death. Once when he entered the pulpit, he found a letter
laid upon the cushion, which threatened him with 'a certain,
sudden, and unavoidable stroke, unless he desisted from
preaching and pursuing the offenders by law.' It was his
determination, formed with the advice of some members of
the Government, to prosecute the offenders, that made them
assail him in this cowardly way; and it is certain there were
some with audacity and wickedness enough to give the stroke.
For some unusual purpose a man followed him into the pulpit
of the Tabernacle while the Long Acre trouble was at its worst;
and it was generally supposed that he was an assassin. Whitefield dared the worst, and let the prosecution go on, until its
preparation to enter the King's Bench terrified his enemies.
One of them also had previously come under better influences,
and regretted the part he had taken in paying ruffians to commit violence.

The letters to the Bishop of Bangor are important for more
than the information they give of the rioting. They give us a
last explanation and vindication of the course Whitefield had
followed for so many years, and which he followed to his
death. The letters of the bishop to Whitefield were not
published, because Whitefield thought that it would be a
breach of courtesy to proclaim their contents, and his lordship,
fearing exposure, had signified his intention to use his right as
a peer to hinder them from appearing; but it is easy to see
what their substance must have been, from the answers they
received. Dr. Pearce had charged Whitefield with unfaithfulness to the Church of England, and the reply was :—

'For near these twenty years past, as thousands can testify, I have con-
scientiously defended her homilies and articles, and upon all occasions
spoken well of her liturgy. Either of these, together with her discipline,
I am so far from renouncing, much less from throwing aside all regard to,

that I earnestly pray for the due restoration of the one, and daily lament the wanton departure of too, too many from the other. But, my lord, what can I do? When I acted in the most regular manner, and when I was bringing multitudes even of Dissenters themselves to crowd the churches, without any other reason being given than that of too many followers after me, I was denied the use of them. Being thus excluded, and many thousands of ignorant souls, that perhaps would neither go to church nor meeting-houses, being very hungry after the gospel, I thought myself bound in duty to deal out to them the bread of life. Being further ambitious to serve my God, my king, and my country, I sacrificed my affections and left my native soil, in order to begin and carry on an orphan-house in the infant colony of Georgia, which, through the Divine blessing, is put upon a good foundation. This served as an introduction, though without my design, to my visiting the other parts of his Majesty's dominions in North America ; and I humbly hope that many made truly serious in that foreign clime will be my joy and crown of rejoicing in the day of the Lord Jesus.

'Your lordship judgeth exceeding right when you say, "I presume you do not mean to declare any dissent from the Church of England." Far be it from me ; no, my lord, unless thrust out, I shall never leave her, and even then (as I hope whenever it happens it will be an unjust extrusion) I shall continue to adhere to her doctrines, and pray for the much wished-for restoration of her discipline, even to my dying day. Fond of displaying her truly Protestant and orthodox principles, especially when Church and State are in danger from a cruel and Popish enemy, I am glad, my lord, of an opportunity of preaching, though it be in a meeting-house; and I think it discovers a good and moderate spirit in the Dissenters, who will quietly attend on the Church service, as many have done and continue to do at Long Acre Chapel, while many, who I suppose style themselves her faithful sons, by very improper instruments of reformation, have endeavoured to disturb and molest us.'

Another extract from the letter cannot be read without great pain by any one who holds that the acceptance of creeds or the subjection to canons ought to be made in simple, literal honesty, without qualifications or reservations of any kind. Whitefield's answer to the bishop might be irrefragable if treated upon the ground on which he placed it; but truth should not be made dependent upon the customs of any class of men, otherwise the law of God is made void by human tradition. Neither were matters mended by his appealing so solemnly to the Almighty, as he did in the following words :—

'But, my lord, to come nearer to the point in hand—and for Christ's sake let not your lordship be offended by my using such plainness of speech—I would, as in the presence of the living God, put it to your lordship's conscience whether there is one bishop or presbyter in England, Wales, or Ireland, that looks upon our canons as his rule of action? If they do, we are all perjured with a witness, and consequently in a very bad sense of the word irregular indeed. When canons and other Church laws are invented and compiled by men of little hearts and bigoted principles on purpose to hinder persons of more enlarged souls from doing good, or being more extensively useful, they become mere *bruta fulmina;* and when made use of only as cords to bind up the hands of a zealous few, that honestly appear for their king, their country, and their God, like the withes with which the Philistines bound Samson, in my opinion they may very legally be broken. . . . As good is done, and souls are benefited, I hope your lordship will not regard a little irregularity, since at the worst it is only the irregularity of doing well.'

Impossible as it is to withhold sympathy from an irregular well-doer, who was singled out as the object of pastoral warnings and the mark of scoundrels' brickbats, while card-playing, gambling, idle clergymen were passed by without rebuke or punishment, there is no gainsaying that he was irregular. To judge his conscience is not our office; but it would have made one inconsistency the less in his life had he severed himself from a Church with which he could hold but a nominal connection so long as he persisted in his irregularities; and it would have been a yet happier thing had no Church been so rigid in its forms as to make the warmest zeal and the tenderest love in its communion things which it could not tolerate, and yet remain true to its constitution. It is strange when the best Christian becomes the most objectionable member of a Church.

Early in 1756, the year which our narrative has now reached, a great change passed over Whitefield's personal appearance.

The graceful figure which was familiar on many a common
and park and market-cross of England, which Londoners
knew so well as he rapidly walked their streets, and country
people recognised as he dashed along their lanes, attended by
a knot of brethren on horseback, in haste to meet some
mighty congregation, or rode slowly along, pondering his next
sermon or silently communing with God—that figure which
was associated with the godly young man who entranced and
awed his countrymen—was now changed, when he was forty-
two years old, into the heavy, corpulent, unwieldy form, which
several painters and engravers have preserved for us in their
likenesses of the great preacher.[1]　The observation of the
common people who heard him gladly has pictured him in
happy lines, as they knew him in his earlier and in his later
days.　It is the bold and active young preacher whom we see
when we hear him described by a poor man as one who
'preached like a lion.'　It is the stout man of middle age
whom we see when another describes him as 'a jolly, brave
man, and sich a look with him.'[2]　And no doubt his kindly
face and rounded form did make him seem 'a jolly, brave
man'; but the truth is, that this change was owing wholly to

[1] These likenesses were a great bugbear to him; he especially disliked
that in which he is represented with his hands lifted above his head, an
attitude which he seldom assumed, and but for a moment.　He used to
say that he should hate himself were he 'the sour-looking creature' they
represented him to be.　They all agree in painting him with a massive
chin and a large mouth, pinched tight at the corners, and long, flexible
lips, capable of expressing anything—the orator's lips.

[2] The words are those of an aged Oxfordshire peasant, and were spoken
in answer to the question, whether he remembered Whitefield's appearance.
'Ay, sure,' said he, 'he was a jolly, brave man; and what a look he had
when he put out his right hand thus, to rebuke a disturber as tried to stop
him, under the pear-tree.　The man had been very threatening and noisy;
but he could not stand the look.　Off he rode, and Whitefield said,
"There he goes; empty barrels make most din."'　An American said he
was 'a cheery, a very cheery old gentleman.'

disease. It was neither less work nor less care that made him seem so hale. As for work, he says : 'I have been enabled to preach twice and thrice a day to many, many thousands for these two months last past. And yet I cannot die. Nay, they tell me I grow fat. I dread a corpulent body; but it breaks in upon me like an armed man.' Preaching failed to cure, it rather increased, his complaint. When advised by a physician to try a perpetual blister for an inflammatory quinsey, he changed the receipt and tried perpetual preaching; and he vigorously and perseveringly applied the same remedy to corpulency, flux, and asthma, but not with the same success. He was doomed to carry a heavy burden of flesh.

He had care as well as work. It had been his plan to give those who helped at the orphan-house no certain income, or a very slender one : he said that if they loved him they would serve him disinterestedly; he asked nothing for his own exhausting toils but food and raiment, and judged that others should be equally devoted. This surrounded him with syco-phants, who pretended to be as high-minded as he wanted to see them, and who humoured his impatience of contradiction, but who at the same time served themselves in an under-handed way. He could be roughly honest himself, and might well have borne with it among the managers of his institution; the smooth deceit which crept into office turned upon him and pierced him, when its time came.

When Whitefield had got one permanent chapel in London, he began to feel that it would be useful to have a second, in another part of the city. The foundation-stone of Tottenham Court Chapel was accordingly laid by himself on May 10, 1756, and the building opened for worship on November 7th, the same year. It became the mother of many chapels, and the birthplace of many souls. It was now becoming a difficult question for the increasing number of Methodists, who, like

Whitefield and Wesley, nominally adhered to the Established Church, and called themselves Churchmen, to determine their standpoint. Churchmen they might be in name and spirit and faith, but Churchmen in modes of action they were not. As Methodists they were no part of the Church of England, neither would she recognise them; yet they were not Dissenters. They did not feel the objections of the Independents to Episcopacy; they did not feel the scruples of Baptists about the baptism of infants; they did not feel the repugnance of Quakers to forms and sacraments of every kind; they did not feel the abhorrence of Presbyterians to prelates and the liturgy. Neither State nor Church had made any provision for this new people. The action of the Church had already been taken; it now remained for the State to determine its mode of procedure. It quietly let Methodism fall into the ranks of Dissent, politically considered. There was a Toleration Act, and the worshippers in the new tabernacles and chapels that were beginning to multiply might avail themselves of its protection. Hence it has followed that this movement, which arose at Oxford, which was impelled and guided by duly ordained clergymen, and which might have crowded the Church of England with vast congregations of devout and holy people, has become more and more identified with the oldest and most extreme forms of dissent in this land. Whitefield's chapels and those of the Countess of Huntingdon are all Independent chapels, the use of the liturgy in some of them not hindering either minister or congregation from declaring that they regard the union of State and Church as an unholy alliance, damaging to the Church and burdensome and useless to the State. Even the society which Wesley established, and the members of which he so solemnly counselled to abide loyal to the Church of which he was a minister, has gradually gone the way of all dissenting societies; it has also declared firmly that it will not return to the ancient fold, to which it has been invited back. It is thus happening that Methodism, which never contemplated any severance from the Church at all, is aiding to bring about the dissolution of a bond which has existed ever since the Reformation. Its numbers are multiplied by tens of thousands; its chapels throng every town, and stand in every village in England; its ministers and lay preachers and helpers are legion; baptism and the Lord's Supper are duly administered within its pale; its adherents are married and buried by their own spiritual teachers. A denomination or denominations constituted and managed in this way are not likely to long for other pastures and another fold. Nor is their unwillingness to be absorbed, or appended as an auxiliary, decreased by some petty annoyances, remnants of former days, to which they are subjected. Their social disadvantages in villages and country districts, the injustice with which their children are forced into High Church day schools, and the rudeness which too often shocks and pains them at the parish churchyard, serve to excite their anger and hostility. As Englishmen they cannot help asking themselves what is their fault, what their sin, that they should be thus treated; and when they see that it is only their love of Methodism and their attendance upon its services, they cleave all the more closely to their denomination. How distant does all this seem to be from the day when Whitefield strove to put his new chapel in Tottenham Court Road under the protection of the Countess of Huntingdon, and thus to preserve it for the Church; and when the Countess herself was annoyed at nothing so much as at the idea of one of her ministers becoming a Dissenter. Berridge of Everton wrote to her twenty years after the opening of this chapel, and seven after the death of Whitefield, in a strain which shows that even at that time, although she had practically been a Dissenter for forty years, she disliked her position, and was impatient when any one told her the bare truth about it. But Berridge was an honest man, and minded little how any one resented his plain speaking. His language to the Countess was :—

‘ However rusty or rickety the Dissenters may appear to you, God hath His remnant among them ; therefore lift not up your hand against them for the Lord’s sake, nor yet for consistency’s sake, because your students are as real Dissenting preachers as any in the land, unless a gown and band can make a clergyman. The bishops look on your students as the worst kind of Dissenters ; and manifest this by refusing that ordination to your preachers which would be readily granted to other teachers among the Dissenters.’

There are other passages in the same letter which describe, almost with the accuracy of prophecy, the course of future events in Methodism and in the Establishment, and which might afford food for profitable thought even yet.

With regard to his new chapel, Whitefield wrote to Lady Huntingdon to say that they had consulted the Commons about putting it under her ladyship’s protection, and that the answer was :—

‘ No nobleman can license a chapel, or in any manner have one put in his dwelling-house ; that the chapel must be a private one, and not with doors to the street for any persons to resort to at pleasure, for then it becomes a public one ; that a chapel cannot be built and used as such without the consent of the parson of the parish, and when it is done with his consent, no minister can preach therein, without licence of the bishop of the diocese.’

‘ There seems then,’ he says, ‘ to be but one way, to license it as our other houses are ; and thanks be to Jesus for that liberty which we have.’ That licensing does not seem to have been made at once, for it was in 1764 that as owner, both of the Tabernacle, Moorfields, and Tottenham Court Road Chapel, he registered them in the registry of the Dean and Chapter of St. Paul, London, as 'meeting-places of certain congregations of Protestant Dissenters from the Church of England calling themselves Independents.' He thus became the owner of two Independent chapels, and was practically an Independent minister, while remaining a clergyman of the Church of England.

There was the same crush of hearers, when the place was opened, as there had been at the Tabernacle. Many great people came, and begged that they might have a constant seat. A neighbouring physician called it 'Whitefield's soul-trap,' and by that name it was commonly known among the foolish scoffers. Among the distinguished visitors who were accommodated in Lady Huntingdon's pew, Lord Chesterfield might not unfrequently be seen; and once his rigid decorum and self-possession were as much overpowered by the eloquence of the preacher as if he had been a peasant at a Cambuslang preaching or a Welsh miner among a host of his countrymen shouting, 'Gogoniant bendith iti!' Whitefield, who was unrivalled in description, could easily make his hearers see with his eyes, and feel with his heart; and on this occasion he was giving a vivid and horrifying picture of the peril of sinners. He carried his audience out into the night, and nigh to a dangerous precipice, where in the feeble light might be seen, dim and staggering, the form of an old man, a blind beggar, deserted by his dog. The old man stumbles on, staff in hand, vainly endeavouring to discover his way. His face is towards the cliff; step by step he advances; his foot trembles on the edge; another moment and he will lie mangled in the valley below, when up starts the agonised Chesterfield, crying as he bounds forward to save him, 'Good God! he is gone!'

Oratory so perfect and so exciting could not fail to bring some actors among the motley throng that listened to him.

Foote and Garrick might sometimes be seen side by side; their opinion was that the sermon was preached best when preached for the fortieth time. All its weaknesses were cut off, and all its ineffective parts suppressed; all its impressive passages were retained, and improved to the uttermost, and his memory holding with unerring accuracy what he wished to say, his tone and look and gesture were adapted to its utterance with perfect art. Yet he was not bound by memory, but seized upon any passing circumstance, and turned it to account. The heavy thunder-cloud hanging on the horizon, and the flash of lightning which rent its bosom, were, for his field congregations, his most vivid emblems of the coming day of wrath. A scoffer's levity would point his stern rebuke; and a penitent's tear seen in some bedimmed eye would prompt a word of loving encouragement.

It was more than the oratorical display which attracted to the 'soul-trap' Shuter, who was pronounced by Garrick the greatest comic genius he had ever seen. Shuter had a warm, kind heart, and must have felt his better nature moved by the humanity of the teaching of Whitefield. It was he who came to the rescue of a remarkable play which was rejected by Garrick, Powel, and Colman; Goldsmith thanked him with tears in his eyes for having established the reputation of his 'Good-Natured Man,' when they had deemed it unfit for production on the stage. He also acted in 'She Stoops to Conquer.' At the time of his first coming to hear Whitefield he was acting the part of Ramble in 'The Rambler.' The name of the play tempted Whitefield into that playing upon words to which he was somewhat addicted, and in the use of which he did not always exhibit the best taste. Seeing Shuter sitting in the front of the gallery—they were by this time known to each other personally—he fixed his eye upon him, and exclaimed in his warm invitation to sinners to come to the

Lord Jesus : ' And thou, poor Ramble, who hast long rambled from Him, come thou also. Oh, end thy ramblings by coming to Jesus.' Shuter went to Whitefield at the close of the service, and said to him : ' I thought I should have fainted—how could you serve me so ? ' But neither this pointed appeal, nor many others to which he listened, succeeded in drawing him from his unsatisfying life to a nobler career. His part in the production of Goldsmith's plays, which appeared two years before Whitefield's death, shows that he continued to follow his old calling. There is, however, an anecdote told of him which proves that the old thoughts and feelings were not extinguished, if they were not sufficiently strong to rule him. The Rev. Mr. Kinsman, who was an intimate friend of his, and had tried hard to wean him from his profession, met him one day in Portsmouth, and said to him that he had been preaching so often, and to such large congregations, that his physician advised change of air for his health.

' And I,' said Shuter, ' have been acting till ready to die ; but oh, how different our conditions ! Had you fallen, it would have been in the service of God ; but in whose service have my powers been wasted? I dread to think of it. I certainly had a call once, while studying my part in the Park, and had Mr. Whitefield received me at the Lord's table I never should have gone back ; but the caresses of the great, who, when unhappy, want Shuter to make them laugh, are too seducing. There is a good and moral play to-night ; but no sooner is it over than I come in with my farce of " A Dish of all Sorts," and knock all the moral on the head.'

When his friends rated him as a Methodist, because they had seen him with Mr. Kinsman, he said : ' A precious method is mine ; no, I wish I were ; if any be right, they are.' Lady Huntingdon gives us yet another glimpse of this kind-hearted actor. Writing from Bath to Lady Fanny Shirley, she says :—

' I have had a visit from Shuter the comedian, whom I saw in the street, and asked to call on me. He was wonderfully astonished when I announced

my name. We had much conversation; but he cannot give up his profession for another more respectable. He spoke of Mr. Whitefield with
much affection, and with admiration of his talents. He promised to come
some other time, when he had more leisure for conversation. Poor fellow!
I think he is not far from the kingdom.'

Much has been said of Whitefield's efforts for his orphan-
house, and of the success with which he pleaded its claims;
but let it not be thought that he never sent the collection-box
round for any other object. He would help others when debt
and anxiety pressed upon himself, the money which would
have freed him being cheerfully sent to meet other wants. He
often preached for the French Protestants in Prussia, who
had suffered much at the hands of the Russians, and collected
as much as fifteen hundred pounds for them (one pound then
was equal to four now). Many of the nobility attended his
chapels while he was making this effort, and the King of
Prussia sent him his thanks for it. At another time he
collected in his chapels, on one day, five hundred and sixty
pounds, for 'the relief of the German Protestants and the
sufferers by fire at Boston.' But on this occasion he resorted
to a strange stratagem. At the close of the sermon, he said:
'We will sing a hymn, during which those who do not choose
to give their mite on this awful occasion may sneak off.' Not
one stirred; he then ordered the doors to be closed, and,
descending from the pulpit, held the plate himself![1] It was
a common thing to make a collection for the orphan hospital
in Edinburgh, when he visited Scotland. He also made a
levy on the generosity of the Glasgow people, and taught them
practical charity, as he did all who heard him. Franklin's

[1] We are not quite sure that this anecdote is authentic; it is inserted
here upon the authority of 'Sketches of the Life and Labours of the Rev.
George Whitefield,' issued by the Committee of the General Assembly of
the Free Church of Scotland.

story of the man who borrowed money for the collection at Philadelphia is matched by a story of Whitefield's power in this Scotch city. An officer, who knew Whitefield's influence, laid a wager with another who was going to hear him with a prejudiced mind, that he would feel himself obliged to give something, notwithstanding his dislike. The wager was accepted; and the challenged man went to church with empty pockets. But Whitefield so moved his heart that he was fain to borrow from his neighbour, and his bet was lost.

In May, 1757, Whitefield was the most highly honoured man in Edinburgh, the next month he was mobbed and stoned in Dublin. Several Scotch towns had previously made him a freeman; and this year he received the marked respect of the ministers of the General Assembly and of the Lord High Commissioner. From the aristocracy of Scotland he went to the Ormond and Liberty Boys of Ireland, and at their hands received the last violence to which he was to be subjected. It was their custom to meet and fight on Oxmanton Green, on Sunday, but when Whitefield had appeared once on the ground, and then came a second time, they turned their strength against him, after he had preached to a vast multitude, and stoned him as, all alone, he was returning home. He writes to a friend that every step he took a fresh stone struck him, and made him reel backwards and forwards, till he 'was almost breathless, and all over a gore of blood.' He thought he should have gone off ' in this bloody triumph to the immediate presence of his Master.' Hatless, wounded, and bleeding, he found a brief shelter in a minister's house, and some friends bringing him a coach, he rode ' in gospel triumph through the oaths, curses, and imprecations of whole streets of Papists,' and without further injury reached Wesley's room. This assault, of which he bore the scar all his life, was entirely owing to his having exhorted all ranks to be faithful to the

Lord Jesus Christ, and to King George, not to his having spoken against Popery.

To escape the danger of open-air preaching was to encounter the danger of ministering in two large chapels all the winter through ; and in the winter 1757–58 Whitefield suffered so much that he was put upon 'the short allowance,' as he called it, of preaching but once a day, and thrice on a Sunday. With so little to do, he began to examine things that were near him ; and finding that round his chapel there was a most beautiful spot of ground, he designed a plan for building twelve alms-houses upon it. Some other 'good folks' agreed with him, and soon one hundred pounds of the necessary four hundred were in his hand. The houses were to be for godly widows, who were to have half a crown a week from the sacrament money. The cost of building them was defrayed by private subscriptions, the public being kept in ignorance of the scheme until the whole sum was promised. In June, 1758, the houses received their first inmates, and stood as 'a monument that the Methodists were not against good works.'

The summer travels of 1758 were begun at Gloucester, and continued into Wales ; and it is grievous to mark the increasing difficulties under which they were undertaken. No trifle ever hindered this willing traveller, but, although he is only forty-four, he is compelled to say to a friend :—

'This tabernacle makes me to groan. The one-horse chaise will not do for me ; as it will not quarter, I am shaken to pieces. Driving likewise wearies me, and prevents my reading ; and if the road be bad my servant that rides the fore-horse is dirtied exceedingly. I have therefore sent to Mr. S——'s about the postchaise, and desired him to beg the favour of you, my dear sir, to look at it, and let me know your thoughts. This is giving you trouble, but you are my friend.'

Possibly the weakness of the body added to the fervour of the spirit, and increased the interest of the congregations.

When he visited Scotland in 1759—his eleventh visit—he exhibited his disinterestedness in a very marked way, by refusing, either for himself personally or for his orphan-house, the estate, both money and lands, valued at seven thousand pounds, of a Miss Hunter, which she offered him.

From the account already given of the kindly feeling of Shuter, the comedian, for Whitefield, and of the visits paid by the chief of actors to the Tabernacle and Tottenham Court Chapel, it might be supposed that actors were among Whitefield's friends; that is to say, that they admired his talents, and respected his character and his calling, while refusing to yield to his warnings and entreaties to seek another profession; but such was not the case. To be inferior to him in histrionic talent would not calm the fretful temper which most of them had. Garrick would doubtless have been better pleased had the public called Whitefield the Garrick of the pulpit, and not himself 'the Whitefield of the stage.' He could not always disguise his pleasure when another actor was burlesqued and mimicked, and his feelings would hardly be more generous towards a Methodist preacher. Dr. Johnson, guided no doubt by what he saw and knew of the actors of his day, never made a truer remark than when he observed, that the stage made 'almost every other man, for whatever reason, contemptuous, insolent, petulant, selfish, and brutal.' To these qualities he might have added—for a description of the staff of actors who are the most brilliant in the history of the English stage— envious, faithless, deceptive. Foote first of all entertained the play-house goers by imitating Whitefield's appearance and manner of speaking. Finding himself so successful, he next wrote a comedy, called the 'Minor,' which affected to kill Methodism by ridicule, and took the chief part in it himself. There is not one happy line in it, and it is as destitute of wit as of piety. There was something in the impudence of the

opening sentence worthy of both author and performer :
‘ What think you of one of those itinerant field-orators, who,
though at declared enmity with common sense, have the
address to poison the principles and, at the same time, pick
the pockets, of half our industrious fellow-subjects ? ’ [1]

Whitefield, on hearing of the merriment of the town at his
expense, simply said, ‘ All hail such contempt ! ’ But his
friends were not content to remain inactive. The Rev. Mr.
Madan wrote to Garrick on the intended representation of the
play at Drury Lane. Lady Huntingdon waited upon the
Lord Chamberlain, the Duke of Devonshire, and applied for
its suppression altogether—a most proper request, apart from
anything that was levelled against Methodists ; for its impurity
condemned it. Yet his lordship could only assure her that
had the evil tendency of the play been found out before it was
licensed, licence would have been refused ; as it was, he could
do nothing immediately. The Countess next appealed to
Garrick, who promised to use his influence in excluding it for
the present, and added ‘ that had he been aware of the offence
that it was calculated to give, it should never have appeared
with his concurrence.’ Nevertheless the offence was continued, yet not to the detriment of Whitefield’s ministry, which
drew crowds of the aristocracy. Foote showed his brutality
by bringing the play upon the stage at Edinburgh within two
months after Whitefield’s death ; but its indecency, combined
with the heartlessness of caricaturing a man who had never
entered the city but to bless it, and who was just dead, emptied
the theatre after the first night, and made many a pulpit

---

[1] The favourite dish of the pocket-picking Mr. Squintum, as Foote,
alluding to Whitefield’s defect, called the greatest of the field-orators, was
a cow-heel. He would cheerfully say, as he sat down to it, ‘ How surprised
would the world be, if they were to peep upon Dr. Squintum, and see
a cow-heel only upon his table.’

thunder out rebukes. Edinburgh had more self-respect than London.

Whitefield was this same year brought into contact with the notorious Earl Ferrers, cousin of Lady Huntingdon. He was tried by his peers for the murder of his steward, Mr. Johnson. His execution was delayed from April 16th to May 5th, an interval which he spent in careless self-indulgence, and in indifference to all the religious solicitude shown in his behalf. Lady Huntingdon restrained him a little, and kept him from appearing utterly shameless. He twice received Whitefield very politely; but his heart was unmoved. His last words before the bolt was drawn were: 'O God, forgive me all my errors; pardon all my sins.'

An unusually sad and weary tone is perceptible in nearly all Whitefield's letters of 1761, nor did he write many. For weeks he did not preach a single sermon; the ability to say but a few words was gratefully received as a little reviving in his bondage. He was beginning to know what nervous disorders are, and was thankful when his friends were prudent, and did not press him to preach much. His prayer was for resignation, so long as the Lord Jesus enforced silence upon him. As to the cause of his weakness and sickness, he thought it was the loss of his usual voyages, which certainly had always been an acceptable cessation of the toils of preaching, if they often brought the quieter and less exhausting toils of writing. Thus he proceeded slowly from place to place, getting as far north as Edinburgh, where he had to say, 'Little, very little, can be expected from a dying man.' It was his old enjoyment, field-preaching, which revived him again. The open sky above his head, the expansive landscape, and the sight and sound of all nature's charms, refreshed him, as an imprisoned Indian would live a new life at the sight and touch of the prairie. 'How gladly would I bid adieu to ceiled

houses and vaulted roofs!' he exclaimed when he resumed his
open-air work.   Yet his revival was only temporary ; winter
prostrated him as much as ever, and he was glad to make
arrangements for sailing to America the following summer.
The condition and wants of Bethesda, and his own feeble
health, seemed to tell him that he must attempt another
voyage.   He accordingly persuaded his friends, Mr. Robert
Keen, a woollen-draper in the Minories, and Mr. Hardy, to
accept the office of trustees to the two London chapels and all
his other concerns in England.   He told them that their compliance with his request would relieve him of a ponderous load
which oppressed him much.   When they accepted the responsibility, he entreated Mr. Keen not to consult him about anything, unless absolutely necessary ; for, he added, 'the Lord,
I trust and believe, will give you a right judgment in all
things.'   In this confidence he was not mistaken ; his friends
proved true to him and to the cause which he served.   But
before we see him on board ship at Greenock, where he embarked for his eleventh voyage, there is one assailant to be
answered (there was a constant fusillade of pamphlets kept up
against him), and a faithful labourer to be laid in his grave.

The assailant was Dr. Warburton, who since 1759 had filled
the place of good Bishop Benson, as Bishop of Gloucester.
Where Whitefield had found kindness and help he was now to
encounter fierce and uncompromising hostility.   Warburton
was totally opposed to the doctrines of Methodism, and the
success they had gained in the land was a sufficient reason for
his attempting to demolish them.   Even before the death of
the charitable Doddridge, he showed his dislike of enthusiasm
in a characteristic way by rating Lady Huntingdon and
Doddridge in Lady Huntingdon's house, where he was paying
the dying man a farewell visit before his departure for Lisbon.
Neither the politeness due from guest to hostess, nor the con-

sideration due to a feeble friend, could restrain his vehement temper. On another occasion he provoked a skirmish at Prior Park—afterwards his own residence—where he met Dr. Hartley, Dr. Oliver, Mr. Allen, and Lady Huntingdon. Dr. Hartley having spoken in laudatory terms of Whitefield's abilities, and respectfully of his doctrines, Warburton remarked, 'Of his oratorical powers and their astonishing influence on the minds of thousands, there can be no doubt : they are of a high order ; but with respect to his doctrines, I consider them pernicious and false.' The conversation grew into a debate, and the debate became so warm that Warburton, pressed by argument and sorely ruffled in temper, hastily left the room, no doubt leaving as many marks as he carried with him. He was now to strike a heavier and more effective blow at 'the false and pernicious doctrines,' which were spreading and triumphing on every hand.

The work he wrote was called a vindication of the office and operations of the Holy Spirit from the insults of infidelity and the abuses of fanaticism. As by Bishop Gibson, at whose hands Warburton had received ordination to the priest's office, so by Warburton, the fanatics were more warmly assailed than the infidels. Indeed, the word used by Warburton is less courteous than Gibson's ; with Gibson the Methodists were 'enthusiasts' ; with Warburton they are 'fanatics.' Nay, fanatics on the title-page is changed into 'fools' in the preface ; it was more than he could do to treat a Methodist with fairness and charity.

His book might have done one great service to the Church had it been devoted only to the discussion of a question which he introduces as but a stepping-stone to his conclusions against the infidels and the fanatics, namely, the inspiration of Holy Scripture. His sober, thoughtful view of that great subject might have saved Christianity from many a reproach had it been commonly adopted by the believers of our faith. But the conclusion he wanted to reach was something subversive of the Methodistical belief concerning the operations of the Holy Ghost upon the heart of man; substantially the same view which Bishop Gibson had advanced against 'enthusiasm,' but supported by a greater show of reasoning.

To these views Whitefield wrote an answer, in the form of a letter to a friend, which he called 'Observations on some fatal mistakes in a book lately published, and entitled, &c.' He fairly and exactly summed up the bishop's reasoning by saying that, in effect, it robbed the Church of its promised Comforter, and thereby left us without any supernatural influence or Divine operations whatsoever. Left in this forlorn state, and yet told by the bishop that charity is the one thing which is to abide in the Church for ever, Whitefield asks with pertinence and force: 'Now, can human reason, with all its heights; can calm philosophy, with all its depths; or moral suasion, with all its insinuating arts, so much as pretend to kindle, much less to maintain and blow up into a settled, habitual flame of holy fire, such a spark as this in the human heart?' Upon our ability to do without the Holy Ghost he remarked with a pungency which Warburton must have felt keenly: 'Supposing matters to be as this writer represents them, I do not see what great need we have of any established rule at all, at least in respect to practice, since corrupt nature is abundantly sufficient of itself to help us to persevere in a religion attended with ease and honour. And I verily believe that the Deists throw aside this rule of faith entirely, not barely on account of a deficiency in argument to support its authenticity, but because they daily see so many who profess to hold this established, self-denying rule of faith with their lips, persevering all their lives long in nothing else but an endless and insatiable pursuit after worldly ease and honour.'

He proceeds : 'The Scriptures are so far from encouraging us to plead for a diminution of Divine influence in these last days of the gospel, because an external rule of faith is thereby established, that, on the contrary, we are encouraged by this very established rule to expect, hope, long, and pray for larger and more extensive showers of Divine influence than any former age hath ever yet experienced.'

It is not without interest to observe that Whitefield's first and last discussion was with a bishop, and upon the doctrine of the Holy Ghost. Years of labour had only strengthened his persuasion that the Comforter still abides personally with believers, and that without His action upon the heart no man can be led into the new life in Christ Jesus.

Before Whitefield sails we must notice the death of his friend Grimshaw, which occurred on April 7, 1763. Probably they met at Leeds, as Whitefield travelled north in March, for he seldom got so near Haworth without affording himself the pleasure of preaching there. No such startling and appalling, as well as happy, effects had ever attended his ministry as were felt there. It was as if the very voice of God were speaking, when once he cried out to a man who had seated himself on the tower of the church : 'Man, I have a word for thee ;' that man was afterwards found among Grimshaw's converts. More solemn was the effect of his words on another occasion. He was standing on the scaffold which used to be erected for these outside gatherings ; worship had been offered by the congregation ; the time for the sermon had come ; all eyes were turned upon him and all ears waiting for his first words, when he was seen to spend a few moments in silent prayer. Silently they waited ; then looking round upon them, he lifted up his hands and earnestly invoked the presence and working of the Holy Ghost. A little while longer, and he announced with solemn voice and manner the solemn text : 'It is appointed

unto men once to die, but after this the judgment.' He
paused, and while he did so 'a wild shriek of terror arose from
amidst the mass.' Some confusion followed, but Whitefield
exhorted the people to remain still, while Grimshaw pressed
into the crowd to see what had happened. Hastening back
in a few minutes, he said as he approached the scaffold:
'Brother Whitefield, you stand amongst the dead and the
dying; an immortal soul has been called into eternity; the
destroying angel is passing over the congregation; cry aloud
and spare not!' The people were then told that one of their
number had died. A second time the text was announced:
'It is appointed unto men once to die.' Again, from the spot
where Lady Huntingdon and Lady Margaret Ingham were
standing, arose a second shriek; and a shudder of awe ran
through every heart when it was known that a second person
had died. Not overcome by the terror of the scene, but
strengthened by the secret Helper whose grace he had implored,
Whitefield commenced again, and proceeded, 'in a strain of
tremendous eloquence,' to warn the impenitent of their perilous
position. Fear and eager interest were in all hearts as the
silent, motionless congregation listened to his word.

Such preaching as this might lead to the opinion that
Whitefield was always either solemn or vehement; but really
no one could have tried more ways than he; and faithful as
he was, he was not always faithful enough for the stern preacher
of the moors. It was common for him to expose the mistakes
and pretensions of professors of religion, and getting on that
topic before Grimshaw's congregation, it occurred to him that
his remarks could hardly be appropriate to them; he therefore
proceeded to say that as they had long enjoyed the ministry
of a faithful pastor, they must surely be a sincerely godly people,
when Grimshaw interrupted him, and cried out, 'Oh, sir, for
God's sake do not speak so; I pray you do not flatter them;

I fear the greater part of them are going to hell with their eyes open ! '

If Grimshaw was not mistaken in this judgment, which was probably spoken early in his ministry, a great change must have passed over his congregation through his labours. He afterwards assured Romaine that not fewer than twelve hundred people were in communion with him ; most of whom, in the judgment of charity, he could not but believe to be one with Christ. The church could not hold the number who some-times came to communicate, and one congregation would with-draw for another to fill its place. In one instance, when Whitefield was present, thirty-five bottles of wine were used in the ordinance.

The complaint which carried Grimshaw off was putrid fever, caught by him in visiting his flock, among whom it was work-ing most fatally. For one-and-twenty years had he proved himself a good minister ; not one soul was there in all the district of his travels with whose spiritual condition he was unacquainted ; and after he died no parishioner could hear his name without tears.

It may have been Grimshaw that Whitefield was specially thinking of when he said, ' Others can die, but I cannot.' Weak and weary he preached in Scotland several times. Ready to fall, as it seemed, yet able to do something, he sailed for America the sixth time on June 4, 1763, and after a twelve week's voyage landed in Virginia. The war between England and France had kept him absent from America eight years.

' Jesus,' he says, ' hath made the ship a Bethel, and I enjoyed that quiet-ness which I have in vain sought after for some years on shore. Not an oath to be heard, even in the greatest hurry. All hath been harmony and love. But my breath is short, and I have little hopes since my last relapse of much further public usefulness. A few exertions, like the last struggles of a dying man, or glimmering flashes of a taper just burning out, is all that can be expected from me.   But, blessed be God, the taper will be lighted up again in heaven.'

From Virginia he proceeded northwards to Philadelphia, New York, and Boston ; and was so much strengthened by the cold as to be able to preach thrice a week.   There was such a flocking of all ranks in New York to his preaching as he had never seen there before.   It was in this city that he gained one of his greatest oratorical conquests ; and a comparison of the anecdote with that which relates Chesterfield's excitement will serve to show his mastery over all classes of people.   On this occasion he was preaching before the seamen of New York—

'when suddenly, assuming a nautical tone and manner that were irresistible, he thus suddenly broke in with, "Well, my boys, we have a clear sky, and are making fine headway over a smooth sea, before a light breeze, and we shall soon lose sight of land.   But what means this sudden lowering of the heavens, and that dark cloud rising from beneath the western horizon ? Hark ! don't you hear distant thunder ?   Don't you see those flashes of lightning ?   There is a storm gathering ! every man to his duty !   How the waves arise and dash against the ship !   The air is dark !   The tempest rages !   Our masts are gone !   The ship is on her beam ends !   What next ?" '

This appeal instantly brought the sailors to their feet with a shout, ' Take to the long boat !'

His power to engage the attention of ship-builders was as great as that of exciting sailors, one builder declaring that he could build a ship from stem to stern every Sunday under the sermon at the parish church, but could not get a plank down when Whitefield preached.

Still, his success was not uniform, only he would have success if it could be gained.   If the fault were in his own heart, he would pray, while he preached, for help from above.   If the fault were in his hearers, he would correct it; if they were thoughtless, he would charge them with it as they sat; if they were stupid and uninterested, he would ask them whether he were preaching to men or to stones. Dr. Young is said to have sat down and wept when his royal hearers slept during his sermon; but Whitefield would have done something very different—most likely what he did to a small American congregation on a rainy day. A curious student from Princeton (New Jersey) College was present, and has told the story. The first part of the sermon made no impression upon the student, and he began to say to himself, 'This man is not so great a wonder after all. His ideas are all commonplace and superficial—mere show, and not a great deal even of that.' The congregation seemed as uninterested as himself, one old man who sat in front of the pulpit having fallen sound asleep! Whitefield now stopped; his face darkened with a frown; and changing his tone, he cried out, 'If I had come to speak to you in my own name, you might rest your elbows on your knees, and your heads upon your hands, and sleep; and once in a while look up and say, "What does the babbler talk of?" But I have not come to you in my own name. No: I come to you in the name of the Lord of Hosts'—here he brought his hand and foot down with a force that made the building ring—'and I must and will be heard!' The congregation started, and the old man awoke. 'Ay, ay,' said Whitefield, fixing his eyes on him, 'I have waked you up, have I? I meant to do it. I am not come here to preach to stocks and stones; I have come to you in the name of the Lord God of Hosts, and I must, and I will, have an audience.' There was no more sleeping or indolence that day.

Other things besides preaching filled his mind when, after a long delay in the north of the colonies, caused by bad health and the unsettled state of the Indians, he travelled to Bethesda, and reached it, as he had so often done before, in time to spend Christmas with the orphans. It had long been his wish to add to the orphanage a college like New Jersey, for the training of gentlemen's sons ; and now, along with the pleasure which he felt in seeing the peace and plenty of his cherished retreat, he had the satisfaction of thinking that his second project would be accomplished. He memorialised the governor, James Wright, Esq., setting forth in his petition that in addition to his original plan, which he had carried out these many years at great expense, he had long wished to make further provision for the education of persons of superior rank, who might thus be fitted for usefulness, either in Church or State ; that he witnessed with pleasure the increasing prosperity of the province, but saw with concern that many gentlemen, who would have preferred having their sons educated nearer home, had been obliged to send them to the northern provinces ; that a college in Georgia would be a central institution for the whole of the southern district, and might even count upon many youths being sent from the British West India Islands and other parts ; that a considerable sum of money was soon to be laid out in purchasing a large number of Negroes, for the further cultivation of the orphan-house and other additional lands, and for the future support of ' a worthy, able president, professors and tutors, and other good purposes intended ' ; he therefore prayed his Excellency and the members of his Majesty's Council to grant him in trust two thousand acres of land on the north fork of Turtle River, or lands south of the river Altamaha. This memorial was supported by an earnest 'Address of both Houses of Assembly,' which bore the signature of James Habersham as president. His Excellency gave a favourable answer, and referred the matter to the home authorities ; and Whitefield returned to support it.

Work and sickness had wrought a striking change in his appearance when he ended his twelfth voyage. That his health must have been grievously broken is evident from his touching appeal to his friends Keen and Hardy: 'Stand, my friends,' he said, 'and insist upon my not being brought into action too soon. The poor old shattered barque hath not been in dock one week, for a long while. I scarce know what I write. Tender love to all.' Asthma had now firmly seated itself in his constitution, and he felt sure that he should never breathe as he would, till he breathed in yonder heaven. Wesley was painfully struck when he met him towards the close of the year in London. 'I breakfasted,' he says in his journal, 'with Mr. Whitefield, who seemed to be an old, old man, being fairly worn out in his Master's service, though he has hardly seen fifty years; and yet it pleases God that I, who am now in my sixty-third year, find no disorder, no weakness, no decay, no difference from what I was at five-and-twenty, only that I have fewer teeth and more grey hairs.' A month later Wesley again wrote in his journal: 'Mr. Whitefield called upon me. He breathes nothing but peace and love. Bigotry cannot stand before him, but hides its head wherever he comes.'

The silver cord was not even yet to be loosed, although the body appeared to be ready for the grave, and the soul for heaven. Lady Huntingdon was increasing the number of her chapels. She had one at Brighton, which was partly due to Whitefield's preaching under a tree behind the White Lion Inn; she had another at Norwich; and a third at Tunbridge Wells; and when she had got one finished at Bath, Whitefield must needs open it. He went and preached one of the sermons on October 6, 1765. It was a chapel in which many of the witty and the learned were to hear his expositions of truth. It had also a strange corner, called 'Nicodemus's Corner,' into which Lady Betty Cobbe, daughter-in-law of the Archbishop of Dublin, used to smuggle bishops, whom she had persuaded to go and hear Whitefield, but who did not want to be seen in such a place as an unconsecrated chapel. The curtained seats just inside the door were both convenient and secret.

And how was the plan for a college at Bethesda prospering? First of all Whitefield waited a long time, to give the home authorities the fullest opportunities for maturing their thoughts; but by delay they intended hindrance, not help. He therefore memorialised his Majesty, praying that since the colonists were deeply interested in the scheme, and were impatiently waiting for information, something might be done. Now came the intricacies of 'red-tape.' The original memorial of Whitefield, supported by the 'Address' of the colonial Houses of Assembly, was remitted to the Lords Commissioners for Trade and Plantations, and they sent it to the Archbishop of Canterbury, who effectually frustrated its intention by a bigoted demand that the charter of the college, were one granted, should contain a clause making it obligatory to appoint none but a member of the Church of England to the office of head-master. To this demand Whitefield offered respectful but uncompromising opposition. He would have no exceptional privilege for a Churchman; he would not have the daily use of the liturgy enjoined; he would not have one doctrinal article entered in the charter. His letter to the archbishop stating and defending his views is as noble and catholic a production as ever came from his pen, while its references to himself and his toils are as pathetic as they are modest. Why did he object to a compulsory clause respecting the master? Was he opposed to the Church of England? By no means; the majority of the wardens were sure to be of that communion, and their choice would be sure to fall upon a master like them-selves in belief; but choice and compulsion were very different things.   Did he dislike the liturgy?   No; he loved it, and had injured himself by his frequent reading of it in Tottenham Court Chapel; moreover, it had been read twice every Sunday in the orphan-house from the day of the first institution of the house.   Did he disbelieve the doctrinal articles?   No : on the contrary, his acceptance of them was as literal and honest as man could give, and he had preached and upheld them everywhere.   The whole question turned upon freedom or compulsion.   As for the orphan-house, Whitefield thought that an institution to which Dr. Benson had made a dying bequest, and for which he had offered his dying prayers, had some claim upon the archbishop also.

All that he could say could not move either the archbishop or the Lord President; for was not the memorialist a Methodist? and was he not pleading for liberty of thought and action?   In reply to their remarks upon the disputed points, Whitefield said that, in addition to all the reasons already given, his truthfulness was at stake, and he might not trifle with it. From the first, whenever he had been asked 'upon what bottom the intended college was to be founded,' he had repeatedly and readily replied, 'Undoubtedly upon a broad bottom'; he had even gone so far as to say from the pulpit that it should be upon 'a broad bottom and no other,' and how could he now withdraw from his word?   More than that, most of the money which he had collected for the orphan-house had been given by Dissenters, and could he be so basely ungrateful as to deny them admission to the very place which their liberality had created and sustained?   If it were asked by what warrant he had said that the college should stand only on a liberal charter, he replied, 'Because of the known, long-established, mild, and uncoercive genius of the English Government; because of his Grace's moderation towards Protestant Dissenters; because of the unconquerable attachment of the

Americans to toleration principles; because of the avowed habitual feelings and sentiments of his own heart.' He wrote as feeling that his very piety and salvation were involved in the position he assumed, and his last words to the archbishop are well worth preserving :—

'If I know anything of my own heart, I have no ambition to be looked upon at present, or remembered for the future, as a founder of a college; but I would fain, may it please your Grace, act the part of an honest man, a disinterested minister of Jesus Christ, and a truly catholic, moderate presbyter of the Church of England. In this way, and in this only, can I hope for a continued heartfelt enjoyment of that peace of God which passeth all understanding, whilst here on earth, and be thereby prepared to stand with humble boldness before the awful, impartial tribunal of the great Shepherd and Bishop of souls at the great day.'

His plan was defeated. In order to uphold his reputation in America, he published his correspondence with the archbishop, and sent it to the Governor of Georgia for circulation. To come as near his idea as possible, he now proposed to add a public academy to the orphan-house, and to form a proper trust, to act after his decease, or even before, with this proviso, that no opportunity should be omitted of making a fresh application for a college charter, 'upon a broad bottom, whenever those in power might think it for the glory of God and the interest of their king and country to grant the same.' Thus his beloved Bethesda would not only be continued as a house of mercy for orphans, but be confirmed as a seat and nursery of sound learning and religious education to the latest posterity. Great and worthy aspirations, which were doomed to disappointment!

In 1768 six students of St. Edmund Hall, Oxford, were expelled from the university for holding Methodistical tenets, for taking upon them to pray, read, and expound the Scriptures, for singing hymns in private houses, and for being tradesmen before entering as students. But their judges did not escape public censure. It was to be expected that the Methodists would be against them ; they were also opposed by men of equal standing in the Church with themselves. Whitefield could not let the matter pass without notice ; and he wrote and published a letter to Dr. Durell, the vice-chancellor, besides showing the students much private sympathy. As to the charges, what evil or crime worthy of expulsion, he asked, could there be in having followed a trade before entering the university? and whoever heard of its being accounted a disparagement to any great public character that he had once been a mechanic? Why, David was a shepherd, and even Jesus of Nazareth was a carpenter. But the delinquents had been found guilty of praying. And how could that, he demanded, disqualify them for the private or public discharge of their ministerial functions? But it was extempore prayer that they had used. Extempore prayer a crime! It was not a crime to be found in any law book, neither had any one been called before the bar of any public court of judicature to answer for it for at least a century. Expelled for extempore praying! Then it was high time there were some expulsions for extempore swearing, which was surely the greater sin of the two. But these men sang hymns. Yes, he replied, and so did David; and this very exercise of praise are we taught by St. Paul to cultivate. Praise! Well, Catholic students might sing ; then why not Protestants? Ought Protestants to be less devout than Papists? And if the Duke of Cumberland allowed his pious soldiers to sing, why should the Vice-Chancellor of a University forbid his pious students? Or was there more harm in hearing a psalm-tune than in listening to the noise of box and dice, which was not an unknown sound even at Oxford?

Thus far his polemics. We must now follow him to other engagements. As if with an expectation of soon dying, he now began to collect his numerous letters ; and to them we are indebted, along with his journals, for the best story of his life. He felt that another voyage to America, whither he must go again on account of Bethesda's affairs, would probably be the last ; and he begged his friends Keen and Hardy to let him have his papers and letters, that he might revise and dispose of them in a proper manner.

It was in June and July, 1768, that he paid his fourteenth and last visit to Edinburgh, always a dear city to him. He thanked God for ordering his steps thither. The congregations in the orphan-house park were as large and attentive as those which he addressed when he was called 'a godly youth' by his friends, and a 'minister of the devil' by his enemies. Great was their affection for him, and his only danger was that of 'being hugged to death ;' for there were friends of twenty-seven years' standing, and spiritual children of the same age, who remembered the days of old. They were seeking after their first love ; and the Spirit of God seemed to be moving amongst them. He often got into the open air upon what he was beginning fondly to call his 'throne'; and indeed he was a king of men when there. 'O to die there !' he exclaimed ; then checking himself, he added, 'Too great, too great an honour to be expected !' No doubt the parting was as painful as any he had ever known ; and he was wont to call parting days 'execution days.'

Soon after his return to London, Mrs. Whitefield was seized with an 'inflammatory fever,' and died on August 9, 1768. He preached her funeral sermon from Romans viii. 20, 'For the creature was made subject to vanity, not willingly, but by reason of Him who hath subjected the same in hope.' Speaking of her fortitude, he observed :—

'Do you remember my preaching in those fields by the old stump of a tree? The multitude was great, and many were disposed to be riotous. A first I addressed them firmly ; but when a desperate gang drew near, with the most ferocious and horrid imprecations and menaces, my courage began to fail. My wife was then standing behind me, as I stood on the table. I think I hear her now. She pulled my gown, and, looking up, said, "George, play the man for your God." My confidence returned. I spoke to the multitude with boldness and affection. They became still, and many were deeply affected.'

He afterwards called her death an 'unexpected breach,' and said that he felt the loss of his 'right hand' daily.

He might quickly have followed his wife to the grave, for within a month of her death he burst a vein by hard riding and frequent preaching. Rest and quietness were enjoined upon him until the flux was quite stopped. The fact is, he had been in Wales, and it was not easy to keep himself within bounds among the fiery, rapturous Welsh. Moreover, he had been attending a significant ceremony—the opening of a college for the education of godly young men who aspired to be ministers. The Countess of Huntingdon had for some time purposed founding such an institution ; and on the anniversary of her birthday, August 24, 1768, Trevecca House, in the parish of Talgarth, South Wales, was dedicated by her to a new purpose, and was afterwards known as Trevecca College. Whitefield opened both the college and the chapel attached to it ; and on the following Sunday, he preached in the court before the college, to a congregation of some thousands. The college was removed to Cheshunt, Herts, August 24, 1792.

The winter of 1768–69 was spent by Whitefield in London ; it was the last but one he lived to see. He was well enough to preach frequently; it was always with the same power of the Spirit ; and as we shall not again find him among his London friends, it may be best now to notice some of his habits and characteristics which have not yet been mentioned. We know how neat and punctual he was in his younger days, and he was not different as an old man. It was a great fault for his meals to be but a few minutes late ; and he would suffer no sitting up after ten o'clock at night, and no lying in bed after four in the morning. He would rise up abruptly in the midst of a conversation at ten at night, and say, ' But we forget ourselves. Come, gentlemen, it is time for all good folks to be at home.' Whether any one or no one sat down to table with him, and whether he had but bread and cheese or a complete dinner, the table must be properly spread. His love of exactness and order was the same in business trans-actions ; every article was paid for at once, and for small articles the money was taken in the hand. His temper was soon ruffled, but quickly appeased. Not being patient enough one day to hear an explanation of a fault from some one who was studious to please, he gave much pain, and saw it by the tears which he started ; this instantly touched him with grief, and bursting into tears himself, he said, ' I shall live to be a poor peevish old man, and every one will be tired of me.' His commands were given kindly, and he always applauded when a person did right.

It is painful to learn that in his later years his confidence in mankind was much shaken. Always true to his friends in all fortunes, he yet was doomed to feel the treachery of many ; and on that account he seemed to dread outliving his useful-ness. The same experience made him exacting, and almost harsh, with young men who wanted to be ministers. To curb their vanity, as he would say, he would place them in humiliating circumstances, and then refer to the young Roman orators, who, after being applauded, were sent upon trifling errands. He would keep them in suspense, and afford them little or no encouragement. One man, who answered him that he was a tailor, was dismissed with, ' Go to rag-fair, and buy old clothes ;' and very likely rag-fair was his proper destination. He said of another who had preached in his vestry from the text, 'These that have turned the world upside down, have come hither also.' 'That man shall come no more here; if God had called him to preach, He would have furnished him with a proper text.' He judged rightly; for the man afterwards became an inconsistent clergyman; he too would have been best at rag-fair.

Tormented as he must have been with all kinds of visitors and all kinds of requests, had he kept an open door, he wisely suffered but few to see him freely. 'Who is it? what is his business?' he would demand before his door was opened; and if the door was opened, he would say, 'Tell him to come to-morrow morning at six o'clock, perhaps five, or immediately after preaching; if he is later, I cannot see him.'

Knowing that he sometimes preached an hour and a half or two hours, it prepares us for long prayers also; and perhaps if others had prayed as well as he preached he might have borne with them. But he hated all unreality. In the middle of an immoderately long prayer by the master of the house where he was once staying, he rose from his knees and sat down in the chair; when the drawler concluded, he said to him with a frown, 'Sir, you prayed me into a good frame, and you prayed me out of it again.'

We have seen that he was like old Mr. Cole in his use of anecdotes, nor were they always without a touch of humour. He was no more afraid of his congregations smiling than weeping; to get the truth into their hearts and heads was his object. His observant habits gathered illustrations from all quarters; and the last book he had read was sure to colour his next sermon.

He always ascended the pulpit with a pale, serious face, and a slow, calm step, as if he had a great message for the expectant thousands. Much preaching made him, not more familiar with his awful themes, but more solemn; and towards the close of life, he sometimes entreated his friends to mention nothing to him which did not relate to eternity.   On Sabbath morning his preaching was explanatory and doctrinal ; in the afternoon it was more general and hortatory ; and in the evening it was more general still.   In the morning he was calm and conversational, occasionally making a modest show of learning ; in the evening he was oratorical, and attempted by every art of persuasion and every terror of denunciation to save his hearers from sin and its punishment.   Then his perfect elocution and graceful gestures were in full play, his uttermost acting never appearing unnatural or improper.   It is difficult to believe that any preacher could successfully put a fold of his gown over his eyes to express grief, yet Whitefield invariably did it when he was depicting in his own vivid way the downfall of Peter, and grieving over it.

He seemed to have no particular time for preparing for the pulpit, although before entering it he loved to have an hour or two alone ; and on Sunday mornings he generally had Clarke's Bible, Matthew Henry's Commentary, and Cruden's Concordance within reach.   It was remarked also that at this time his state of mind was more than usually devout ; but ordinarily, indeed, the intervals of conversation were filled up with private ejaculations of praise and prayer, notwithstanding his love of pleasantry, which he did not care to suppress.   His was an honest, real life from beginning to end ; he was himself at all times and everywhere.

He did not love to be known and observed wherever he went.   If he ever was fond of popularity, he was weary of it long before he became old, and often said that he almost 'envied the man who could take his choice of food at an eating-house, and pass unnoticed.'

It is said that when he wrote his pamphlets, he shut himself up in his room, and would see no one until his work was done. Besides the productions of his pen already noticed, he wrote a 'Recommendatory Preface to the Works of John Bunyan,' which would have been more appropriately called a recommendation of Puritans and Puritan divinity ; it contains not one discriminating remark on the writings of the dreamer. Early in his ministry he began some 'Observations on select passages of Scripture, turned into catechetical questions,' which are much like questions that an ordinary Sunday school teacher would put to his class ; but they were soon discontinued. A more elaborate work was 'Law Gospelised,' which means 'an attempt to render Mr. Law's "Serious Call," more useful to the children of God, by excluding whatever is not truly evangelical, and illustrating the subject more fully from the Holy Scriptures.' We never hear of Law in this evangelical garb now, though we do hear of him without it. He has been preferred ungospelised. 'A Communion Morning's Companion,' which he compiled, contained extracts from Bishop Ken and Bishop Wilson and fifty-nine sacramental hymns and seventeen doxologies taken from several authors ; the book was a public favourite. Whitefield also published 'Pious Aspirations for the use of Devout Communicants,' a book of quotations from a work of Professor Rambach, of Giessen University. Whitefield published several prayers, some of which are most appropriate in petition and language. Their titles are a leaf of Church history, and the petitions contained in some are as plain an index to passing conditions of life as are the peculiarities of the psalms. They were composed for persons desiring and seeking after the new birth, for those newly awakened to a sense of the Divine life, for those under spiritual desertion, for those under the displeasure of relations for being religious ; then come the cases of servants, Negroes, labourers, rich men, the sick, travellers, sailors, and persons in a storm at sea.

In 1753 Whitefield published 'Hymns for Social Worship,' a collection of hymns from various authors, 'more particularly designed for the use of the Tabernacle Congregation in London.' He drew most of its hundred and seventy hymns from Watts, and many from the Wesleys. The book, which was quickly followed by Wesley's 'Hymns and Spiritual Songs' and a Moravian Hymn Book, passed through thirty-six editions in forty-three years. It contained a preface addressed to the 'Courteous Reader,' and is as like the author as Wesley's famous preface to his book of 1779 is like him. Whitefield himself has left no great hymn to the Church, though the Methodist revival gave the English Church in all its branches the greater number of its best hymns. Watts, John and Charles Wesley, Doddridge, Cennick, Olivers, Toplady, and others, all of them either taking an active part in the movement or coming within the range of its influence, have expressed for us the humblest grief of our repentance, the fullest trust of our faith, and the brightest expectation of our hope; but Whitefield has given us not a verse worth retaining. Emotional, like Charles Wesley, he yet had none of that fervid poet's music. One gift in a supreme degree is enough for any man; and as a preacher he was the greatest of all his brethren, the most competent of his contemporaries being judges.

The only direct association of Whitefield's name with the names of the brilliant and gifted men of his time has already appeared in the narrative of his preaching triumphs. It was principally statesmen—Pitt and Fox among the number, never Burke—who went to hear him. Hogarth disgraced his genius by some indecent caricatures of him; Pope by abusing him in the Dunciad. Not one of the celebrated Literary Club, Garrick excepted, was ever seen in the 'soul-trap.' Oglethorpe makes a kind of link between the Club and the Tabernacle. A friend of Whitefield, he was also a friend of Goldsmith; and some-

times he and Topham Beauclerc would turn in of an evening
to drink a glass of wine with 'Goldy,' at his chambers in Brick
Court, Middle Temple—the chambers which he bought with
the proceeds of the play that Shuter lifted into popularity. But
the easy ways of many of these sons of genius, their wine-
sipping, when they could get it, their comfortable suppers at
the 'Turk's Head,' their gaiety and their sins, sufficiently explain
how it was that in all Whitefield's career not one of them crossed
his path. They talked about him, as they talked about everything and everybody; they theorised about his popularity;
Johnson was sure that it was 'chiefly owing to the peculiarity
of his manner. He would be followed by crowds were he to
wear a night-cap in the pulpit, or were he to preach from a tree.'
For a while; but the night-cap would not have made grasping
men give of their beloved money to the orphan-house, nor
hardened sinners go home as gentle as lambs, nor worldly
wretches, who had been living only for the body and for this
life, begin to lift up their abject souls to look towards the
splendours and joys of a heavenly kingdom!

We turn again with him to the places which he had loved
to frequent, and where his form has become familiar to us. It
is the last interview between Whitefield and Wesley that
Wesley records in his journal on Monday (their old meeting
day), February 27, 1769. He says: 'I had one more agreeable conversation with my old friend and fellow-labourer,
George Whitefield. His soul appeared to be vigorous still,
but his body was sinking apace; and unless God interposes
with His mighty hand, he must soon finish his labours.' And
this is a pleasant picture of the now aged, grey-headed
evangelists, who in their youth had fired the nation with
religious enthusiasm, which is sketched by Charles Wesley in
a letter to his wife: 'Last Friday I dined with my brother at
George's chapel. Mrs. Herritage was mistress, and provided

the dinner.   Hearty Mr. Adams was there ; and to complete
our band, Howel Harris.   It was indeed a feast of love.   My
brother and George prayed : we all sang an hymn in the chapel.'
They were never all together again in this world.   Their last
hymn in ' George's chapel ' carries the soul up to that house
in the heavens, and we seem to hear it renewed again there.

The parting solemnities were exceedingly awful, when, early
in September, 1769, Whitefield, accompanied by Cornelius
Winter, took his last farewell of his English friends.   His
thirteenth voyage much resembled his first ; it was hindered
by similar delays ; it was made dangerous by similar high gales.
He took to his old employment when sailing, of reading the
History of England, composing sermons, and writing letters.
The greatest respect was shown him by both captain and
passengers ; and all attended service.   He only wanted some-
body about him with ' a little more brains,' he said, and then
his comforts would have been complete.

His reception at Charleston was very hearty, and he
preached the day after landing.   Bethesda was in a satisfactory
condition ; he admitted ten orphans in the spring of 1770.
They were what he called his prizes.   The peace and happiness of the place were his daily joy ; and thus Bethesda, after
all the trouble it had cost him, after all his prayers, and tears,
and pleadings for it, was to minister largely to the comfort of
his last days.   His health continued better than it had been
for years ; and when summer approached he started on his
old preaching circuit in the north.   Invitations crowded in
upon him ; and he travelled from place to place as if the
vigour of his youth were renewed.   During one month, July,
he travelled five hundred miles, riding and preaching during
the heat of every day.

How like the language of his youth is that which he penned
at New York to his friend Keen :—

'O what a new scene of usefulness is opening in various parts of this new world ! All fresh work where I have been. The Divine influence hath been as at the first. Invitations crowded upon me, both from ministers and people, from many, many quarters. A very peculiar providence led me lately to a place where a horse-stealer was executed ; thousands attended. The poor criminal had sent me several letters, hearing I was in the country. The sheriff allowed him to come and hear a sermon under an adjacent tree. Solemn ! solemn ! After being by himself about an hour, I walked half a mile with him to the gallows. His heart had been softened before my first visit. He seemed full of solid, Divine consolations. An instructive walk ! I went up with him into the cart. He gave a short exhortation. I then stood upon the coffin, added, I trust, a word in season, prayed, gave the blessing, and took my leave.'

This was not the first execution he had been present at. He pressed all things into the service of the pulpit, and was wont to make even the final scenes of a criminal's career give effect to the urgency and solemnity of his appeals and warnings. At the close of a sermon, and after pausing for a moment, he would say, *with his eyes full of tears* and his heart almost too big for words : ' I am going now to put on my condemning cap. Sinner, I must do it ; I must pronounce sentence upon you.' Then, like a peal of thunder, fell the terrible curse, ' Depart from Me, ye cursed, into everlasting fire, prepared for the devil and his angels.'

It was now eventide with him ; only one week of life remained. There was a hush and quietness gathering round the close of his marvellous ministry, which seemed to tell of coming rest for the weary and broken servant. Opposition was silent ; none spoke or wrote a word against him. The people, as if they expected to see his face no more, clung to him, and were unwilling to let him leave their towns and villages, through which he was still attempting to travel on his evangelistic work. But it was not always he could meet them when they had assembled together ; for the body was being shaken to its fall. They were, he said, but 'poor efforts he could make to serve his Lord.   O for a warm heart !   O to stand fast in the faith—to quit ourselves like men and be strong !'   To the letter which contains this prayer, he sub-scribed himself, as was now his way, 'LESS THAN THE LEAST OF ALL, GEORGE WHITEFIELD.'   It was the last he penned, and well did it harmonise with one of the strongest wishes he had ever made known to God—the wish to be humble.

On Friday, September 28th, he preached at Portsmouth, and on the following morning started for Boston, travelling by way of Exeter and Newbury Port, in order to fulfil an engage-ment at the latter place on the Sunday.   But the people of Exeter could not let him pass without his giving them a sermon ; and he yielded to their entreaties.   He had ridden fifteen miles that morning, and, as he was more than usually uneasy, one remarked to him before going out to preach, 'Sir, you are more fit to go to bed than to preach.'   Whitefield remarked, 'True sir ' ; then turning aside, he clasped his hands together, and looking up, said, 'Lord Jesus, I am weary in Thy work, but not of Thy work.   If I have not yet finished my course, let me go and speak for Thee once more in the fields, seal Thy truth, and come home and die.'   The Lord heard his request.   He went out, and, taking his stand on a hogshead for a pulpit, preached in the fields for nearly two hours to a large congregation, at first slowly and with great effort, then with all his wonted animation and power, 'his countenance,' says a spectator, 'shining like the unclouded sun.'   Then he dined, and went forward to Newbury Port with a dear old friend, the Rev. Jonathan Parsons.   In the evening he was tired, and after an early supper, of which he partook very sparingly, begged Mr. Parsons, at whose house he was staying, to have family prayer, so that he might retire to rest at once.   Meanwhile the pavement in front of the house and the hall became crowded with people who wanted to hear some

words of grace and truth from his lips; but he felt himself unequal to the task of addressing them, and said to another
clergyman, 'Brother, you must speak to these dear people; I
cannot say a word.' To his friend and companion, Mr.
Richard Smith, who slept in the same room with him, he said,
'I will sit and read till you come to me.' But there were the
waiting people to be passed, as, with candle in hand, he went
to his bedroom; and his heart strove with him to say something. He halted on the staircase, turned towards them, and
began an exhortation. Tearful eyes were lifted up to him,
while his words flowed on and ceased not 'until the candle,
which he still held, burned away, and went out in its socket.'

When his friend entered his room, Whitefield was found
reading the Bible, with Watts' psalms lying open before him.
After committing himself into the hands of God, he went to
rest, and slept, with the window half-open, till two in the
morning, when an attack of asthma seized him. Yet he talked
of his work as if many days more were left to him; he must
have two or three days' riding without preaching, and then he
would be all right, or, he thought, his preaching the next day
would make him better—his old remedy, a 'pulpit-sweat'—he
used to sweat through and through—would relieve him; he
would rather wear out than rust out. It had long been his
habit to rise in the night and pray; and this night, weary and
panting, he sat up in bed and prayed God to bless his preaching on the past day, and his forthcoming services on the
Sunday; to bring more souls to Christ; to give him the
direction in the way he should take, whether he should winter
at Boston, or hasten to the south; to remember Bethesda and
his dear family; to smile on the congregations at the Tabernacle and Tottenham Court Chapel, and on all his English
friends. He lay down again to sleep; but in an hour he called
his friend for help. 'My asthma—my asthma is coming on,'

he said.　At five o'clock he rose to open the window wider for more air.　A few minutes afterwards he turned to his companion, and said, ' I am dying.'　He ran to the other window, panting for breath, but could get no relief.　They seated him in his chair, wrapped his cloak round him, and did their utmost to restore him.　But the end was come.　The device on his seal, of wings outspread for flight, and the motto it bore, '*Astra petamus*,' had long expressed his ardent desire to pass even beyond the stars; and at six o'clock on Sunday morning, September 30, 1770, he entered heaven itself.

The end was conformable to his hope and prayer.　He was an evangelist and died in a foreign land, although not among strangers.　He was a field-preacher, and preached his last sermon in the fields.　He had feared outliving his usefulness, and was permitted a reviving of his strength before he departed at the comparatively early age of fifty-six, and after thirty-four years of exertion.　He had expected to die silent ; for he said, ' It has pleased God to enable me to bear so many testimonies for Him during my life, that He will require none from me when I die.'　And so it was.

His dying prayer for the salvation of souls was also answered that very day.　When he preached at Portsmouth on the previous Friday, a young sail-maker named Benjamin Randall heard him, and was, as he had often been before, greatly impressed with his words and tears.　Randall, however, was hard and bitter even against the man who fascinated him.　But about noon on the Sunday a stranger rode into the town, and halting at the different corners in the main street, cried in a clear but subdued voice, ' *Whitefield is dead ! Whitefield is dead ! He died at Newbury Port this morning at six o'clock.*'　A voice also cried in the young man's soul, ' Whitefield is dead. Whitefield is in heaven, but I am on the road to hell.　He was a man of God, and yet I reviled him, and spoke reproachfully of him. He taught me the way to heaven, but I regarded him not. O that I could hear his voice again ! But ah, never, no, never shall I again hear it till in the judgment of the great day he shall appear as a swift witness against me.' He yielded himself to God.

On Tuesday, October 2nd, Whitefield was buried, according to his wish, in front of the pulpit of Mr. Parsons, in the Presbyterian Church at Newbury Port, the mighty host of mourners present, six thousand members and ministers of many denominations, fitly representing the catholicity of his heart and the magnitude of his labours. When the coffin was placed close to the mouth of the vault, the Rev. Daniel Rogers, of Exeter, one of his sons in the faith, ascended the pulpit, offered prayer, and confessed before all his vast obligations to him whose body they were about to commit to the grave. His emotion conquered him, and as he cried out, ' O my father, my father ! ' and stood and wept, the people mingled their tears with his. They tried to sing a hymn, but weeping choked many voices. A sermon was then preached ; the coffin was lowered into the vault ; another short prayer was offered ; and the congregation, still in tears, passed along the streets to their homes.

The outward demonstrations of grief were numerous and sincere. The bells of Newbury Port were tolled, and the ships in the harbour fired their guns, and hung their flags half-mast high. Funeral sermons were preached in the principal cities of America. In Georgia all the black cloth in the stores was bought up for mourning by the sorrowing people. They hung the church at Savannah in black, and the Governor and Council led the procession which attended to hear the funeral sermon. In London, where the news of his death was received on November 5th, the same grief was felt and expressed. The *London Chronicle* of November 19th says that the multitudes which went to hear his funeral sermon by Wesley, in Tottenham Court Chapel and the Tabernacle, exceeded all belief; and in churches and chapels of all orders there were similar commemorations of him.

Lovers of absolute, unvarying consistency, and lovers of real or apparent contradictions, may measure him by the room he had for diverse things. He loved privacy, but always lived in public; he was the foremost philanthropist of his time, but owned fifty slaves to maintain his orphans, and bequeathed them in his will to Lady Huntingdon in trust for the same use; he was slim in person, but occasionally stormed in his preaching as if he were a giant; he was weak, but worked to the last, and crowded a long life into a short one; he was the favourite preacher of colliers and London roughs, but was an equal favourite of peers and scholars; he believed in a limited atonement for sin, but proclaimed the love of God with a tenderness which made all feel that Christ had died for them; he was a clergyman of the Church of England, and also practically an Independent minister, but, at his own request, lies buried in a Presbyterian church; he was a Calvinist in doctrine, but chose an Arminian to preach his funeral sermon. Nominally narrow and exclusive, he was really one of the most liberalising influences of his age, and beneath his apparent inconsistencies and behind his ever-changing life there was a true unity. From his first sermon to his last he had one motive—the love of Christ—and one aim—the salvation of souls. Nor through all his distractions did he ever turn aside for a moment from his great work. The hostility of mobs, the bitterness of controversy, the unfaithfulness of friends, the opposition of the clergy and bishops, the seductions of popularity and the praise of the titled, all failed to make any impression upon his resolution to preach Christ to every soul that he could reach.

Two questions are almost sure to be upon the reader's

tongue. First, what became of the orphan-house? Secondly, where are the results of his preaching? These shall now be answered.

I. The orphan-house, with everything connected with it, was left to the Countess of Huntingdon, Mr. Habersham to act in her absence from America. Arrangements had been made in Whitefield's lifetime for carrying on an academy along with the orphanage. It became also a home, whence missionaries, sent from England by Lady Huntingdon, started on mission work among the Indians and the settlers. It was accidentally burnt down about two years after the death of Whitefield, and rebuilt, but not upon the original site. Other changes of fortune happened to it, one of which was the appointment of Franklin, its early opponent, as a trustee, because he was 'an honest man.' Its original charter appointed its continuance as long as there were three members to celebrate the anniversary, which falls on St. George's Day. This provision might once have sealed its fate. Three members, 'a Protestant, a Catholic, and an Israelite,' who apparently constituted the whole board at that time, were all prisoners of war on board a British man-of-war when St. George's Day came round. Remembering the charter, they begged permission of the captain to go ashore and celebrate the anniversary under an oak tree in Tunbury, Georgia. He consented, and the ceremony was duly performed. Mr. Joseph S. Fay succeeded, during the time he was president of the institution, in repurchasing the old site, and placing the orphanage upon it again. In 1870 a new building was begun, making the fourth since Whitefield laid the first brick of Bethesda with his own hand.

Whittier falls into a strange mistake when, in his fine poem, 'The Preacher,' he says—

'Alas for the preacher's cherished schemes !
Mission and church are now but dreams ;

> Nor prayer nor fasting availed the plan
> To honour God through the wrong of man.
> Of all his labours no trace remains
> Save the bondman lifting his hands in chains.'

Hallowed traces of his labours remain in every place he visited; the reproachful bondman only is gone; and had the liberal-minded Quaker known and realised all the facts, he would have penned a glowing tribute to Christ's abounding love, which forgives our sins and mistakes, and fulfils for us in nobler forms our purposes and prayers.

II. The results of Whitefield's work may be classed as indirect and direct. Little can be affirmed positively of the bearing of his work upon political and social life, but it must have corresponded to the religious effect. Men like Pulteney, Chatham, and Fox were not uninfluenced in their political action by the words they heard at Lady Huntingdon's; while among the people Whitefield saved to the nation thousands of its finest men and women. In America he saw, during his last visit, the beginnings of the War of Independence, and sympathised with the feelings of the colonists. Whether he would ultimately have sided with them no one can say; he was spared the pain of the strife; but there can be no doubt which side his converts were on and which part they played. One of the men whom he greatly influenced was the Rev. Alexander Craighead, and he again is said to have aroused the Presbyterian patriots who framed the Mecklenburg Declaration, which was copied only one year later by the Philadelphia Declaration of Independence. Thus Calvinism became once more the stone of stumbling on which tyranny has so often been broken.

1. Among indirect results must be placed the impetus which he undoubtedly gave to philanthropic work. His preaching to prisoners and his constant pleadings for orphans, for perse-

cuted Protestants on the Continent, and for other distressed persons, accustomed all classes of people to kindly thoughts and generous deeds for the wretched and the forlorn.   If his collections be taken in present equivalent, they will appear enormous.   He created, not altogether, but largely, the feeling upon which philanthropy in its active forms must live.   The benevolent objects of present religious work received recognition in every city and village, when the connection between acceptance with God through our Lord Jesus Christ and the necessity for good works was repeatedly and clearly pointed out.   Justification was the introduction to feeding the hungry, clothing the naked, and housing the orphan.

It is equally significant that the great missionary movements of our time followed closely upon the Methodist reformation ; and in that reformation who was there among the hosts of preachers and evangelists to be compared with Whitefield for missionary enterprise ?   Whose foot ranged over so wide a circuit ?   Whose sympathies were enlisted for so many objects ?   If he did not go to the heathen who worship idols of wood and stone, he went to those who were debased by the lowest vices ; and when, under his leadership, the Church had conducted them to a holy life and pure enjoyments, her attention was next directed to the heathen beyond. Whitefield accustomed the Church to the idea of aggression upon the kingdom of darkness ; he taught her that all lost and forgotten people are the inheritance of her Lord.   The Church Missionary Society, the child of the evangelical fervour of the followers of Whitefield—Newton, Thornton, Scott, and Venn— is the strongest foreign missionary society in the world, and the history of its first century's work just completed would have been a book exactly after Whitefield's heart.

Again, it needs but a simple statement of facts to show that Whitefield's preaching and his catholic spirit (the latter more than the former) have tended in no small measure to produce in England, as they first did in America, a true love of spiritual freedom and an honest reverence for religious equality. In his labours among all denominations he affected no condescension, he never played the patron. All were equally, truly brethren. Neither to benefit himself, nor to forward any of his plans, would he place one denomination before another. His conduct with regard to Bethesda College proves indisputably that he believed in religious equality, and would not support or countenance anything else.

Could nothing more than this be said, then Whitefield has not lived in vain; since the power of a life consists not so much in the formation of parties and sects and schools as in the anticipation of the truest and holiest things of future days, and in the preparation of the world for their advent. Churches may be cemeteries of the dead railed off from the living, or loving messengers of Christ going about doing good. Whitefield found them generally the former, and left them the latter. He was a breath, an inspiration, which to this day thrills evangelical Christendom.

2. Still, the demand is sure to be made for facts and figures. What did he accomplish? is the question asked. The answer is :—

(1) That his converts were to be found wherever he had travelled, nay, even beyond that extensive range, and were to be counted by tens of thousands. His preaching was remarkable for challenging the strongest characters, and either conquering them or else rousing their active opposition; neutrality was not easy in his presence. Among his converts were Thomas Olivers, author of the hymn 'The God of Abraham praise'; Samuel Davies, of the Presbyterian Church in Virginia; Thomas Rankin, of Dunbar, one of Wesley's best helpers; Robert Robinson, the famous Baptist minister of

Cambridge, and author of 'Come, Thou Fount of every blessing'; Andrew Kinsman, Whitefield's 'dear Timothy,' a mighty preacher of the Word; Cornelius Winter, the spiritual father of William Jay, of Bath; Henry Tanner, a useful preacher at Exeter; John Edwards, of Dublin, who preached in many parts of England, Scotland, and Ireland; John Fawcett, a Yorkshire preacher, author of 'Blest is the tie that binds' and 'Lord, dismiss us with Thy blessing'; Thomas Adams, of Minchin Hampton, the fearless witness, the able minister, the faithful friend; Samuel Cooper, one of the most popular preachers in America.

(2) That a great number of his converts were ministers properly trained for their ministerial work, who handed the truth down to children's children. Such, *e.g.*, was James Hervey, the once popular author. In the neighbourhood of Boston in America alone there were at one time twenty ministers who owned him as their spiritual father. Some of the ministers had a spiritual history not less wonderful than his own.

(3) That he was the first of the evangelical clergy in the Church of England; and had they formed a separate sect, instead of a party in a church, no one would have asked what are the results of his labours. This is the party which holds Whitefield's legacy to mankind strictly in the letter—sometimes not more than that. Other parties, again, to whose faith and practice he would have taken serious exception, have imbibed his spirit of zeal and love, and closely resemble him in all that makes his character lofty and his life beautiful. The whole Church of England has been moved by the wave which first lifted on its breast only a small section of her people, though parties have drifted in different directions.

(4) That he helped to revive and increase the Churches of the Dissenters. His own chapels belong to them, and in Yorkshire at least it is affirmed, on competent authority, that all the

chapels in which his preaching and that of other evangelicals was welcomed continue to this day to be centres of spiritual influence, while such as rejected it have declined or become extinct. Whitefield's lay-preachers supplied many of their pulpits. In many favourite Nonconformist preachers, down even to a generation ago, if not now, it is not difficult to trace the influence of his popular oratory—the doctrinal solidity, the pungent application, the tender and passionate appeal, the solemn warning. Nonconformist ministers proclaim our Lord's atonement for sin, while possibly differing as to the nature of the atonement; they insist upon a personal and vital union of spirit with Jesus Christ; they invoke the help of the Holy Ghost, feeling that without His power upon preacher and hearer no spiritual good can be done. But they say little about predestination, and nothing at all about Christ's having died for an elect world.

(5) That the Church of Scotland was made alive again by his numerous visits to Scotland, and by his impassioned appeals to the slumbering and the dead. Scotch journeys were nearly always an unmixed joy to Whitefield because of the good he did; and it is noticeable that, sixty years ago, the foremost ministers and the great bulk of the members of the Scotch Church assumed the position of the English Dissenters, and made of themselves 'a Free Church.'

(6) That the Church in Wales, of all denominations, received a remarkable impetus from Methodism, and that Whitefield was the first to join hands with the earnest men of the Principality. The early representations of the Methodists as to the religious condition of the country cannot be relied upon, but the following comparative table was carefully prepared by Dr. Rees, and published in his volume on Nonconformity in Wales. It gave the number of Nonconformist congregations in Wales as 110 in 1716, 105 in 1742, 171 in 1775, 993 in

1816, 2,927 in 1861. It is now 3,456, besides the congregations connected with 91 Wesleyan Methodist, and 32 Primitive Methodist, circuits. The great increase between 1775 and 1816 was owing to the separation of the Calvinistic Methodists from the Established Church, which took place in 1811; and from 1816 to 1899 the increase is the result of the zeal and labours of the Churches, crowned with the blessing of God. Broadly stated, the result of Methodism in Wales has been the changing of a nation of ignorant, irreligious Churchmen into a nation of conscientious Nonconformists, who adhere to their convictions in spite of much persecution and disadvantage. Whitefield neither desired nor sought the Nonconformity; but, as in the case of Scotland, an intense religious life would have freedom of action.

(7) That in America he founded the Presbyterian Church of Virginia, and helped more than any man to triple the ministers of the New York Synod within seven years, and to bring into existence a hundred and fifty Congregational Churches in less than twenty years. He gave a welcome in 1769 to two of Wesley's preachers who were sent to America—Richard Boardman and Joseph Pilmoor—and his preaching prepared the way for the formation of the Methodist Episcopal Church, one of the strongest churches in the world. His labours materially aided the building of Princeton College and Dartmouth College. They also produced the same effect upon Church government in America, which we have seen to have been produced in Scotland, England, and Wales. The spiritual life would not be fettered; and the union between Church and State was broken.

What did Whitefield accomplish? It is true that he did not organise his converts into a new denomination, but some will think that he did a nobler service by encouraging them to join any existing Church to which their beliefs and sympathies

might draw them.   He was chiefly the means of rejuvenating
the Episcopal, the Independent, the Presbyterian, and the
Baptist Churches ; even the Society of Friends was quickened
by his labours, and he frequently preached for Wesley's
societies.   The catholic spirit of the work is perhaps more
than the work itself.   He also founded churches and inaugu-
rated religious revolutions by a sermon.   His last sermons,
as we have seen, touched the heart of a young man named
Randall; his death sealed all the holy impressions as with the
mark of God ; and that young man shortly afterwards founded
in the United States the Free-will Baptist Church, a Church
always opposed to slavery, and now nearly one hundred
thousand members strong.   His works do follow him.   Only
this year (1900) the pastor of Tottenham Court Road Chapel
received a donation towards the cost of rebuilding that structure
from a gentleman in Australia who had been converted in
that colony by reading one of Whitefield's sermons.

Could his hand add one word to this record of his life and
its fruits, it would be this—'Grace ! Grace ! Grace !'   For
his sake, then, and especially for the sake of Him who came
bringing grace and truth with Him, it shall be inscribed as the
last word here—GRACE.

INDEX.